ISBN: 9781313006811

Published by:
HardPress Publishing
8345 NW 66TH ST #2561
MIAMI FL 33166-2626

Email: info@hardpress.net
Web: http://www.hardpress.net

A DEFENCE OF
FUNDAMENTAL TRUTH.

AN EXAMINATION OF MR. J. S. MILL'S

PHILOSOPHY

BEING

A DEFENCE OF FUNDAMENTAL TRUTH.

BY

JAMES M{c}COSH, LL.D.

PROFESSOR OF LOGIC AND METAPHYSICS, QUEEN'S COLLEGE, BELFAST; AUTHOR OF 'THE
METHOD OF DIVINE GOVERNMENT,' 'INTUITIONS OF THE MIND,' ETC.

London:
MACMILLAN AND CO.
1866.

EDINBURGH : T. CONSTABLE.

PRINTER TO THE QUEEN, AND TO THE UNIVERSITY.

CONTENTS.

CHAPTER I.

IF any one competent to offer an opinion on such a subject were asked, Who are the most influential philosophic thinkers of Britain, in this the third quarter of the nineteenth century? he would at once and unhesitatingly name Sir William Hamilton and Mr. John Stuart Mill. For the last twenty or thirty years the former has had great authority in Scotland, and considerable power in Oxford and among the Dissenting colleges of England; has been much admired in the United States of America; has been favourably known in France, and heard of even in Germany, where few British metaphysicians attain a name. Mr. Mill has qualities which specially recommend him to the English mind, and of late years he has got a firm hold of the rising thought of Oxford and Cambridge, where young minds, in the recoil from the attempt to impose the mediæval forms upon them, have taken refuge in the Empiricism and Utilitarianism so lucidly expounded by him; while writers bred at the great English Univer-

A

sities have, in certain portions of the London press,
been constantly and apparently systematically quoting
him, or referring to him, as possibly the only philosopher known to them, or at least appreciated by them.
It should be added that he is known in France as the
English representative of their own Positive School;
and his clear logical expositions have been esteemed
by not a few in Germany, anxious to escape from the
inextricable toils of Kant and Fichte, Schelling and
Hegel.

These two men are alike in the greatness of their
intellectual power, and in the range of their attain-
ments. But they differ widely in their peculiar mental
endowments and predilections, in the manner in which
they have been trained, and the influences under which
their opinions have been formed. Hamilton is known
to have received a thoroughly complete collegiate education in classics and philosophy; to have afterwards
had his logical powers sharpened by the study of law,
and his extensive information widened by his researches
when Professor of History; while his pursuits were
made finally to centre in mental science by his appointment as Professor of Logic and Metaphysics in
the University of Edinburgh. Receiving his early college training in Glasgow, where the influence of Reid
was predominant, he retained through life a profound
reverence for the common sense philosopher. Com-
pleting his academic education at Oxford, he fell under
the sway of Aristotle, and found in him much that was
congenial to his own intellectual nature, and was led to

study his philosophy not only in his own writings, but
in the pages of his commentators, and in the modification of his logic constructed by the schoolmen. In the
course of his multifarious reading he could not but fall
in with constant references to Emmanuel Kant as a profound thinker, and, as he entered upon the study of his
works, could not but be impressed with the vast logical
power of the German metaphysician. These three,
Reid, Aristotle, and Kant, are the men who have
exercised the greatest influence on the studies and the
ughts of the Scottish philosopher. But in his vast
. rare reading he delighted to find truth scattered
ᵉ gold dust in the pages of forgotten writers of all
ꜱ and countries, and, rejoicing in the discovery, he
ᵢ magnified its value as he hastened to bring it
ᵢ to the public view in an age and country which
Ɪed to him greatly deficient in scholarship.
is intellectual features stand out very prominently.
scerning eye might have seen from the beginning
his independent and impetuous mind would impel
to follow a course of his own ; and that, while pro-
ly destined to lead, he would not be led—certainly
ꞮꞮd not be driven by others. He is evidently moved
strong internal appetency to master all learning,
ᵉ spent his life in accumulating stores which, after
ꞮꞮ immeasurably beneath his high ambition. Along
his he has a masterly capacity of retention and
of arrangement. His skill in seizing the opinions
of the men of all ages and countries : the ancient Greeks,
the philosophic fathers of the Church, the schoolmen,

the thinkers of the age of the Revival of Letters,—such as Scaliger, and of the continental metaphysicians from the days of Descartes to about the year 1830, has never been equalled by any British philosopher. His powers of logical analysis, generalization, and distribution are scarcely surpassed by those of Aristotle or Thomas Aquinas or Kant. I have to add, that while he has also superior powers of observation, he has, like most metaphysicians, often overridden and overwhelmed them by logical processes, and hastened by dissection, division, and criticism to construct prematurely a completed system of philosophy—such as is to be built up, only as systems of physical science are formed, by the careful inductions of successive inquirers conducting their work through successive ages. In this respect he has imbibed the spirit of Kant, and has not followed the examples set by the more cautious school of Reid and Stewart.

His manner and style are very decided and very marked. Any man of sharp discernment could easily recognise him at a great distance, and detect him under the most rigid *incognito*. To some ears his nomenclature may sound uncouth and crabbed, being coined out of the Greek or borrowed from the Germans ; but these persons forget that chemistry and geology and anatomy have all been obliged to create a new terminology, in order to embody the distinctions which they have established. Hamilton is certainly without the power of poetical or oratorical amplification for which Brown and Chalmers of the same University were distinguished ;

and he is deficient in the aptness of illustration in which such writers as Paley and Whately excel; still his manner of writing has attractions of its own. His phraseology, if at times it sounds technical or pedantic, is always carefully explained and defined, and is ever scholarlike in its derivation and articulate in its meaning. His style is never loose, never tedious, never dull; it is always clear, always terse, always masculine, and at times it is sententious, clinching, and apothegmatic. In reading his works the reader need entertain no fear of being led into a Scotch mist, or being met by a fog from the German Ocean. Not unfrequently dogmatic, at times oracular, resolute in holding by his opinions when attacked, and on certain occasions, as in his assaults on Luther, Brown, Whately, and De Morgan, giving way to undue severity and passion, he is ever open, manly, and sincere. He uses a sharp chisel and strikes his hammer with a decided blow, and his ideas commonly stand out before us like a clean cut statue standing firmly on its pedestal between us and a clear sky. Indeed we might with justice describe his style as not only accurate, but even beautiful in a sense, from its compression, its compactness, its vigour, and its point. His thoughts, weighty and solid as metal, are ever made to shine with a metallic lustre. At the places at which his speculations are the most abstract and his words the baldest, he often surprises us by an apt quotation from an old and forgotten author; or a sudden light is thrown upon the present topic by rays coming from a hundred points. If we have not the flowers or the riches, we are at the same time without the sultriness of a tropical climate; and in the arctic region to which he carries us, if the atmosphere feels cold at times, it is always healthy and bracing, and the lights in the sky have a bright and scintillating lustre.

Mr. Mill's characteristics are of a different kind. It is understood that he received no collegiate education; but it is clear that he has been instructed with care, and I should suppose upon a system, in the various branches even of academic learning. If not so technically erudite as Hamilton, it is evident that he is well acquainted with the various departments of physical science; that he is extensively read in all historical and social questions; and that he is competently conversant with the opinions of philosophers and logicians in different ages. His thinking has many of the qualities of a self-educated man : that is, it is fresh and independent, but, at the same time, it is often exclusive and angular, in consequence of its not being rubbed and polished and adjusted by being placed alongside of the philosophic and religious wisdom of the great and good men of the past. Taught to think for himself from his boyhood, he has prepared opinions on all subjects; he has published many of these in his writings, and has evidently many more to advance in due time, as circumstances may seem to require, and the world is able to bear them. He received, I rather think, his first intellectual impulse from his own father, of whom he always speaks with profound reverence—a circumstance creditable alike to the father and the son. But Mr. James

Mill, though a clear and independent, was by no means (so I think) a comprehensive or profound thinker. The title of his philosophical work, *Analysis of the Pheno-mena of the Human Mind,* indicates its character and its contents ; it is an analysis of the operations of the mind into as few elements as possible, and preceded by no careful observation of the nature and peculiarities of the mental phenomena which he seeks to decompose. One so trained could not but have his attention drawn to the speculations of Dr. Thomas Brown, who, largely following the Sensational School of France, had shown his ingenuity in deriving the complex phenomena of the mind from a few ultimate laws. Like the older Mr. Mill (in this respect unlike Dr. Brown), the younger Mr. Mill delights to trace ideas to sensations ; like Brown and James Mill, he represents all our mental states as "feelings," and like them he generates our ideas by means of suggestion or association.

These are evidently Mr. Mill's immediate predecessors in psychology. In historical speculation he was early seized with an admiration of the general principles of the philosophy of M. Auguste Comte, who was becoming known to a select few at the time when the character of the young Englishman was being formed ; and M. Littré claims Mr. John Mill as the first who gave " a public adhesion to the method of the positive phi-losophy." Not that he has followed the founder of the Positive School in every respect ; in particular, he has been prevented by his adherence to his father's meta-physics from following M. Comte in his denunciations

of all attempts to study the human mind by consciousness. But he was led by the influence of this teacher
to regard it as impossible for the mind to rise to first or
final causes, or to know the nature of things ; and to
adopt his favourite method of procedure, which is by
deduction from an hypothesis, which he endeavours to
show explains all the phenomena. Though a fairly
informed man in the history of philosophy, he has
attached himself to a school which thinks it has entirely
outstripped the past ; and so he has no sympathy with,
and no appreciation of, the profound thoughts of the
men of former times : these are supposed to belong to
the theological or metaphysical ages, which have for
ever passed away in favour of the positive era which
has now dawned upon our world. Bred thus in a
revolutionary school of opinion, his predilections are in
all things in favour of those who are given to change,
and against those who think that there is immutable
truth, or who imagine that they have discovered it.
His expressed admiration of Coleridge may seem to
contradict this statement, but it does so only in appearance, for he has no partiality for any of the favourite
principles of that defender of transcendental reason ; it is
clear that he delights in him chiefly because his speculations have been acting as a solvent to melt down the
crystallized philosophical and theological opinions of
England. The school of Comte has hitherto had no
analyst of the mind (the founder of it was a phrenolo-
gist, and studied the mind through the brain) ; and Mr.
Mill may be regarded as, for the present, the recognised

metaphysician of the school, and will hold this place till he is superseded by the more comprehensive system, and the bolder speculative grasp of Mr. Herbert Spencer.

With an original clearness of intellectual apprehension, his whole training has disposed him towards distinct enunciations and practical results. Engaged for many years in a public office, he has acquired habits which enable him to understand the business of life and the condition of society. He is particularly fitted to excel in the exposition of those *media axiomata* upon which, according to Bacon, " depend the business and fortune of mankind." With an English love of the concrete, he has a French skill in reducing a complex subject into simple elements, and a French clearness of expression. He is ever able to bring out his views in admirable order, and his thoughts lie in his style like pebbles at the bottom of a transparent stream, so that we see their shape and colour without noticing the medium through which we view them. I have to add, that in his love of the clear, and his desire to translate the abstract into the concrete, he often misses the deepest properties of the objects examined by him ; and he seems to me far better fitted to co-ordinate the facts of social science than to deal with the first principles of fundamental philosophy. As to his spirit, there are evidences of a keen fire, of enthusiasm, perhaps of passion, burning within, but the surface is ever still and ever green.

These two eminent men, whose systems evidently stood all along so widely apart from each other, have now been brought into violent collision by the publication of Mill's *Examination of Sir William Hamilton's Philosophy.* Such a collision was inevitable. Hamilton was the ablest and most learned, I do not think the wisest or most consistent, defender of intuitive or *a priori* truth in our country in the past age. It was felt to be absolutely necessary, in these circumstances, by the British section of the school of M. Comte, that the fundamental positions of Hamilton should be removed out of the way of the advancing deductive empiricism. I rejoice that the attack has been made by Mr. Mill himself, so that we see all that can be advanced by the acutest representative of the experiential or sensational philosophy in our age and country. It is to be hoped that the formidable assault will be met by some disciple of Hamilton who has caught the spirit and who understands the system of his master. As the result, the student of philosophy will be in circumstances to decide what he should receive with gratitude, and what he should refuse or reject with regret, in the philosophy of the last of the great Scottish metaphysicians.

In the title of his work, Mr. Mill announces it as an examination of "the principal philosophical questions discussed in his writings;" and in his introductory remarks he declares, "My subject, therefore, is not Sir W. Hamilton, but the questions which Sir W. Hamilton discussed." It is this circumstance which makes the work so important in the view of the students of mental science generally, and which has induced me to review it. In examining his opponent, Mr. Mill has taken the opportunity of developing his own philosophic system, and has put us in a position to judge of its principles and results. It is true that we had the germs of that system embedded in his treatise on *Logic*, and germinating there. No doubt he is continually telling us in that work that he avoids metaphysics, but there is a metaphysical system underlying and running throughout all the deeper discussions. He refers, and evidently adheres to a large extent, to a sensational theory of the origin of our ideas in his chapter, " Of the Things denoted by Names ;" he seeks to undermine all intuitive truth in his chapters on " Demonstration" and " Causation ;" and he has exposed with a special zest the errors of the *a priori* school in his book on " Fallacies." He has thus been preparing those who have studied his logic for accepting his metaphysics. In these circumstances I rejoice that in his recent work he has furnished us with the means of thoroughly estimating his theory of the mind, of which we had only hints and glimpses in his logical treatise. It is this theory which I profess to examine in this volume.

In performing this special task it is not necessary to enter into the controversy between Mill and Hamilton. Far more important questions than the merits of the individuals have been started. I certainly do not feel that it is a duty devolving on me to offer a defence of the philosophy of Hamilton. Since the year 1854, when I reviewed his doctrines of the " Relativity of Knowledge" and of " Causation," in an appendix to the fourth edition of my work on the *Method of the*

Divine Government, I have been opposing certain of his favourite principles. I offered my strictures with excessive reluctance, as feeling a profound reverence for the vast erudition and logical power of the Edinburgh professor, and cherishing a lively gratitude for the services he had rendered to philosophy in refuting old and widely-received errors and establishing important truth. I advanced my criticisms while he was yet alive, and I have continued them in articles in reviews, and in my work on *The Intuitions of the Mind,* while his reputation was at its greatest height, and his disciples were indignant at any attempt to dispute the infallibility of their master.

Hamilton, as it appears to me, was never able to weld into a consistent whole the realistic matter he got from Reid with the subjective forms he took from Kant. In his review of M. Cousin, he took up a negative position, which did not leave him free to follow thoroughly the positive revelations of consciousness. In his *Discussions* he developed a theory of causation which prevented him from rising from the phenomena of the world to a belief in the existence of Deity; and he expounded a doctrine as to the relativity of knowledge which makes us perceive objects under forms, and with additions imposed by the perceiving mind, which landed him avowedly in a system of nescience. Kant is claimed, with some truth, by M. Littré as in fact a precursor of the school of Comte. I have felt all along that Hamilton adopted principles from the Critical Philosophy, which made it impossible for him to stand up for the trustworthiness of our faculties and the reality of things, which yet as a follower of Reid he seemed to be establishing. I declared openly and repeatedly, and in a number of places, that the admissions he made would sooner or later be followed to their logical consequences ; that without meaning it, he was preparing the way for a nihilist philosophy ; and that it would be seen that he had not left himself ground from which successfully to repel the attacks of scepticism. When Dr. Mansel published his famous Bampton Lectures, *On the Limits of Religious Thought*, notwithstanding my great reverence for his erudition, his acuteness, and his high character, I immediately opposed his application of Hamilton's doctrine of the unconditioned to our knowledge of God and of good and evil, which I represented as being fraught with disastrous logical consequences. As having anticipated Mr. Mill in many of his objections to Hamilton's philosophy, and having advanced others against doctrines which Mr. Mill applauds and turns to his own uses, and believing it to be impossible to defend fundamental truth from the positions assumed by Hamilton, I feel that it is not for me to propose to defend the philosophy of the Scottish metaphysician from the assaults of Mr. Mill.[1]

At the same time, I cannot give my adherence to many of the objections which have been taken by his new opponent. Notwithstanding incongruities in some parts of his system, he has furnished more valu-

[1] I have placed in an *Appendix* to this volume a summary of the objections I have taken to Sir William Hamilton's Philosophy.

able contributions to speculative philosophy than any
other British writer in this century.   No man has ever
done more in clearing the literature of philosophy of
commonplace mistakes, of thefts and impostures.   He
has shown that it is dangerous to quote without con-
sulting the original, or to adopt without examination
the common traditions in philosophy ; that those who
borrow at second-hand will be detected, and that those
who steal without acknowledgment will sooner or
later be exposed.   He seems to experience a delight in
stripping modern authors of their borrowed feathers,
and pursuing stolen goods from one literary thief to
another, and giving them back to their original owner.
More than any other Englishman, Scotchman, or Irish-
man, for the last two centuries, he has wiped away
the reproach from British philosophy that it is narrow
and insular.   For years past ordinary authors have
seemed learned, and for years to come will seem learned,
by drawing from his stores.   In incidental discussions,
in foot-notes, and notes on foot-notes, he has scattered
nuts which it will take many a scholar many a day to
gather and to crack.   It will be long before the rays
which shine from him will be so scattered and diffused
through philosophic literature—as the sunbeams are
through the atmosphere—that they shall become common property, and men will cease to distinguish the
focus from which they have come.   By his admirable
powers of division and subdivision he has placed the
philosophic systems of various ages and countries into
appropriate compartments, which enable us at once to

see the form and the nature of each. Mr. Mill regrets
that he " did not write the history of philosophy." I am
not sure whether the Scottish professor had all the quali-
fications necessary for such a work ; whether, in particular, he could always enter sympathetically into the
spirit of the times in which the philosopher lived, and
whether he could have given us an easy and continuous
narrative. But every student should be grateful to him
for what he has actually performed ; for arranging under
proper heads, and stating, always with admirable brevity,
and commonly with unimpeachable accuracy, the
opinions of philosophers, ancient and modern, on most
of the topics of speculative interest which still continue
to be agitated. Looking to his original contributions to
philosophy, his defence of the principles of common
sense is characterized at once by extensive learning, by
unsurpassed logical acumen and consummate judgment.
His immediate theory of sense-perception, if it does not
remove all difficulties, appears to me to be more consistent than any other with the facts both of psychology
and of physiology. His logic is too Kantian in its
manner and spirit, and will require to be carefully
sifted : but I believe it is the most important addition
made in our day to the analytic of the laws of thought.
I am persuaded that his distribution of the mental
faculties, given in the second volume of his *Metaphysics*,
is upon the whole the best we yet have, and any
one who would improve it must make extensive use
of it. Nor is it to be forgotten that he has introduced fresh topics into British philosophy, and has

always thrown light upon them even when he has not succeeded in settling them.

I am sure Mr. Mill means to be a just critic of his rival. But from having attached himself to a narrow and exclusive school of philosophy and of history, he is scarcely capable of comprehending, he is certainly utterly incapable of appreciating some of Hamilton's profounder discussions. It could be shown that not a few of the alleged inconsistencies of Hamilton arise from misapprehensions on the part of his critic. I have observed that some of the supposed contradictions are merely verbal, and originate in his using a phrase in its usual acceptation, perhaps to a promiscuous class in one place, and employing it in a more technical sense after explanation in another. Nor is it to be forgotten that the writings published by himself appeared in the form of articles in reviews, and of notes and appendices to works edited by him; and that his *Lectures*, which contain his complete system, though carefully edited by Professors Mansel and Veitch, had not the advantage of being reduced to thorough consistency by himself. It has to be added, that, being willing to take a thought that struck him as true or important from any quarter, he was not always able to join the materials he had gathered into a harmonious structure. Hence his philosophy takes the appearance of a squared and diamonded mosaic, in which it is not always easy to discover the unity of the plan. But I verily believe that Hamilton had after all a complete system, which, with some hiatuses and incongruities, and some fatal errors adopted from Kant, is, as a whole, consistent, and contains valuable truth. His critic, from his training and sectarian predilections, is incapacitated for forming a due estimate of many of his higher excellences, and everywhere examines him from his own standpoint, which is very narrow, and by his own experiential system, which is lamentably defective. But I leave the work of defending Hamilton to his pupils and disciples, and I rejoice to believe that in many points, and these very important ones, their defence will be triumphantly successful.

In that curious retribution which we often discover in the affairs of this world, we find that those who are severe in judging others, may come in the end to be severely judged themselves.[1] The late Sir W. Hamilton was often harsh, at times I think unjust (not intentionally) in his censures on those who had possession of the philosophic ear of the country at the time when he was forcing himself into public notice in opposition to the spirit of the age. In saying so, I do not refer so much to his able and manly, though not altogether successful, criticism of M. Cousin, or to his non-recognition of any special merit in Mr. James Mill (of which his son com-

---

[1] Have we an illustration of this in the manner in which Plato, who is supposed to have treated the Sophists with injustice, is himself treated in his turn by Mr. Grote, in his *Plato and the other Companions of Socrates ?* The exposition of the Search Dialogues in that able and learned work is admirable, but the positive doctrines of Plato are examined from the standpoint of M. Comte, Mr. Mill, and Professor Bain ! Is there no living Archer Butler among British scholars to defend Plato's high aspirations, and to show that he had glimpses of great verities which have never disclosed themselves to the view of the ancient Sophists or modern Positivists ?

plains), so much as to the censorious manner in which he refers to Dr. Brown and Archbishop Whately, who, if not very profound or erudite, were certainly fresh, acute, and honest thinkers. He has now been repaid for all this in his own coin, by one who has a great admiration of Whately, and who has sprung from the school of Brown and Mill, and who writes as if he had public wrongs to avenge, and an accumulation of accepted errors to scatter. The time will come, I doubt not, when the avenger may himself have to suffer for the excess of punishment he has inflicted. But I beg to say that this is not the spirit in which I have written this review. I have really no pleasure in exposing the inconsistencies, the misunderstandings, and mistakes, to be found in Mr. Mill's *Examination*, or any of his other works. Acuter minds, or more pugnacious spirits, or earnest souls irritated as they see the evils which must arise from the prevalence of a philosophy which undermines fundamental truth, will, I suspect, rejoice to do this, and may be tempted to do it in excess. But I have no personal antipathies to gratify, no wrongs to avenge. The deepest feeling which I entertain towards Mr. Mill is that of admiration of his talents, and gratitude for the clear exposition which he has given of many important principles.[1] My aim in this work is simply to defend a portion of primary truth which has

---

[1] Simply to illustrate this, I may mention that the part of his *Logic* which treats of induction, has a place in my college classes, and on my recommendation, joined to that of the corresponding professors in Cork and Galway, has a place in the examination for the Bachelor's and Master's degree in the Queen's University in Ireland.

been assailed by an acute thinker who has extensive influence in England.

Some of his admirers claim for Mr. Mill, that he is the genuine philosophical descendant of Locke. I acknowledge that in some respects he resembles our great English metaphysician. He is like him in his clearness of thought and diction. Both are careful to avoid, as far as possible, abstruse arguments and technical phrases. Both have a name in other departments as well as mental philosophy,—Locke having thought profoundly on political questions, and Mr. Mill having given us one of the best works we have on political economy. Both have written on toleration or liberty, and defended views in advance of those generally entertained in their own times. I am inclined further to admit that Mr. Mill has quite as much influence in our day in England as Locke had in his. But with these points of likeness there are important points of difference. Locke had an originality, a shrewdness, a sagacity, and a high-principled wisdom and caution which have not been equalled by the later speculator. Locke avows extreme enough views in opposing the doctrines of professed metaphysicians, but he is saved by his crowning sense, and his religious convictions, acquired in Puritan times, from taking up positions adverse to the sound sense of mankind. Vehement enough in opposing a doctrine of innate ideas supposed to be held by philosophers, and labouring in vain to derive all our ideas from sensation and reflection, we do not find him falling back on such extreme positions as those of Mr.

Mill, when he endeavours to draw our higher ideas out of sensation by means of association, and maintains that we can know nothing of mind except that it is a series of sensations, aware of itself, or of matter, except that it is a possibility of sensations. I believe that Locke abandoned, without knowing it, some important fundamental truths ; but he resolutely held by many others, as that man has high faculties working on the original materials, and that in particular he has an intuitive knowledge " which is irresistible, and, like bright sunshine, forces " itself immediately to be perceived, as soon as ever " the mind turns its view that way, and leaves no room " for hesitation, doubt, or examination, but the mind is " presently filled with the clear light of it" (*Essay*, B. iv. c. 2). Mr. J. S. Mill is the successor and the living representative of an important British school, but it is that of Hobbes, of Hartley, of Priestley, of David Hume, and of James Mill. I have studiously left Thomas Brown out of this list, because, while adopting much from Hume, he carefully separates from him on the subject of intuition, maintaining that we have original and irresistible beliefs in our personal identity, and in causation. It will be seen as we advance how close the philosophy of Mr. J. S. Mill comes to that of Hume. I rather think Mr. Mill is scarcely aware himself of the extent of the resemblance, as he seems to have wrought out his conclusions from data supplied him to some extent by Brown, but to a greater extent by Mr. James Mill, both of whom drew much from the *Treatise of Human Nature*. But even on the supposition that Mr.

Mill is the Locke of the nineteenth century, it would be necessary to examine and correct his views. For while the *Essay on the Human Understanding* evolved much truth, and exercised, upon the whole, a healthy influence, it contained very grave defects and errors, which issued in very serious consequences both in France and in this country ; in the former landing speculation in a miserable sensationalism, and in the latter originating the wire-drawn attempts to fashion all our ideas out of one or two primitive sources by means of association. I have already intimated that I believe the errors of Mr. Mill to be far more numerous and fundamental than those of Locke ; and should his sensational and nescient system come to be adopted, it will be followed, both in theory and in practice, with far more fatal results than any that ensued from the combined idealistic and realistic philosophy expounded in Locke's great work.

Among a considerable portion even of the reading and thinking people of England, there is a strong aversion to all professedly metaphysical speculation,—which they regard as a net of sophistry spread out to catch them. But in avoiding an avowed and elaborate discussion of fundamental truth, it often happens that they are taken in by a plausible smartness, which is really metaphysics, but bad metaphysics,—treating every profound subject in a superficial way. In this respect some of our countrymen act very much like those excessively cautious and suspicious persons to be met with in the world, who are so afraid of everybody cheating them, that they become the dupes of those

more designing schemers who are ever warning them
against the dishonesty of others.   There are readers of
Hobbes, who, on perceiving how free he is from mysticism,
and how readily he seems to explain all our ideas by
sensation, and all our actions by selfishness, are tempted
to think that this man who speaks so clearly and dog-
matically must be speaking truly.   They are about as
wise as the excessively far-sighted individuals who so
easily account for all extraordinary actions on the simple
principle that all mankind are fools, or rogues, or mad-
men!   The Englishman is thus often led astray by a
deception which pretends to be simplicity itself.   I
abhor as much as any man the introduction of metaphysics into the discussion of commonplace or practical
subjects.   But there is another error, quite as common,
and to be equally dreaded, and that is the introduction
of superficial metaphysics furtively, by those who would
gain your confidence by telling you that they avoid
metaphysics.   If we are to have metaphysics, let them
avow that they are metaphysics, and let the investigation be conducted scientifically and systematically.   By
all means let us have clear metaphysics, just as we
would wish to have clear mathematics and clear physics.
But clearness to the extent of transparency is of no value,
provided it be attained, as in the case of the French sensational school, only by omitting all that is high or deep
in man's nature.   I certainly do not look on Mr. Mill
as a superficial writer.   On the contrary, on subjects
on which he has not been led to follow Mr. James Mill
or M. Comte, his thoughts are commonly as solid and

weighty as they are clearly expressed. But, speaking exclusively of his philosophy of first principles, I believe he is getting so ready an acceptance among many for his metaphysical theories, mainly because, like Hobbes and Condillac, he possesses a delusive simplicity which does not account for, but simply overlooks, the distinguishing properties of our mental nature.

CHAPTER II.

THE METHOD OF INVESTIGATION.

M. Cousin brings it as a charge against Locke, that in his *Essay on the Human Understanding*, he treats of the origin of ideas before inquiring into their nature. Locke thus announces his method : " 1*st*, I shall in- " quire into the original of those ideas, notions, or what- " ever else you please to call them, which a man observes, " and is conscious to himself he has in his mind, and the " ways whereby the understanding comes to be furnished " with them" (Introd. s. 3.) Upon this, his French critic remarks that there are here "two radical errors in regard " to method : 1*st*, Locke treats of the origin of ideas be- " fore having sufficiently studied these ideas ; 2*dly*, he " does more, he not only puts the question of the origin " of ideas before that of the inventory of ideas, but he en- " tirely neglects this last question" (*Lectures on Locke*, ii.) M. Cousin seems to lay down an important principle here, and to be so far justified in blaming the English philosopher for neglecting it. In order to be able to settle the very difficult question of the origin of our ideas, we must begin, and, I believe, end, with a careful inspection of their precise nature. In the very passage in which Locke proclaims his mode of procedure, he speaks of inquiring into the original of those ideas which a man "observes, and is conscious to himself." The observation by consciousness should certainly precede any attempt to furnish a theoretical decomposition of ideas. I am convinced that in the construction of his theory, that all our ideas are derived from sensation and reflection, Locke did not patiently and comprehensively contemplate all that is in certain of the deepest and most characteristic ideas of the human mind. I do not ground this charge so much on the fact that he treats, in the First Book, of the Origin of Ideas, before coming, in the Second Book, to discuss the Nature of Ideas, as on the circumstance that in the Second Book he is obliged to overlook some of the profoundest properties of our ideas, in order to make them fit into his preconceived system. But we find Mr. Mill justifying Locke, and condemning Cousin. " I accept the question as M. Cousin " states it, and I contend that no attempt to determine " what are the direct revelations of consciousness can be " successful or entitled to regard, unless preceded by " what M. Cousin says ought to follow it—an inquiry " into the origin of our acquired ideas " (*Exam.* p. 145).

Mr. Mill at this place examines Sir W. Hamilton's constant appeals to consciousness. Sir William would often settle by consciousness alone questions which I suspect must be solved by a more complicated and difficult process. It is thus, for instance—that is, by an appeal to consciousness—that he would determine that we know immediately an external or material world.

In language often of terrible severity, he charges Brown, and nearly all philosophers, with disregarding consciousness : " But it is thus manifestly the common interest of " every scheme of philosophy to preserve intact the integrity of consciousness. Almost every scheme of philosophy is only another mode in which this integrity has " been violated " (*Metaphysics*, vol. i. p. 283). Mr. Mill shows successfully (as I think) that the question between Hamilton and his opponents is often not one of the testimony of consciousness, but of the interpretation of consciousness : " We have it not in our power to ascertain, " by any direct process, what consciousness told us at the " time when its revelations were in their primitive purity. " It only offers itself to our inspection as it exists now, " when these original revelations are overlaid and buried " under a mountainous heap of acquired notions and per- " ceptions" (pp. 145, 146). Mr. Mill then goes on to explain his own method, which he calls the Psychological : " And here emerges the distinction between two different " methods of studying the problems of metaphysics, form- " ing the radical difference between the two great schools " into which metaphysicians are fundamentally divided. " One of these I shall call for distinction the Introspective " method, the other the Psychological." He rejects the Introspective method : " Introspection can show us a " present belief or conviction, attended with a greater or " less difficulty in accommodating the thoughts to a dif- " ferent view of the subject ; but that this belief or con - " viction or knowledge, if we call it so, is intuitive, no " mere introspection can ever show." He therefore resorts to the other method : " Being unable to examine " the actual contents of our consciousness until our " earliest, which are necessarily our most firmly knit " associations, those which are most intimately inter- " woven with the original data of consciousness, are fully " formed, we cannot study the original elements of mind " in the facts of our present consciousness. Those origi- " nal elements can only come to light as residual pheno- " mena, by a previous study of the modes of generation " of the mental facts which are confessedly not original, " —a study sufficiently thorough to enable us to apply " its results to the convictions, beliefs, or supposed in- " tuitions which seem to be original, and determine " whether some of them may not have been generated " in the same modes, so early as to have become insepar- " able from our consciousness before the time at which " memory commences. This mode of ascertaining the " original elements of mind I call Psychological, as " distinguished from the simply Introspective mode " (pp. 147, 148). These quotations furnish a sufficiently clear view of his account of the two methods, and of his reasons for rejecting the one and adopting the other.

I have long been of opinion, and I have endeavoured to show elsewhere,[1] that Sir William Hamilton's use of " consciousness" is very unsatisfactory. He avows that he employs the phrase in two distinct senses or appli- cations. First, he has a general consciousness, discussed largely in the first volume of his *Metaphysics*. This he

[1] Particularly in a review of Hamilton's *Metaphysics* in the *Dublin University Magazine* for August 1859.

tells us cannot be defined (vol. i. p. 158) ; " but it com-
prehends all the modifications, all the phenomena of the
thinking subject" (p. 183).   " Knowledge and belief are
both contained under consciousness" (p. 191).   Again,
" consciousness   is   co-extensive   with   our   cognitive
faculties;"   " our   special   faculties   of   knowledge   are
only   modifications   of   consciousness" (p. 207).   He
shows that consciousness implies discrimination, judgment, and memory (pp. 202-206).   This is wide enough ;
still he imposes a limit, for consciousness " is an immediate, not a mediate knowledge" (p. 202).   Already,
as it seems to me, inconsistencies are beginning to creep
in ; for whereas he had before told us that consciousness includes " all the phenomena of the thinking subject," now he so modifies it as to exclude " mediate
knowledge," which is surely a modification of the thinking subject.   Throughout these passages he uses the
phrase in the wide, loose sense given to the German
Bewusstsein by the school of Wolf.   He stoutly maintains, what no one will deny, that this general consciousness is not a special faculty ; but when he comes to
draw out a list of mental powers, in the second volume
of his *Metaphysics,* he turns to the Scottish use of the
phrase, and he includes among them a special faculty
which he calls consciousness, but to which, for distinction's sake, he prefixes *self,* and designates it self-
consciousness.   It is the office of this special faculty to
" afford us a knowledge of the phenomena of our minds"
(vol. ii. p. 192).   It is an inevitable result of using the
phrases in such ambiguous senses, that we are ever in

danger of passing inadvertently from the one meaning to the other, and making affirmations in one sense which hold good only in another. Hamilton is ever appealing to consciousness, as Locke did to idea, as Brown did to suggestion, and as Mr. Mill does to association, but without our being always sure that the various affirmations are made in the same sense of the term. His appeal to consciousness, both in establishing some of his own positions and in summarily setting aside those of his opponents, is often far too rapid and dogmatic. He represents the principles of common sense as being emphatically "facts of consciousness," whereas they are not so any more specially than our acquired and derived beliefs, which are equally under consciousness. In fact, these principles are not before the consciousness as principles. The individual manifestations are of course before the consciousness (though not more so than any other mental exercise), but not the principles themselves, which are derived from the individual exercises by a reflex process of abstraction and generalization. Consciousness cannot decide directly which of our convictions are intuitive. Consciousness reveals only the present state of mind, and it cannot say whether it is original or derived. That state is probably a very complex one, and may embrace secondary beliefs mixed up with the primary ones ; and if we are to separate these and fix on the true primitive convictions, we must subject the whole to a process of analysis. Again, consciousness can reveal to us only the singular, only the present state as an individual perception ; but

in psychology, as in every other science, we are in search
of the principle, and if we would gather the law out of
the particulars we must generalize. In order, then, to
the discovery even of an " intuitive principle," there
must be what Bacon calls " the necessary rejections and
exclusions," or what Dr. Whewell calls the " decomposition of facts," and then the co-ordination of the facts
into a law by induction. In order, then, to the construction of metaphysics, more is required than a simple
exercise of consciousness or introspection ; there is need
of discursive processes to work the facts into a science.[1]
It is of the utmost moment to remove these misapprehensions out of the way, as Mr. Mill, with his usual
acuteness, has taken advantage of them ; and after he
has shown that introspection cannot do everything, he
leaves upon us the impression that it can do nothing.

But consciousness, after all, is the main instrument
in determining what are first principles. Let us endeavour to ascertain its precise province. The method
followed by Mr. Mill in his psychology (and also in his
political economy) is evidently what he calls the deductive, and which he represents in his *Logic* (B. iii.
chap. xi. sect. i.) as consisting of three operations :
" The first one of direct induction ; the second of ratio
cination ; and the third of verification." Now, of these
three steps the first and the third are, properly speaking, inductive ; they depend entirely on observed facts.
In physical science the agent of observation is the

[1] I may be permitted to mention that I have fully wrought out these
cautionary rules in *The Intuitions of the Mind*, Part First.

senses, aided, it may be, by artificial instruments, and corrected by careful methods as enjoined by modern accuracy. In mental science the observing agent is consciousness. We bend back the mental eye, and observe what is passing within as it passes. As this is often a very difficult and delicate operation, more particularly when thought is rapid and feeling intense, we must resort to other operations, but in which consciousness is still the main instrument. We must by memory bring up the past as much as possible in its entirety, and notice all that is in it. Not only so; in order to correct the narrowness of our personal observations, we must look to external quarters; we must gather what are the convictions of other men from their deeds, ever passing under our notice, and as recorded in history; and from their conversation and their writings, as the expression of human thought and sentiment. This may not be introspection in the narrow sense of the term; still it is inspection of the soul of man, and it may be referred in a general way to self-consciousness, for it is by what we feel within ourselves that we are enabled upon evidence to comprehend the experience of others.

But let it be observed that consciousness, understood in this enlarged sense, has to take the first step, and the final step in the process. It has to observe and gather the original facts which suggest the law. It has again to collect and notice the verifying facts which establish the law. In comparison with these, the intermediate step, the ratiocination, is a subordinate and a dependent one. If the commencing and closing inductions are conducted improperly, the reasoning which issues from them or leads to them will only bind the blunders more closely together. Thus, if in the original observations part of the light has been obstructed, consequential deductions will only widen the shadow,—as the mistake of a wrong datum is only increased by multiplying it. We see this strikingly illustrated in most of our rational systems of philosophy,—as, for instance, in that of Spinoza, who began with an ill-observed account of substance, and ended in the bogs of a horrid pantheism. Again, if in the final observations the facts are mutilated in order to fit them into an ingenious hypothesis, the error is thereby confirmed, and the system-builders feel themselves justified in adhering the more resolutely to a creation of their own minds. We see this exhibited in the history of most of those systems of empiricism which, as Bacon characterizes them, leap and fly at once from particular facts to universal principles, which are supposed to explain all the phenomena, and can easily get instances quoted to support them, found by " a vague and ill-built" observation.

In conducting this work of observation by consciousness, there is a constant temptation to oversight, to hasty conclusions and distorted representations. In physical investigation there is less room for conscious or unconscious deception, as modern research insists on having the phenomena weighed or measured in some way : that we cannot apply such a corrective to the alleged facts of consciousness, constitutes one of the disadvantages under which psychology labours. No doubt, we have immediate access at once to the facts as being in our minds—and this seems to entitle every man to be a metaphysician ; but, from the impossibility of employing a numerical test, there is room for great looseness in the observation and inaccuracy in the statement, and these issue in augmented errors in the results reached by deduction. In these circumstances, there is great need in mental science of intellectual shrewdness, to keep us from mistaking one fact for another, and still greater need of high moral qualities, such as a spirit of self-restraint and caution, of integrity and candour. In particular, great pains must be adopted to guard against taking a part, and overlooking and rejecting the rest, because it may not fit into a pre-conceived theory to which the individual may have committed himself. In order to secure this we must as it were go round the mental phenomena and view them on all sides, and in all their aspects, both in our own minds and in those of others. We must mark their various properties, adding none and subtracting none, lessening none and magnifying none, disguising none and correcting none, but making each stand out in its own form, in its proper action, and with its natural accompaniments. We ought, as Hamilton expresses it, to exhibit each " in its individual integrity, neither distorted nor mutilated, and in its relative place, whether of pre-eminence or subordination " (Appendix to *Reid's Works*, p. 747). Till this careful and candid observation has been completed, we are not at

liberty to begin to analyse or theorize. When we
venture on these processes, all we can do is to dissect
the concrete, to generalize the individual, or find out the
producing cause. But the errors will only multiply
upon us in these steps if we have not commenced with
accurate observations.

Sir W. Hamilton says, "Philosophy is wholly dependent on consciousness" (*Reid's Works*, p. 746). This
is going too far, as philosophy cannot be constructed
without discursive processes. But Mr. Mill has committed a far more serious error, when he says that
" Locke was therefore right in believing that the origin
of our ideas is the main stress of the problem of mental
science, and the subject which must first be considered
in forming the theory of the mind" (p. 147). M. Cousin
seems to me to be altogether right when he lays it down
as a rule, that in psychology we must begin with a
painstaking inquiry into the actual nature of our ideas.
Mr. Mill has thus reversed the order of things, placing
that which is first last, and that which is last first—
putting the theory of ideas before the observation of the
ideas, which evidently holds out great temptations to
him to determine their nature by his theory.

Not that we are precluded from making an inquiry
into the origin of ideas. This is a very fair subject of
investigation, provided always that we acknowledge its
difficulties and its uncertainties, and proceed in a .
cautious manner, and in the proper method. But even
here the main agent must be consciousness, in the sense
which has been explained, that is, as giving us directly

a knowledge of our own mental operations, and indirectly an acquaintance with those of others. In order
to the successful resolution of ideas into their originals,
we have two objects, or classes of objects, to look at.
We have first to consider the ideas or convictions which
we would seek to account for, and, secondly, the elements into which we would resolve them. The first of
these operations must be done by consciousness exclusively. Even in the other and more complicated and
perplexing inquiry, introspection must be the main
agent. No doubt, it is possible that some light may be
thrown on the origin of certain ideas by the brain and
nerves, and in this physiological investigation the instruments must be the eye and the microscope. But
no unconscious action can account for conscious ideas.
The attempt to explain ideas must always proceed by
deriving the more complex from the simpler mental
phenomena. But in the determination of the precise
nature of the simpler mental affections, we are again
thrown back on consciousness. Suppose that the attempt be, as in the school of Mr. Mill, to get our ideas
from sensations, and associations of sensation, we must
begin to determine what sensations are, and what the
laws of association are, by the internal sense. I am quite
willing to adopt Mr. Mill's psychological method, but
only on the condition that we take introspection as our
main instrument of observation.

Mr. Mill tells us that " the proof that any of the
alleged Universal Beliefs or principles of Common Sense
are affirmations of consciousness, supposes two things—

that the beliefs exist, and that they cannot possibly have been acquired" (p. 147). I have no objection to accept these two conditions, with an explanation of the one and a correction of the other.

As to the *first rule*, there are some points which consciousness can settle at once. It lets us know what is our present idea or conviction. This is altogether competent to it, this in fact is its office; its revelations carry their own evidence with them, and from them there is no appeal. This is admitted by Mr. Mill: "Introspection can show a present belief or conviction." "If consciousness tells me that I have a certain thought or sensation, I assuredly have that thought or sensation" (p. 141). Now, in the mature mind there are a vast number and variety of ideas and convictions. We have perceptions, apprehensions, and beliefs, about matter and mind, about time and space, about things changing and things abiding, about the near and the remote, the past and the future, about activity and efficiency, about priority and succession, about cause and effect, about right and wrong, eternity and immensity. Now, it is the office of consciousness to reveal all that is in these ideas, and psychology should begin with attending to its revelations. Mr. Mill refers particularly to the alleged universal beliefs. The word "belief" is unfortunately a very vague one, and may stand for a number of very different mental affections. When I am speaking of first or intuitive principles, I use the term to signify our conviction of the existence of an object not now present, and thus I distinguish "primitive faith" from

" primitive knowledge," in which the object is present. But however wide we may make the application of the phrase, it does not embrace all that is before consciousness. Thus we are capable of immediate knowledge ; we have such in every exercise of self-consciousness, and I maintain also in all perception through the senses. The mind, also, is ever pronouncing judgments, declaring, for instance, that things agree, or that they differ, or that this change indicates a cause. We have not only intellectual operations, we form moral perceptions, and pronounce moral judgments,—as when we decide that kindness is a virtue and cruelty a sin. If we would construct a science of psychology, we must survey carefully these apprehensions, beliefs, and decisions. If we would establish or dis-establish any metaphysical point, we must view, firstly and finally, and all throughout, what is in the mind's notion and conviction. Or if, what is more to our present review, we would resolve any idea into simpler elements, we must determine all that is in the idea by a searching introspection. Consciousness has thus not only to settle that certain ideas or beliefs, or convictions "exist," but ascertain for us all that is in them. Now, it has been repeatedly brought as a charge against the school to which Mr. Mill belongs, that, so far as the deeper notions and beliefs of the mind are concerned, they have never carefully observed, weighed, and measured the phenomenon which they seek to explain by means of such elements as sensations. I believe that this accusation is just, and I hope to substantiate it in the course of this review.

Mr. Mill's *second rule* of proof can be admitted only with a restriction. I allow that it is not so easy a matter as Sir W. Hamilton imagines to determine what is a first principle; and that this cannot be done by an immediate introspection. But is it not demanding too much to require that we are not to accept any beliefs as universal till it has been shown "that they cannot possibly have been acquired"? The burden of proof seems rather to lie on those who maintain they are acquired. . Were any man of science to affirm that hydrogen is not an element, chemists would be quite prepared to listen to him, but they would insist, as a condition of their giving a positive assent, that he should decompose the substance, and until this is accomplished they would continue to regard hydrogen as at least provisionally an elementary body. On a like principle, we should be quite ready to attend to Mr. Mill when he maintains that he can resolve our idea of moral good into simpler elements, but until he brings forward his components, and shows them to be quite sufficient to produce the result, we may surely be allowed to hold that our sense of duty is an ultimate principle.

But instead of thus throwing the *onus probandi* from one side to another, I think it better to avow broadly that the question is not to be settled by possibilities or impossibilities, by *may be* or *cannot be*, but by the ordinary rules of evidence. On the one hand, persons are not to be allowed to imagine that they have resolved an alleged fundamental idea into something else, unless they can explain all that is in the idea by means of some principle competent to produce the idea with all its peculiarities. On the other hand, we are not to assume a conviction to be ultimate till it has been tried by clear and sufficient tests. Such tests, I believe, can be had. Almost all philosophers have appealed to them. We shall find Mr. Mill implicitly admitting them. We shall be able, I hope, to reach a precise expression of them as we advance. Following these general principles, the following rules of proof may help at once to guide and guard inquiry :—

I. *No one is to be allowed to imagine that he has made a successful resolution into simpler elements, of an idea, belief, or conviction, unless he can explain all that is in the mental phenomenon.* It is necessary to enunciate this rule, from the circumstance that it has so often been violated. Hobbes, and the sensational school of France, were able to derive all our ideas from sensation, simply by refusing to look at and to weigh such ideas as those which we have of substance and power, moral good and infinity, so different from mere sensitive affections. It has been shown again and again against Hume, that all our ideas are not copies of impressions,—that we have convictions of the existence of things, of personal identity, and of power, which cannot be traced to impressions, whatever be the meaning attached to that vague phrase. I am convinced Mr. Mill has been guilty of like over-sights, when he would draw all our ideas, even those we have of mind and body, extension, personal identity, causation and moral obligation, from sensations, and associations of sensations : he can appear to himself and his admirers to be successful, solely by not noticing the characteristic qualities of these profound and peculiar ideas. In these dissections, this school of mental anatomists destroys the life, and then declares that it never existed. Mr. Mill defines mind as a series of sensations : we shall see that the phenomenon to be explained is the consciousness of self; that even in sensation we are conscious of self. He describes our conviction of personal identity as a series of sensations, with the mind being aware of itself as a series : I shall show that we know in consciousness a present self and in memory a past self, and that in comparing the two we declare them to be the same. He makes body the possibility of sensations : it will be proven, that in his hypothetical explanation, he utterly fails to render any account of that idea of externality which we attach to matter. He resolves our idea of extension into length of time, and length of time he makes identical with a series of muscular sensations : it will not be difficult to establish the essential difference of the three phenomena which are thus confounded. In treating of ethical questions, he shows that we might be led to do good by motives derived from pleasure and pain : but he has failed to account for the very peculiar ideas involved in such phrases as "duty," "ought," "obligation," "sin," and "reproach."

It has been resolutely maintained by the profoundest philosophers of all ages, that there are certain convictions in the mind which have the characters of self-evidence and necessity. These constitute the "residual, phenomena," which cannot be explained by a gathered

experience, and to account for which we must call in a
new cause. We know, or believe, or judge so and so, on
the bare contemplation of the objects; we must do so,
we cannot do otherwise. Mr. Mill has looked at this
mental phenomenon, and has endeavoured to account
for it in accordance with his general theory by two
principles, which it can be shown miss, and utterly fail
to account for, the peculiarities of our conviction. We
may here look at these for a moment, as illustrating the
importance of our rule, reserving the more thorough discussion of them to future chapters.

It is alleged by the whole school, that our belief in
certain general principles, supposed to be ultimate, can
be accounted for by experience. But the word "experience" is a very uncertain one, and may cover a
number of very different mental actions and affections.
Everything that has been within our consciousness, all
that we have seen or felt, may be said in a vague general
sense to have fallen under experience. In this sense our
intuitions of sense and consciousness, our original beliefs and primitive judgments, all come within our experience. But thus understood, experience can explain
nothing, can be the cause of nothing. The thing experienced may, but not the experience, that is, the mere
consciousness or feeling. As to the thing experienced,
it should not be called experience; and as to what it
may produce, we must determine this by looking at the
nature of the thing, and not at our experience of it.
But there is a sense, and this a very important one, in
which experience can furnish us with a principle, and

this may be mistaken for an intuitive one. Thus we
have observed, not once, or twice, or thrice, or ten
times, but a hundred, a thousand times, that our friends
have been in the habit of speaking the truth, and we
expect them to do so in time to come as they have done
in time past. There have been metaphysicians who
regarded our trust in testimony as an original instinct
of our nature. But it is surely quite competent for
persons to attempt to show that the conviction can
be explained by an early, a lengthened, and a uniform
observation ; and they may be allowed to be successful
when they have proven that the experience is capable
of producing the conviction entertained. Let it be
observed, that when thus employed experience means
an induction of instances to establish a general rule or
law. And I take this opportunity of stating, that when
I have occasion to refer to this power of experience, I
call it a *gathered experience*, to distinguish it from a mere
individual feeling. I admit freely that a gathered experience can generate a strong conviction, such as the
trust we put in testimony, and our belief in the uniformity, or rather uniformities, of nature ; that is, it will
account for all the marks of our convictions on these
subjects, for their gradual formation, for their extent
and their limits,—as when we allow that our friends
may at times commit mistakes in their testimony, or
that there may have been miraculous occurrences in
the midst of the regularities of nature. But then, it is
said that there are, and I hope to show that there are,
convictions of a very different nature, which are as strong

in early youth, and in early stages of society, as in later
life and in more advanced communities, and which
allow of no limitation or exception. As examples, we
may give mathematical axioms, as that two straight
lines cannot enclose a space, and moral maxims, as that
ingratitude for favours deserves reprobation. Our convictions of this description spring up on the bare contemplation of the objects, and need not a wide collection
of instances ; and their necessity and universality cannot be accounted for by a gathered experience. The
school to which Mr. Mill belongs explains the phenomena only by failing to distinguish between two sorts
of convictions, and neglecting to mark the characteristics
of those which announce themselves as self-evident,
necessary, and universal.

But Mr. Mill has another principle, by which he thinks
he can explain the necessity and the unlimited expectation ; this is the law of the association of ideas.
When we have often thought of two things together,
the idea of the one comes invariably, in the end necessarily, to call up the other. Thus Martinus Scriblerus,
having never seen a lord mayor without his fur gown
and gold chain, could never think of a lord mayor
without also thinking of his appendages. But here
again Mr. Mill has missed the characteristic of the
mental phenomenon. " If we find it impossible by any
trial to separate two ideas, we have all the feeling of
necessity the mind is capable of" (p. 264). But this is
to confound two things which are very different, the
association of two ideas, so that the one calls up the

other, with the judgment, which declares that the two
things are necessarily related. When he heard the lord
mayor named, Martin could not but think of his gown
and chain ; but he did not therefore decide that the
mayor and his wig had always been together, that they
would always be together, that it had never been otherwise, and could not be otherwise. The laws of association may account for the rise of one idea along with
another, or immediately after another, but they do not
come near explaining the self-evidence and necessity of
certain cognitions, beliefs, and judgments, which may rise
on the contemplation of single objects perceived for the
first time, or on the immediate comparison of two
objects.

II. *In resolving an alleged fundamental idea or conviction into certain elements, we must assume only known
elements, and we must not ascribe to them more than can
be shown to be in them.* To illustrate what I mean : It
is quite competent to any one to attempt to explain
chemical action by mechanical causes, or vital action by
mechanical and chemical forces. But if he understand
the problem which he hopes to solve, and grapple with
it fairly, he must not give to mechanical action, or
mechanical and chemical action combined, more than
is in them. The whole attempt would be denounced
as a mere pretence if he gave a chemical affinity to
the mechanical power, or a power of assimilation and
absorption to the mechanical and chemical action.
Now we are surely entitled to impose a like restriction

upon the analyst of the human mind. It is perfectly competent to him to attempt to resolve such convictions as those of identity, causation, and moral good, into any other principle. But we can require of him to specify the principle, to prove that it actually works in the mind, to unfold its nature and its laws, and to show from its ascertained action that it is quite sufficient to produce the conviction. In particular, he must not be allowed, when he starts with an element, to add new properties to suit his purpose as he goes along. Or if he does so, he must formally announce the introduction of the new power, specify its nature, and honestly avow it to be a new element.

This is a rule which has been habitually neglected by that school of metaphysicians who delight to reduce all the operations of the mind to a very few principles. Locke succeeded, to his own satisfaction, in deriving all our ideas from sensation and reflection, but it has been shown by distinguished philosophers, British and Continental, that in accounting thus for such ideas as substance, and time, and power, he changed, without perceiving it, the sensations and reflex perceptions into something entirely different. It can be proven that Mr. Mill is ever falling into a like error. The operation by which he derives all our ideas and beliefs from a few elements, is a sort of jugglery, in which he alters the elements without its being discovered; and it may be added, that in the product which he shows, he has not the real phenomenon which he professes to have explained.

The main elements which he employs are sensations and associations of sensation. But he works up sensations into convictions of mind and body, of space and time, of personality and personal identity, of infinity and obligation to do good, which are not contained in the nature of sensations, and which could be imparted to them only by a new power superinduced, which power would require to have a place allotted to it in his system, and its laws enunciated, and its significance estimated. Again, it will be shown that Mr. Mill has made an unwarrantable use and application of the laws of association. These are the laws of the succession of our ideas, and nothing more. Give us two ideas, and place these two ideas together in the mind, and association will tend to bring them up once more in union. But it is not the office of association to give us the ideas which must first be furnished to it. We shall see that Mr. Mill is for ever giving to association a power, which does not belong to it, of generating new ideas by an operation in which we see sensations go in, and a lofty idea coming out, solely by the idea being surreptitiously introduced, without any person being expected to notice it. The process carried on by this whole school of analysts is like that of the alchemists, who, when they put earth into the retort, never could get anything but earth, and could get gold only by introducing some substance containing gold. The philosopher's stone of this modern psychology is of the same character as that employed in mediæval physics. If we put in only sensations, as some do, we have never any thing but sensations, and a "dirt philosophy," as it has been called, is the product. If we get gold (as certainly Mr. Mill does at times), it is because it has been quietly introduced by the person who triumphantly exhibits it.

III. *Tests may be furnished to try intuitive truths.* From the days of Aristotle down to the present time, it has been asserted that there are first truths, the support of other truths, while they themselves require no support. Profound thinkers have systematically or incidentally been striving to give us the marks of such truths. Amidst considerable difference of nomenclature and confusion of thought and statement (such as we might expect in the first efforts to catch and express the exact truth in so difficult an investigation), there has been all along a wonderfully large amount of agreement in the criteria fixed on. These have been such as self-evidence, necessity, and universality. Some have fixed on one, and some on another of these, as their favourite testing principle, and have overlooked the others. Some have employed two, overlooking the third. But these three are, in fact, the tests which, in a loose or more stringent form, have been announced or applied by the great body of deep and earnest thinkers. It could be shown that Aristotle had at least glimpses of all of them. In modern times, Locke formally propounded the self-evidence, referring incidentally from time to time to the necessity and universality. Reid was in the way of referring, not always in a very clear or satisfactory way, to all the three. Leibnitz brought out prominently the necessity; and Kant, followed by Sir W. Hamilton, conjoined necessity and universality—all three overlooking the self-evidence, in consequence of their keeping away very much from realities, and dwelling among mental forms.[1] We shall find Mr. Mill employing all of them, without, however, fully apprehending their character or seeing their significance.

As we proceed, we shall gather these tests into heads, and establish their validity, and give them their proper expression. We shall show that association of ideas, which is supposed to work such wonders, cannot give these characters to any apprehension or proposition. No experiential or derived truth can stand any one, or at least the whole of these tests. A general truth discovered by a gathered experience, as that night succeeds day, cannot be said to be self-evident. Nor can it be represented as having any necessity in thought, for we can easily apprehend it to be otherwise. Nor can it be described as universal, for the time may come when, in consequence of a change of mundane arrangements, the day or the night may cease.

Following out these principles, I mean, in discussing the questions started by Mr. Mill, to proceed in the following method :—

(1.) I allow him to try his power of analysis, according to his psychological method, on all alleged fundamental truth, without reserving any exception. This is what

---

[1] These tests will be considered, *infra*, Chap. xii. A historical and critical review of them will be found in *The Intuitions of the Mind*, Part I. B. ii. c. 3.

Sir W. Hamilton would not have done, as he regarded consciousness as deciding the whole question at once, and authoritatively and conclusively. I hold that consciousness has a most important part to act. It has to disclose to us what are the ideas and convictions in the mind when it begins to reflect, and what is the precise nature of the elements into which we would resolve them. But I admit that in the mature man all is not intuitive that is spontaneous and apparently instantaneous. And so I freely permit Mr. Mill to attempt to decompose any idea into simpler composites. But as he does so, I claim the right to sit by and watch him, lest he unconsciously change the elements in the process; and at the close I carefully inquire whether he has explained all the characteristics of the idea and conviction.

(2.) When he fails, as I believe it will be found that he does fail, in regard to certain mental principles, then I hold that these principles which the acute intellect of Mr. Mill cannot decompose may be regarded as elementary, at least provisionally so; that is, till some abler man (which is not likely to happen) makes the attempt and succeeds.

(3.) I bring the alleged first truths to the test of self-evidence, necessity, and universality, and when they can stand these criteria, I pronounce them conclusively to be original and primary and fundamental.

CHAPTER III.

MR. MILL'S ADMISSIONS.

THE common impression regarding Mr. Mill's philosophy is that it needs no intuitive principles; that
the author of it does not presuppose or allow that there
is anything innate in the mind. Some of his admirers
give him credit for weaving a rich fabric without any
material except sensations, and with no machinery
except experience. Mr. Mill's cavils against those who
support fundamental truth, and the manner in which
he expounds his own system, are fitted to leave this
impression. He begins the construction of his theory
with sensations; he goes on to fashion them into various
forms by association of sensations; he allows among
the series of sensations a memory of the past, an expectation of the future, and a power of observing coexist-
ences and successions, resemblances and differences
between sensations; and he makes the mind as it advances receive powerful aid from the artificial instrumentality of language. These seem, at least to a cursory
observer, to constitute the matter and the agency by
which he ingeniously constructs the ideas, many of

them so grand and far-ranging, which the mind of man
is capable of forming. But while these seem to be the
original furniture of the mind and the sum of the
assumptions he has to make, we find if we look more
carefully that in rearing his fabric he is ever and anon
calling in other principles, some of them openly and
avowedly, and others unconsciously and furtively; and
that these form when placed together a huge but ill-
fashioned and incongruous body of what are in fact,
whatever he may call them, intuitive principles or
metaphysical truth.

It will be found, indeed, that the mental analysts,
whose ambition it has been to reduce the original
capacities of the mind to a very small number, have
been obliged to bring in a vast body of assumptions
and new elements as they advance. Locke satisfied
himself that he had derived all our ideas from sensation and reflection, but then he called in faculties to
work upon the materials thus furnished; he finds ideas
" suggested " as these powers operate; he gives an important function to "intuition," and supposes the mind
capable of discovering " necessary" relations. Even
Hume, who of all metaphysicians is disposed to make
fewest admissions, remarks in criticising Locke, " I
" should desire to know what can be meant by asserting
" that self-love, or resentment of injuries, or passion be-
" tween the sexes, is not innate " (*Works*, vol. iv. p. 23).
The Sensational School made all our ideas transformed
sensations; but in order to get such ideas as those
of personal identity, power, and duty, they quietly gave

the transforming act a power of transmuting one thing into another. I am now to show how many principles Mr. Mill has been obliged to call in, as he goes along, in order to explain the actual phenomena of the mind on his hypothesis. I must give considerable extracts in order to do justice at once to his views and my argument. The admissions are no doubt candidly made, and they are always clearly stated. Our readers must judge as to how far they affect the apparent simplicity and modify the logical consistency of his system. As I may have occasion to refer to them in the course of the discussion, I number and designate them by the letters of the Greek alphabet.

a. There is an immediate and intuitive knowledge. His language is express. "We do know some things " immediately and intuitively" (p. 126).

β. From the truths known by intuition, others are inferred. "Truths are known to us in two ways; some " are known directly and of themselves, and some " through the medium of other truths. The former are " the subject of intuition or consciousness, the latter of " inference. The truths known by intuition are the " original premisses from which all others are inferred" (*Logic*, Introd. § 4).

γ. Reasoning carries us back to intuition, from which it derives its ultimate premisses. He thus follows up the passage last quoted: "Our assent to the conclusion " being grounded upon the truth of the premisses, we " never could arrive at any knowledge by reasoning, " unless something could be known antecedently to

" reasoning." And in the work more immediately under review : " Unless, therefore, we knew something imme-
" diately, we could not know anything mediately, and
" consequently could not know anything at all" (p. 126).
Elsewhere he says First Principles cannot be proven :
" To be incapable of proof by reasoning is common to all
" first principles : of our knowledge as well as of our
" conduct" (*Utilitarianism*, p. 51).

These statements are very satisfactory as to the existence of intuition, and the place occupied by it, and the
purpose served by it. He does not in these passages
state the grounds on which he admits intuition, nor the
tests by which he would try it. These, however, may
come out incidentally as we advance. Let us inquire
what he represents as exercises of intuition.

δ. *Consciousness is a form of intuition.* This is implied throughout, and will be shown to be so by the
passages quoted under other heads.

ε. *Whatever consciousness reveals is to be received.*
" According to all philosophers the evidence of con-
" sciousness, if only we can obtain it pure, is con-
" clusive" (p. 126). " If consciousness tells me that I
" have a certain thought or sensation, I assuredly have
" that thought or sensation " (p. 141).

ζ. Consciousness and intuitive convictions are arbiters
from which there is no appeal. " The verdict of con-
" sciousness, or, in other words, our immediate and
" intuitive conviction, is admitted on all hands to be a
" decision without appeal " (p. 127).

η. *The truth revealed by consciousness rests on its own*

evidence. " All the world admits, with our author, that
" it is impossible to doubt a fact of internal conscious-
" ness.   To feel, and not to know that we feel, is an
" impossibility.   But Sir William Hamilton is not
" 'satisfied to let this truth rest on its own evidence.
" He wants a demonstration of it.   As if it were not suf-
" ficiently proved by consciousness itself, he attempts to
" prove it by a *reductio ad absurdum* " (p. 132).   He then
criticises, I think justly, Sir William Hamilton's proof,
which he says carries us " round a long circuit to return
" to the point from which we set out."   " He has deduced
" the trustworthiness of consciousness from the veracity
" of the Deity ; and the veracity of the Deity can only be
" known from the evidence of consciousness " (p. 138).
Mr. Mill himself would have the truth " rest on its own
" evidence."   I rejoice in this appeal.   For what is this
ultimate test but that of *Self-Evidence,* so often enunciated, or at least referred to and implied in the writings
of profound thinkers, from Aristotle downwards, and
among others, very expressly by Locke ?   Nothing can
be clearer or more satisfactory than Mr. Mill's language :
" We know intuitively what we know by its own evi-
" dence—by direct apprehension of the fact."

θ. *It is impossible to doubt or deny the facts made
known by consciousness.*   " A real fact of consciousness
" cannot be doubted or denied " (p. 134).   What is this
but the other famous test of first truths, the test of
Necessity appealed to by Plato, Aristotle, Leibnitz, Kant,
and so many other profound thinkers of ancient and
modern times ?   Already, then, we have the two tests of

Self-Evidence and Necessity sanctioned. In the passage quoted under last head he had, as most philosophers have done, mixed them up together as being intimately connected. " It is impossible to doubt a fact of internal " consciousness. To feel, and not to know that we feel, " is an impossibility :" and so he would have the truth " rest on its own evidence." The law of necessity is repeatedly appealed to. " The facts which cannot be " doubted are those to which the word *consciousness* is " by most philosophers confined; the facts of internal " consciousness; the mind's own acts and affections. " What we feel, we cannot doubt that we feel. It is " impossible for us to feel, and to think perhaps that " we feel not, or to feel not, and think perhaps that we " feel " (p. 132). Sir William Hamilton has nowhere made a more decisive use of the law of necessity and principle of contradiction than Mr. Mill has done in these passages.

ι. *No man ever doubted of the facts of consciousness.* " Consciousness in the sense usually attached to it by " philosophers, consciousness of the mind's own feelings " and operations, cannot, as our author truly says, be " disbelieved. The inward fact, the feeling in our " minds, was never doubted, since to do so would be to " doubt that we feel what we feel " p. 141). As in a passage previously quoted, the tests of self-evidence and necessity were joined, so in this the tests of Necessity and *Universality* (universality of conviction) are com bined, and the universality is traced to the necessity. The fact " was never doubted," since to do so would be to doubt that we feel what we feel, which is represented as impossible. We thus find the tests of intuition, as I cursorily sketched them in last chapter, and mean to unfold them more fully in a future chapter, employed by Mr. Mill, and in the very logical order in which I have placed them. He makes an appeal to self evidence; the truth " rests on its own evidence." He tests this by the principle that " to feel, and not to know that " we feel, is an imposibility." And now we find him appealing to catholicity or common consent, and founding it on necessity, the fact " was never doubted," since it " cannot be disbelieved."

κ. *In arguing with the sceptic we are entitled to call in the assurance of immediate knowledge as a test.* " I put " to him (the sceptic) the simplest case conceivable of " immediate knowledge, and ask, if we ever feel any- " thing? If so, then, at the moment of feeling, do we " know that we feel? Or if he will not call this " knowledge, will he deny that we have a feeling, we " have at least some sort of assurance, or conviction, of " having it? This assurance or conviction is what " other people mean by knowledge. If he dislikes the " word, I am willing, in discussing with him, to employ " some other. By whatever name this assurance is " called, it is the test to which we bring all our convic- " tions " (p. 126). This passage has not the logical power of some of Hamilton's arguments, but it is alto-gether after his manner. I have quoted it to show, that Mr. Mill thinks himself justified in appealing to the assurance of consciousness as an ultimate and decisive test.

λ. *The revelations of consciousness, together with what can be inferred from them, constitute the sum of our know-ledge.* " What consciousness directly reveals, together " with what can be legitimately inferred from its reve- " lations, composes, by universal admission, all that we " know of the mind, or indeed any other thing " (p. 107). I do not admit that this statement is correct. unless he make consciousness synonymous with intuition, and include the senses and our primitive beliefs, which also contribute, and this largely, to what we know. I quote it to show how deep a place our author allots to the revelations of consciousness.

These admissions all relate to Consciousness, the word being used, however, now in a wider and now in a narrower sense ; sometimes being coextensive with intui-tion, as when (see ζ.) he speaks of " consciousness, or in " other words, immediate and intuitive conviction ;" and in other passages meaning (see ι.) " consciousness of the " mind's own feelings and operations." In the heads that follow, his admissions relate to facts it may be attested by consciousness, but not beyond it.

μ. *We may be sure of what we see as well as of what we feel.* " What one sees or feels, whether bodily or men- " tally, one cannot but be sure that one sees or feels " (*Logic,* Introd. § 4). This is a satisfactory statement, but he afterwards detracts from it by observing that we often suppose that we see what we do not see, and he is evidently doubtful whether we see anything beyond ourselves. This topic will require to be carefully examined in a future chapter. Meanwhile I bring forward the statement to show, that if it can be proven that we do intuitively see external objects, and that our intuitions of externality and extension are not resolvable into anything simpler, then we must be prepared to grant that the objects exist. Speaking elsewhere of the "first premisses of our knowledge," he says, that " being matters of fact they may be the sub-" ject of a direct appeal to the faculties which judge of " fact, namely, our senses and our internal conscious-" ness" (*Utilitarianism*, p. 51).

v. We know existence, and make assertions about exist-ence. Thus he places existence among his categories, and does not attempt to resolve it into anything else. " Besides the propositions which assert sequence or Co-" existence, there are some which assert simple exist-" ence," etc. (*Logic*, B. i. v. § 5, 6).

ξ. *We are capable of experiencing and knowing sen-sations.* We need not produce passages or references to prove this, for the evidence of it runs throughout his works.

o. *Pleasure and pain are what we feel them to be, and nothing else.* Speaking of these he says of Hamilton, that " he is not so much the dupe of words as to sup-" pose that they are anything else than what we feel " them to be " (p. 479).

π. *Extension is an essential part of the concept of body.* " The truth is, that the condition of space cannot be " excluded ; it is an essential part of the concept of body, " and of every kind of bodies " (p. 327). This is not an adequate statement, but it implies that man has at least one necessary concept as to body, and I shall endeavour to show that this cannot be resolved into sensation or association.

ρ. *There is evidently an ultimate fact in memory.* " Our belief in the veracity of Memory is evidently ulti- " mate : no reason can be given for it which does not pre- " suppose the belief, and assume it to be well-grounded" (p. 174). This statement appears in a foot-note,[1] and

[1] Mr. Mill makes the admission frankly and candidly, but he was driven to it by a criticism of Dr. Ward :—"I would ask of these philosophers " (those who build wholly upon Experience), do they mean by ' experience ' " the experience of the present moment, or do they include past experi- " ence also ? If they say the former, I reply it is obviously false that " they *do* in any sense build their philosophy wholly or chiefly on experi- " ence. But if they answer (as they most certainly will) that they *do* in- " clude past experience as well as present, then again I deny their allega- " tion, that they build their philosophy wholly on experience." " How " can you even guess what your past experience has been ? By trusting " memory. But how do you prove that those various intuitive judgments, " which we call acts of memory, *can* rightly be trusted ? So far from this " being provable by past experience, it must be in each case *assumed* and " *taken for granted* before you can have any cognizance whatever of your " past experience." " As it is most desirable to bring this point quite " clearly home, I will cite and apply a passage in which Mr. Stuart Mill " states his own philosophical doctrine. ' There is no knowledge *a priori* ; " no truths cognizable by the mind's inward light, and grounded on in- " tuitive evidence. Sensation and the mind's consciousness of its own " acts are not only the exclusive sources, but the sole materials of our " knowledge.' Let us test, then, by these principles an act of memory. " I am at this moment comfortably warm ; but I call to mind with great " clearness the fact, that a short time ago I was very cold. What datum " does ' sensation' give me ? Simply that I am now warm. What datum " does ' consciousness' give ? that I have the *present impression* of " having been cold a short time ago. But both these data are altogether " wide of the mark. The question which I would earnestly beg Mr. Mill " to ask himself is this :—What is my ground for believing that I *was* " cold a short time ago ? ' I have the present *impression* of having been " cold a short time ago ;' this is one judgment. ' I *was* cold a short time " ago :' this is a totally distinct and separate judgment. There is no " necessary, nor even any probable, connexion between these two judg- " ments,—no ground whatever for thinking that the truth of one follows " from the truth of the other,—except upon the hypothesis that my mind is

our author does not even try to show how it fits into his system. The justification of the principle will fall under our notice under another head. Meanwhile I call attention to the admission. He declares that memory carries with it its own veracity, and that our belief in that veracity is "ultimate," and "evidently ultimate." I shall endeavour to show that the full facts of memory are not embraced in this brief statement. But there is much stated, and there is more implied. He here concedes fully that there is a "veracity" in at least one other faculty of the mind besides internal consciousness, that there is a "belief" that can be trusted, and that this belief is "ultimate," is in fact "evidently ultimate." He who allows so much might have inquired whether there may not be other beliefs of the same kind, and equally veracious, involved in the exercise of other faculties of the mind. Mr. Mill is constantly and terribly severe in his strictures on the Intuitive School of Philosophy; but it is clear he himself belongs to an intuitive school, without knowing or at least avowing it. Admitting an intuitive consciousness and an ultimate belief, he makes no attempt to show how far they modify his empirical philosophy, and he enters upon no scientific investigation of the

---

" so constituted as accurately to represent past facts. But how will either
" 'sensation' or 'consciousness,' or the two combined, in any way suffice
" for the establishment of any such proposition?" (*On Nature and Grace*,
1860, pp. 26-28). The *Philosophical Introduction* is the work of a
mind of extraordinary acuteness, and has unfolded many important philosophical truths. Published at the same time as the first edition of my work
on *The Intuitions of the Mind*, both Dr. Ward and myself have noticed
curious coincidences in the two works.

nature, the laws, or the mode of operation of these elements of our nature.

σ. The mind, whatever it be, is aware of itself, is aware of itself as a series of feelings, is aware of itself as past and present. The statements he makes are very curious : " Our notion of Mind, as well as of Matter, is " the notion of a permanent something, contrasted with " the perpetual flux of the sensations and other feelings " or mental states which we refer to it" (p. 205). "If " we speak of the Mind as a series of feelings, we are " obliged to complete the statement by calling it a series " of feelings which is aware of itself as past and future." Again, if but a series of feelings, it "can be aware of itself as a series" (pp. 212, 213). I shall have to subject this language to a sifting examination in the two next chapters, where it will be shown that it does not fairly or fully embody the facts of which we are conscious. I quote it at present to show that Mr. Mill is obliged to allow that there is something permanent in mind, and that the mind is in a sense aware of itself and of this permanence.

The above seem to be very much of the nature of those first or original principles which the Intuitive School of Metaphysicians, to which Mr. Mill is so much opposed, are in the way of putting forward. Those that I am now to state seem to be of the nature of laws or faculties operating in the mind. No doubt, as we are ever being told, we prove that they exist by observation. But while it is by experience we discover them and learn their nature, they must

operate prior to our experience, and independent
of it.

τ. *There is a native law of expectation.* He tells us
that the psychological method which he adopts " postu-
" lates, first, that the human mind is capable of Expec-
" tation. In other words, that after having had actual
" sensations, we are capable of forming the conception
" of Possible sensations ; sensations which we are not
" feeling at the present moment, but which we might
" feel, and should feel if certain conditions were present,
" the nature of which conditions we have, in many cases,
" learnt by experience" (p. 190). Almost all metaphysicians have postulated, that the mind has a capacity
and a tendency which prompt it to look forward from
the past and present to the future. They have done so
because internal observation shows that there must be
some such principle, and they have endeavoured to give
the proper expression of it : some describing it (unfor
tunately, as I think) as an expectation that the future
will resemble the past ; others (also unfortunately, as I
think) as a belief in the uniformity of nature ; by
others, more philosophically, as a belief in the identity
of self and of other objects, together with a conviction
that the same agents, acting as a cause, will produce
the same effects. But it does not concern us at present
to inquire what is the accurate and adequate expression
of the law (this discussion will be taken up as we
advance) ; only, I may remark, that Mr. Mill's version
seems to me to be about the most defective and confused I have met with, experience being the arbiter, for

he makes a series of feelings, each one of which must pass away before another appears, expect something of itself. It is satisfactory, however, to find him granting that there is such a law ; and surely he cannot object to others making a like postulate, and endeavouring to give an account of it which they regard as being more in accordance with our conscious experience.

v. There are original laws of association. The psychological theory " postulates, secondly, the laws of the " Association of Ideas." Then follows an enumeration of these laws. It is unnecessary to give it at this place ; it will subsequently fall under our notice and review. It does not seem to me to be the best in our language ; and we shall find that he enormously exaggerates the power of association. I refer to it at present to show that he is admitting at this place a new law, or rather group of laws operating in the mind.

φ. *The mind can form very lofty ideas as to the Infinite and the Absolute.* In this respect he adopts deeper and in some respects juster views than those of Hamilton. " Something infinite is a conception which, like most " of our complex ideas, contains a negative element, " but which contains positive elements also. Infinite " space for instance : is there nothing positive in that ? " The negative part of this conception is the absence of " bounds. The positive are, the idea of space, and of " space greater than any finite space, so of infinite " duration," etc. Again, " Absolute, in reference to any " given attribute, signifies the possession of that attri " bute in finished perfection and completeness. A being

" absolute in knowledge, for example, is one who knows,
" in the literal meaning of the term, everything. Who
" will pretend that this conception is negative or un-
" meaning to us" (pp. 45, 47). This is a very just account,
so far as it goes, of our apprehension of the infinite and
perfect[1]—a better phrase than the absolute. Mr. Mill
does not say that this conception implies any intuitive
capacity ; in fact, he neglects to tell us how it is
formed. Whether ultimate or not, it is acknowledged
that the mind has such a conception ; and Mr. Mill, if
he account for it on his psychological theory, will require to bring in something much deeper than the sensations and associations of sensation, from which he
seems to draw our ideas.

We have yet to look at some other laws which look
excessively like the first or ultimate truths, which
metaphysicians of the Intuitive School have been in the
way of enunciating and employing.

χ. *Beliefs are ultimate when no reason can be given for
them which does not imply their existence and veracity.*
I have already (see ρ.) given the passage which autho-
rizes this law. After stating that belief in the veracity
of memory is evidently ultimate, he adds, " No reason
" can be given for it which does not presuppose the
" belief, and assume it to be well grounded." After an-
nouncing this principle, he might have been expected
to inquire whether it does not sanction other cognitions

---

[1] I have endeavoured to show (*Intuitions of the Mind*, Pt. II. B. ii. c. 3)
that we have a positive notion of some thing as infinite, say space or time,
or Deity, and that we regard that thing as (1.) ever exceeding our widest
image or notion, and (2.) such that nothing can be added to it.

and beliefs, such as those which we have of the externality
and extension of bodies, and the existence of time and
of an abiding self. It can be shown that every attempt
to derive these from other elements presupposes the
ideas and the convictions.

ψ. *There are truths implied in other truths necessarily,
and according to an ultimate law, internal or external.*
He is speaking of logical Proprium, and of its being involved in the attribute which the name ordinarily or
specially connotes; and he affirms, that "whether a
"Proprium follows by demonstration or by causation, it
"follows *necessarily;* that is to say, it *cannot but* follow
"consistently with some law which we regard as a part
"of the constitution either of our thinking faculty or of
"the universe" (*Logic,* B. I. c. vii. § 7). As I understand this statement, it implies that when a Proprium
follows by demonstration, it does so according to a law
which is part of the "constitution" of our "thinking
faculty." The language reminds us of that of Reid and
Hamilton.

ω. *Any assertion which conflicts with the Fundamental
Laws of Thought is to us unbelievable, and this may very
possibly proceed from the native structure of the mind.*
His language is very remarkable. He is speaking of
the three Fundamental Laws of Thought,—those of
Identity, Contradiction, and Excluded Middle, and he
thus comments upon them: "Whether the three so-
"called Fundamental Laws are laws of our thoughts by
"the native structure of the mind, or merely because
"we perceive them to be universally true of observed

" phenomena, I will not positively decide : but they are
" laws of our thoughts, now and invincibly so.   They
" may or may not be capable of alteration by experi-
" ence, but the conditions of our existence deny to us
" the experience which would be required to alter them.
" Any assertion, therefore, which conflicts with one of
" these laws—any proposition, for instance, which
" asserts a contradiction, though it were on a subject
" wholly removed from the sphere of our experience, is
" to us unbelievable.   The belief in such a proposition
" is, in the present constitution of nature, impossible as
" a mental fact " (p. 418).   The language is cautious
and hesitating.   It is evident that he would fain explain
the incapacity of believing contradictory propositions
by his favourite law of association.   We shall see as we
advance that this law cannot explain our peculiar conviction, but meanwhile it is interesting to notice that
he will not decide whether these fundamental principles
may not be " laws of our thoughts by the native structure of the mind."   The hesitation implies a doubt of
the whole system of empiricism.

Some of my readers in looking at these passages thus
brought into convenient (or inconvenient) juxtaposition,
may require to be assured that I have not taken them
from Hamilton's works, instead of the *Examination of
Hamilton* and other works of Mr. Mill.   And were it not
that in the expression of them they have not the homeli-
ness and depth of Reid, nor the clinching logical grasp
of Hamilton, they might be mistaken for utterances of

the two great Scottish metaphysicians. I have allowed Mr. Mill to speak for himself. All that I have done is to cull out the scattered statements as to ultimate truth, and present them *in relievo*, that students of philosophy may mark their significance. I mean to refer to them from time to time in the coming discussion ; but I do not make use of them simply as concessions by Mr. Mill. I would not think it worth while employing a mere *argumentum ad hominem*. I feel no pleasure in pointing out real or seeming incongruities in the metaphysical system of an eminent thinker, who, in other departments, such as political economy and inductive logic, has done so much to advance knowledge. I employ these admissions because they contain important truth, not always in the best form, but capable of being fully vindicated.

Mr. Mill, I believe, would urge that many of the admissions thus made are not separate and distinct from each other, and that several of them might be included under one head. Be it so, it is nevertheless of advantage to have them spread out in the several shapes in which they are presented, the more so that some of these imply very important principles with far-looking results.

The first principles thus avowed in the course of his exposition should have had a formal place allotted them in the system, say at the commencement or the close. Had this been done it would have utterly destroyed the apparent simplicity, and I believe also the symmetry of his system, which would have been seen to be a very complex and heterogeneous one. Seemingly a continuation of the philosophies of Hobbes, Condillac, and Hume, it contains as many assumptions as are demanded by the Scottish metaphysicians, who appeal to fundamental laws of thought, or by the German metaphysicians, who stand up for *a priori* forms.

It will not be difficult to show, as we proceed to take up one special topic after another, that these admissions logically imply vastly more than is conceded in the metaphysical system constructed. In particular, it will be proven that they are made on avowed or implied principles, such as those of the veracity of consciousness, and of ultimate beliefs, such as those of self-evidence, necessity, and universality, which require that vastly more be conceded.

Already it is clear that the question between Mr. Mill and the school he opposes cannot be said to be one as to the existence of intuition. I am not sure that any judicious defender of fundamental truth would demand or postulate a greater number of first principles than those allowed by the most influential opponent of necessary truth in our day. The question is not one as to the reality, but as to the nature and significance of ultimate truth.

Of this I am sure, that the pressing philosophical want of our day is an exposition, with an enumeration and classification of the intuitions of the mind which, we have seen, must be admitted even by those who are supposed to deny them. It is time that those who allow them incidentally should be required to avow them openly and formally, and give a separate place to them. A flood of light will be thrown on metaphysics, and a world of logomachy between rival schools scattered, when we have an earnest attempt, by one competent for the work, to unfold the laws of our intuitions and their mode of operation.

CHAPTER IV.

SENSATIONS.

IN the school to which Mr. Mill has attached him-self, there is a perpetual reference to Sensation. Those who look into their works with the view of discover-ing the deeper properties or higher affections of the mind, are wearied by the everlasting recurrence of the word, and by the perpetual obtrusion of the thing denoted by it.[1] Some members of the school seem to be incapable of comprehending anything but matter, and the sensations excited by matter. I bring no such charge against Mr. Mill. He is clearly capable of mounting into a higher and more spiritual region. But even he is often dragged down to the dust of the earth by the weight of the theory which he has under-

[1] The mental sciences elevate those who study them in proportion as they exhibit the higher faculties and ideas of the mind. This leads me to remark, that in the Competitive Examinations which now exercise so great an influence on the studies of our young men, care should be taken that the Examiners in Morals should not be taken mainly from the Sensational School, and that they be kept from so setting their questions, as to en-courage the reading only of the works of writers belonging to that school. In those departments in which the mental sciences have a place, they are surely meant to stimulate and to test a different order of tastes and talents from those called forth by the physical and physiological sciences.

taken to support. As we are threatened with a revival, under a new and disguised, and somewhat more elevated form, of the Sensational system which wrought such mischief in France at the end of last century, it is essential that we inquire what sensation is, and settle what it can do, and what it cannot do. In other words, let us, with the internal sense as our informant, look carefully at the original matter out of which Mr. Mill draws our higher ideas, with the view of determining whether the seed is fitted to yield such fruit.

What then is Sensation? It is allowed on all hands that it cannot be positively defined. This arises from its being a simple quality, and there is nothing simpler into which to resolve it. All we can do in the way of unfolding its nature, is to bid every man consult his consciousness when any bodily object is affecting his senses or sensibility. But while we cannot furnish an affirmative definition, we can offer some explanations to remove misapprehensions, and some decided denials to oppose accepted errors.

It should be understood that the word is employed to denote an affection of the conscious mind (whatever that may be), and not of the mere bodily frame. It should further be borne in mind that it does not include that knowledge of bodily objects, of their externality and extension, which is now denoted by the phrase 'sense-perception.' It is of special importance to press attention to the circumstance that sensation is not a separately existing object like this stone, this tree, or this bird, but is an attribute of an object. At this point we are coming in collision with Mr. Mill. Elsewhere (*Logic*, B. I. c. iii.) he has an ingenious distribution of nameable things or realities into substances, attributes, and feelings, the last of course including sensations. " Substances are not all that exist : attributes, " if such things are to be spoken of, must be said to exist, " --feelings certainly exist." " Feelings, or states of con- " sciousness, are assuredly to be counted among realities, " but they cannot be reckoned among substances or " attributes." This distribution of realities, especially this separation of feelings from substances or attributes, seems to me to be curious : I have not met with it elsewhere. It is favourable to Mr. Mill's purpose, which we did not so well know when we had only his work on Logic, but with which we are now made fully acquainted by the fuller exposition of his views in the Examination of Hamilton : that purpose being to banish, to as great a distance as possible, substance and attribute, and leave only feelings. We are not yet sufficiently advanced, in these discussions, to deal with the confused metaphysics of substance and attribute. The present topic is sensation, and sensation I maintain is an affection, that is an attribute, of the conscious mind.

But Mr. Mill tells us that " the sensations are all of which I am directly conscious" (*Logic*, B. I. c. iii. § 7). This mode of representing our conscious states was introduced by Hume, who derived his sceptical conclusions from it. He maintained that we are conscious only of impressions and ideas, the ideas being merely fainter impressions. Hume took care never to enter into any explanation as to what he meant by " impression ;" whether it implies, as it should do if it has any meaning, a thing impressing and a thing impressed. The doctrine of the school of Mill is that we are conscious merely of feelings, and among these, the first and all along the main place is given to sensation. Now, in opposition to these defective statements, I maintain that we are conscious, not of a mere impression, but of a thing impressed, not of sensation apart, but of self as sentient. On hearing this statement, metaphysicians will be disposed to ask with amazement, perhaps with scorn, " What! are we really then conscious of self?" And they will tell us that the child has never said to itself, " This is I." If they think it worth while going any further, they may then in condescension, or compassion towards our ignorance, explain to us that the Ego is a metaphysical notion, the product of advanced reflection. But I disarm all this at once, by allowing that we are never conscious of a self, apart from self as sentient, or as engaged in thinking, willing, or some other operation. And I balance this statement by another, that we are just as little conscious of the sensation, or the impression, or the thought, or volition apart from self. The child has never said to itself, " This is I :" but just as little has it said, " This is an impression :" " This is a sensation." We are in fact conscious of both in one concrete act ; ever conscious of self in its present affection, conscious of self as affected. Mr. Mill uses language which implies this when he says (§ 4) that " sensations are states of the sentient mind ;" and every body employs like expressions if he does not happen to be upholding a special theory. He who leaves out either of these elements, is not giving a correct interpretation of consciousness. We may, by abstraction, separately contemplate the two, and important intellectual purposes are served by such a process. Each of the things we thus distinguish in thought has a real existence ; the one as much as the other : the sensation or feeling has an existence, but so has also the self. Not that either has a separate existence, or an independent existence, or an existence out of the other. As the one is an abstract, so is also the other. If you call the one, say the self, a metaphysical entity, you should in consistency describe the other, the sensation, as in the same sense a metaphysical entity. The correct statement is that we are *conscious of the sensation as a sensation of self*, and *of the self as under sensation.* And as we can never be conscious of the self, except as sentient or otherwise affected, so we can never be conscious of a sensation except as a sensation of a sentient self. It is high time, when physiologists and metaphysicians are drawing such perverted conclusions, to put this seemingly insignificant and yet really important limitation upon the common statement.

I am quite willing that Mr. Mill should apply the sharp razor of his Psychological Method to sensation. I have called in consciousness to declare what is in sensation, but I do not allow consciousness to decide at once, and without further inquiry, that sensations are and must be primary and elementary. I freely allow the mental analyst to put them in his crucible, and to try if he can decompose them. No such attempt has been made; I believe no such attempt will ever be made. Mr. Mill and his school acknowledge that they are unresolvable and ultimate. I am glad to have one element allowed,—it may prepare the way for the admission of others on the same title. In particular, the self (I will show in next chapter) may turn out to be quite as unresolvable as the sensations of self.

As so much is made of sensations by this whole school of philosophy, we must be careful to inquire what is really embraced in them, and not allow anything to be drawn from them which is not truly in them. It is necessary in these times to utter even such a truism as this, that a sensation is a sensation, and is nothing more. A sensation is not a thing extended, is not extension, is not space. A sensation being only momentarily under consciousness, is not the same as time, which has a past and a future. A sensation is not matter or body, which is extended and occupies space. A sensation may be preceded by resistance, but is not itself resistance, which implies one body opposing the movement of another. It is important even to make the further statement, that we are conscious of many other mental acts and affections which are not identical with sensations. A sensation is not memory, say the remembrance of my reading Mr. Mill's book at a particular time. A sensation is not expectation, the expectation which I cherish that truth will in the end prevail over error. A sensation is not an imagination, as when I paint a glorious ideal of beauty or of virtue. A sensation is not judgment, even when that judgment is about sensation, as when I decide that the sensations produced by a noise are not so pleasant as those excited by music. Certainly, sensation is not reasoning, as when I argue that mere sentient affections cannot yield our higher ideas and deeper convictions. Sensation is not even the same as emotion, as when I fear that the sensational philosophy is to prevail for a time in this country. A sensation is something far lower than sentiment or affection, as when I would love God and my neighbours,—even those from whom I differ in most important points. A sensation is not a volition, as when I resolve to do my best to oppose prevailing error,—even when countenanced by influential names.

But may not sensation be the cause of something else? I can answer this question only after giving an explanation. In ordinary mundane action, an effect is always the result of the operation of more than one agent or antecedent. " A man," says Mr. Mill, " takes " mercury, goes out of doors, and catches cold. We say, " perhaps, that the cause of his taking cold was ex- " posure to the air. . . . But to be accurate, we ought to " say that the cause was exposure to the air while under " the effect of mercury" (*Logic*, B. III. c. v. § 3). I agree with this doctrine of Mr. Mill (it will be expounded more fully in chapter xiii. of this treatise), and I would apply it to the supposed causative influence of sensations. Sensation may be one of the antecedents which go to make up the cause, but it cannot, pro-

perly speaking, be a cause in itself; it is a condition or
occasion, and can produce an effect only when conjoined with some other agent. A sensation may be the
occasion of something else,—say of a violent derangement
of a bodily organ; but that derangement is not the
sensation, and in accounting for it we must look not
merely to the sensation, but the properties of the organ
affected. A sensation may, in like manner, be the occasion of a new thought arising, but the thought should
not be confounded with the sensation; the sensation
is not even the cause of the thought. Such a sensation in a plant (supposing it to be capable of feeling),
such a sensation in one of the lower animals, would
give rise to no such thought. The sensation can originate the thought only by stirring up a mental capacity in the soul, which mental potency is to be regarded
as the main element in the complex cause. And yet
this essential element is inexcusably, culpably overlooked by the Sensational School, when they derive all
our thoughts from sensations. They make the mere
auxiliary or stimulating condition the producing power,
as if, to use a homely illustration, we should make the
setting of the pointer, which roused the attention of the
sportsman, the cause of the killing of the bird shot by
him. The mind of man, consciousness being the witness, does entertain a vast variety of ideas, some of them
of a very elevating character, such as those we entertain
of God, and good, and eternity. I doubt whether these
are the product of sensations in any sense. Of this I
am sure, that they do not proceed from sensations ex-

cept when sensations are employed and moulded by lofty mental faculties, which faculties, and not the sensations, are the main agents in the production of the effect; and they should have their nature, laws, and modes of action unfolded by any one who would give us a correct theory of our mental operations.

By insisting on such points as these, we lay an effectual arrest on those rash speculations of our day which derive man's loftiest ideas from so low and subordinate an agent as sensation.

CHAPTER V.

MIND, PERSONALITY, PERSONAL IDENTITY, SUBSTANCE.

Mr. MILL admits fully the veracity of consciousness and the reality of the facts attested by it (see δ, ε, η). But his view of the objects of which it is cognisant is very defective. It seems to be derived, through Mr. James Mill and Dr. Thomas Brown, from Hume and the Sensational School of France. Condillac, and those who followed him, designated all the states of the mind by the words *sentir* and *sensibilité*, which conveniently embraced two such different things as sensations excited by outward objects, and mental emotions, such as hope and fear. We have no such pliable word in our tongue, and Brown, who caught so much of the French spirit, had to adopt a narrower phrase when he habitually represents all states of mind as Feelings : thus he speaks of " feelings of relation " and " feelings of appro bation," both of which imply judgment. Mr. James Mill says, " In the very word *feeling*, all that is implied " in the word *consciousness* is involved." And now we find Mr. J. S. Mill declaring " a feeling and a state of

" consciousness are, in the language of philosophy" [that
is, in the philosophy of Thomas Brown and James Mill],
" equivalent expressions : everything is a feeling of which
" the mind is conscious ; everything which it *feels,* or, in
" other words, which forms a part of its own sentient
" existence." Again, " Feeling, in the proper sense of the
" term, is a genus of which Sensation, Emotion, and
" Thought are the subordinate species" (*Logic,* B. I. c. iii.
§ 3). Of course Mr. Mill is at liberty to choose his
own nomenclature, and use it in the signification he
thinks fit to attach to it. But others have an equal
liberty to reject it and give their reasons. It seems to
me an unwarrantable use of the phrase to make Feelings embrace Thought, and I may add Volition ; and
those who so use it will be found, in spite of themselves,
and of all explanations, understanding the word in its
habitual and proper signification ; and when all other
ideas and resolutions are spoken of as " feelings," the
impression will be left that they are part of our sentient
and (at best) emotional nature.

Mr. Mill claims the liberty of examining all the facts
of consciousness, and of resolving them if he can into
simpler elements. I freely grant him this power. Our
sensations, he grants, are simple and original. But I
have argued that when we are conscious of a sensation,
we are always conscious of self as sentient. Now I am
quite ready to allow Mr. Mill or any other to reduce the
self to something more elementary. But I am sure no
components, which did not contain self, could give us
self. Surely our perception of self could not be given

by mere sensations, that is, by sensations in which self is not mixed up. We are as conscious of the self as of the sensation ; and the sensation could as little give us the self as the self could give the sensation. It should not be forgotten that this self appears in all our other mental exercises—thus showing that it is more essential than our very sensations ; it is found in our memories, beliefs, imaginations, judgments, emotions, and volitions. We are conscious of these not separately or as abstracts; but of self as remembering, self as believing, self as imagining, self as judging, self as under feeling, self as willing.

This self is what I call a Person. Thus understood, it is altogether correct to say that we are conscious of ourselves as persons. Not that we are conscious of personality as a separate thing ; we are conscious in one concrete act of this person as sentient, or as thinking, or resolving. I believe that the infant, that the child, does not separate the two. Even the mature man sel-dom draws the distinction unless, indeed, he be addicted to reflection, or has to speak of the *ego* and the *non ego*. It is only on our remembering the self, and finding it necessary to distinguish between the various states of self, and on our discovering that there are other conscious beings besides ourselves, that we ever think of forming to ourselves the abstraction personality, or taking the trouble to affirm that we are the same persons to-day as we were yesterday, or that we are different from all other persons.

So much for our consciousness of our present self, or

F

of ourselves as persons. The truth now evolved enables us to develop the exact psychological nature of our conviction of personal identity. In all our waking moments we have a consciousness of a present self. But in every exercise of memory we have a remembrance of a past self. We remember the event as in past time. We remember it as an experience of self. Thus, in remembering that we visited the London Exhibition, we recollect not merely the Exhibition, but ourselves as seeing it. True, this recollection of ourselves may be very faint in comparison with that of the brilliant objects witnessed; and, from laws of memory to be afterwards referred to, it may very much disappear; still it is there wrapt up in one concrete act with the image of the external things. In this remembrance of ourselves we have more than a recollection of a past thought or a past feeling, say of the feeling we had when visiting the Exhibition, we remember the feeling as a feeling of self. Here, as in so many other cases which will come under our notice, Mr. Mill has failed to apprehend and unfold all that is in the fact of consciousness. " The feeling I had yesterday," is his account (*Logic*, B. I. c. iii. § 2), " is gone never to return ; what I have to-day is another feeling exactly like the former, but still distinct from it." This is not the correct statement. What I had yesterday was a conscious self under one affection, say grief ; what I have to-day is also a conscious self under, it may be, a like affection of grief, or it may be under a different affection, say joy. Having thus a past self brought up by memory, and a present self under consciousness, we compare them and affirm that they are the same. This is simply the expression of the fact falling under the eye of consciousness. Let Mr. Mill, if he choose, try his sharp analysis upon it. If he does so, he will find the edge of his instrument bent back as he would cut it. It is a rock, itself needing no support, but fitted to act as a foundation. It is a self-evident truth, attained by the bare contemplation of the objects ; and no one can be made to come to any other decision, or to allow that he is a different person now from what he was when he recollects himself at some given instant in the past.

We see what is meant by personality and personal identity. We can express both these, without wrapping them in that awful mystery in which they have so often been made to appear. Personality is the self of which we are conscious in every mental act. Personal identity is the sameness of the conscious self as perceived at different times. The phrases do not point to some unknown essence, apart from or behind the known thing. They simply designate an essential, an abiding element of the thing known. As the personality and personal identity appear, we are entitled to insist that they be brought out to view and expressed in every proper science of psychology. One of Aristotle's definitions of the soul is " *that* (τοῦτο) by which we live, and feel, and understand."[1] Some have charged him with introducing an unmeaning phrase when he men-

---

[1] Ἡ ψυχὴ δὲ τοῦτο ᾧ ζῶμεν, καὶ αἰσθανόμεθα, καὶ διανοούμεθα πρώτως· ὥστε λόγος τις ἂν εἴη καὶ εἶδος, ἀλλ᾽ οὐχ ὕλη καὶ τὸ ὑποκείμενον. *De Anima*, II. 2.

tions not only certain qualities of the soul, but a *that*
by which we exercise the qualities. But Aristotle was
far too comprehensive and accurate a thinker to omit
the τοῦτο, by which, no doubt, he meant to designate a
thing, an existence, or rather a thing having existence,
and capable of living, feeling, understanding. As we
advance, we shall see that Mr. Mill is obliged to use
similar phrases to denote the permanent thing that
abides, amid the changes of attribute or exercise. In
ordinary circumstances, no doubt, our attention is
directed most forcibly to the changing element, to
the action and new manifestation, and may allow the
other, which is ever the same, to fall very much into
what Mr. Mill calls " obliviscence." But it is the
office of the careful psychologist to observe it ; to
bring it out from the shade in which it lies ; and to .
give this conscious self, this remembered self, this identical self, the same place in his system as it has in the
mind of man.

We are now in circumstances to judge of Mr. Mill's
account of mind, and his psychological theory of the
nature and genesis of the idea we form of it. In fram-
ing these he has neglected to look carefully and
patiently at the actual facts of consciousness, both in
regard to the idea and conviction, and the elements out
of which he would fashion it. He acknowledges that
mind involves some sort of notion of what Kant calls
Perdurability. He begins, indeed, by telling us that " we
" neither can know nor imagine *it*, except as *represented*
" by the succession of manifold feelings which metaphy-

" sicians call by the name of states or modifications of
" mind" (p. 205). I have put in italics the words which
Mr. Mill uses, must use, to express the facts ; the words
which correspond to the τοῦτο of Aristotle. He goes
on to say, " It is nevertheless true that our notion of
" Mind, as well as of Matter, is the notion of a perma-
" nent something contrasted with the perpetual flux of
" the sensations and other feelings or mental states
" which we refer to it ; a something which we figure as
" remaining the same, while the particular feelings
" through which it reveals its existence change." This
is an inadequate account of the idea and conviction
entertained by us in mature life. We do not *refer* the
mental states to *it*, we know it in a particular state.
We do not figure self as remaining the same, we judge
or decide the conscious self of to-day to be the same as
the conscious self of yesterday remembered by us. It
does not reveal itself *through* feelings, we know *it as
feeling*, the one being as immediate as the other.

Nevertheless his account, though confused and never
exactly hitting the facts, is a very remarkable one. We
must look at it carefully :—" Besides present feelings,
" and possibilities of present feeling, there is another
" class of phenomena to be included in an enumeration
" of the elements making up our conception of mind.
" The thread of consciousness, which composes the
" mind's phenomenal life, consists not only of present
" sensations, but likewise in part of memories and ex
" pectations. Now, what are these ? In themselves,
" they are present feelings, states of present conscious-

" ness, and in that respect not distinguished from sen-
" sations. They all, moreover, resemble some given
" sensations or feelings, of which we have previously
" had experience. But they are attended with the
" peculiarity, that each of them involves a belief in more
" than its own existence. A sensation involves only
" this : but a remembrance of sensation, even if not
" referred to any particular date, involves the sug-
" gestion and belief that a sensation, of which it is a
" copy or representation, actually existed in the past :
" and an expectation involves the belief, more or less
" positive, that a sensation or other feeling to which it
" directly refers, will exist in the future. Nor can the
" phenomena involved in these two states of conscious-
" ness be adequately expressed, without saying, that the
" belief they include is, that I myself formerly had, or
" that I myself, and no other, shall hereafter have, the
" sensations remembered or expected. The fact be-
" lieved is, that the sensations did actually form, or will
" hereafter form, part of the self-same series of states, or
" threads of consciousness, of which the remembrance
" or expectation of those sensations is the part now
" present. If, therefore, we speak of the mind as a
" series of feelings, we are obliged to complete the state-
" ment by calling it a series of feelings which is aware
" of itself as past and future : and we are reduced to
" the alternative of believing that the Mind, or *Ego*, is
" something different from any series of feelings or pos-
" sibilities of them, or of accepting the paradox, that
" something which *ex hypothesi* is but a series of feel-

" ings, can be aware of itself as series" (pp. 212, 213). This surely is an excessively roundabout and far-fetched account of a very clear fact, in order to suit it to an empirical theory. Making the mind " a thread of consciousness," " a series of feelings," he is obliged to give to this thread or series a set of attributes, such as that *it is aware of itself*, in order to make it even in appearance embrace the obvious phenomena. He prefaces the above by an acknowledgment that " the theory has in-" trinsic difficulties [they are those stated] which it seems " to me beyond the power of metaphysical analysis to " remove." The intrinsic difficulties are very much the creation of the theorist. We decline certainly being shut up to the position, that the mind is " a series of feelings aware of itself," for if thus aware of itself, it is more than a series ; the genuine fact is that the mind is aware of itself as abiding. But as little do we consent to take the other alternative, that the mind is something *different* from the series of feelings ; it is *an abiding existence with a series of feelings.*

He adds, " the truth is, we are here face to face with " that final inexplicability at which, as Sir William " Hamilton observes, we inevitably arrive when we " reach ultimate facts." As finding himself shut up to such an issue, he should have exercised more patience in dealing with those who, like Reid, Kant, and Hamilton, have been painfully striving to give an adequate account of these ultimate facts. If he says they are beyond investigation or expression, I meet him with a direct denial. The operations are within consciousness, and we can observe and co-ordinate them. The fact is, Mr. Mill himself has been trying to unfold them, but has given a very insufficient and perplexed rendering. "The "true incomprehensibility perhaps is, that something "which has ceased, or is not yet in existence, can still be in "a manner present: that a series of feelings, the infinitely "greater part of which is past or future, can be gathered "up, as it were, into a single present conception, accom- "panied by a belief of reality. I think, by far the wisest "thing we can do, is to accept the inexplicable fact, with- "out any theory as to how it takes place." This is a most circuitous and inadequate, I believe, indeed, an inaccurate statement of the fact. That which has ceased to exist is not present, it is the remembrance, which is a very different thing, that is present. The future is not gathered into the present, we at the present anticipate the future. We cannot, of course, give a theory of the production of an ultimate fact, but we can state it correctly, and even, I believe, seize and express its law.

Let us inquire what he makes of the fact according to his Psychological Method. We shall find him accumulating statements which bring in new ideas, without his being able to reduce them even to an apparently consistent system, or to resolve them into simpler elements. "The belief I entertain that my mind exists, when it "is not feeling, nor thinking, nor conscious of its own "existence, resolves itself into a belief of a Permanent "Possibility of these states. If I think of myself as in "dreamless sleep, or in the sleep of death, and believe "that I, or in other words my mind, is or will be existing

" through these states, though not in conscious feeling,
" the most scrupulous examination of my belief will not
" detect in it any fact actually believed, except that my
" capability of feeling is not in that interval perma-
" nently destroyed, and is suspended only because it does
" not meet with the combination of outward circum-
" stances which would call it into action : the moment
" it did meet with that combination it would revive, and
" remains, therefore, a Permanent Possibility " (p. 205).
It could be shown that at this place we are brought
very nearly to the doctrine of Hume, who represents
the mind as " a bundle or collection of different perceptions," to which we are led, by certain tendencies, to give
a fictitious identity (see *Works*, vol. i. pp. 318-334). But
we have here to do not with Hume but with Mr. Mill,
who represents mind as a series of feelings, with a belief
of the permanent possibility of its states. It is admitted,
then, that there is more than feelings, more than even
a series of feelings, there is belief. Surely Mr. Mill
might have inquired more particularly into the nature of
this belief, and he might then have seen that it is quite
as noteworthy a phenomenon and quite as essential to
the mind as the very feelings themselves ; he might have
found that it is quite as " ultimate " as the belief in
the veracity in memory is acknowledged to be (see ρ.) ;
or rather he might have found it involved in that ultimate belief.

Observe how mental attributes are growing in number,
without an attempt to reduce them to simpler elements.
He seems to allow that they cannot be resolved into

sensation. "They are attended with the peculiarity that "each of them involves a belief in more than its own pre- "sent existence. A sensation involves only this." There is a 'belief,' a 'permanent' something. Mark that we have now Time. He has stolen in imperceptibly (time always does so), but we should notice him now that he is in; and we are entitled to ask him what he is and whence he has come; and he is far too important a personage to allow himself to be dismissed at our wish. It is a permanent *possibility*, we decide that there *may be* things in this enduring time. Observe what we have now gathered together. We have sensations; we have a series of sensations; we have a belief; we have a belief in time; a belief in time as permanent, and of possibilities in time. These are evidently different from each other, consciousness being witness. The belief is not the same as the sensations, or the series of sensations. The permanence is not identical with the belief. The possibility is different from the permanent. I know no philosopher who has called in so many unresolved instincts to account for our convictions of memory and personal identity as Mr. Mill has done. His psycho- logical method is multiplying, instead of diminishing, ultimate elements. His system, so far from being simple, is in reality very complex; and its apparent simplicity arises merely from his never summing up, or distinctly enunciating, the original principles he is obliged to postulate and assume.

But I would not have objected to his system merely because of its complexity, provided it had embraced all the phenomena. But I deny that he has noticed, or stated correctly, the facts of consciousness. No doubt there is a belief; but it is a belief in my past existence, conjoined with a knowledge of my present existence. There is time, an idea of time, and a conviction of the reality of time ; but it is in the form of a belief that I existed in time past. There is more than a belief, there is an immediate decision, that the present self known is the same with the past self remembered. There is more than an idea of mere possibility, there is the assurance that I did exist at a particular time, and that I who then existed do now exist. I acknowledge, that I have no intuitive certainty that I existed every moment of a dreamless sleep. I have intuitive assurance that I existed when I fell asleep, and that I exist now when I have awoke, and I am led by the ordinary rules of evidence to believe that I existed in the interval. Here it is that Mr. Mill's permanent possibility of feeling comes in : I believe that had I been awakened sooner I should have been consciously active as I now am. But these very possibilities all proceed on an intuitive remembrance of self, and an intuitive decision as to the identity of self.

Mr. Mill labours to prove that his psychological theory leaves the doctrines that our fellow-men exist, and that God exists, and that the soul is immortal, where it found them. For we look on other people's minds as but a series of feelings like our own ; and we may regard the Divine Being as "a series of the Divine thoughts and feelings prolonged throughout eternity ;"

and our immortal existence to be "a succession of feelings prolonged to eternity" (p. 207-211). Now we are
not yet in a position to inquire (which is the all-important question) whether Mr. Mill's theory admits of
the usual arguments for the existence of our fellow-men,
and of God, and of an immortal life ; or whether, if it
cannot adopt the old arguments, it furnishes new ones.
But before leaving our present subject I may remark,
that the common doctrine, which I believe to be the true
one, and which I have endeavoured to enunciate philosophically, is much more in accordance with our
cherished convictions and sentiments than the subtle
one defended by Mr. Mill. As believing that I myself
am more than a series of feelings, that I have a permanent existence amid all mutations, I can, on evidence
being adduced of their existence, take the same view of
my fellow-men, of my friends, and my family ; that is, I
can look upon them as having not only a permanent
possibility of feelings but a permanent personality, round
which my affections may cluster, and which leads me to
treat them as responsible beings like myself. He says
elsewhere (*Logic*, B. III. c. xxiv. § 1) : "My belief that
" the Emperor of China exists is simply my belief that
" if I were transported to the imperial palace or some
" other locality in Pekin, I should see him. My belief
" that Julius Cæsar existed, is my belief that I should
" have seen him if I had been present in the field of Phar-
" salia, or the senate-house at Rome." This is to reverse
the proper order of things, and to confuse all our conceptions. Looking on ourselves as persons with a per-

manent being, on evidence produced of their existence, we take the same view of the Emperor of China and Julius Cæsar, and thus believe that if we were in Pekin we should see the one, and that if we had been in the battle of Pharsalia we should have seen the other. The picture presented of the Divine Being, in this new philosophy, will appear to the great body of mankind to be unattractively bare and unmeaning, or rather in the highest degree shadowy, uncertain, and evanishing ; and they will rejoice when they are invited to contemplate Him instead as Jehovah, I AM THAT I AM, the independent and self-existent One. I am not inclined to urge our conviction of personality and personal identity as in itself a proof of our immortality ; but in constructing the cumulative argument, and cherishing the hope of a life beyond the grave, I feel it satisfactory to regard myself, I believe on sufficient evidence, not as a permanent possibility of feeling, but a permanent being, the same in the world to come as in this.

We may now combine the results which we have reached. In every conscious act we know an existing thing, which when we begin to reflect we learn to call self, manifesting itself in some particular way which we are taught to regard as an attribute. Again, in all remembrance, we recollect self as exercising some particular attribute in time past, and we know self as now remembering ; and on comparing the two we decide that they are the same. This is a bare statement of the facts, as they daily present themselves. I defy Mr. Mill, or any other mental analyst, to reduce these facts of con sciousness to fewer or simpler elements. In all consciousness, I have a knowledge of self as a person; in all remembrance, a recollection of self as a person; and in the comparison of the two a perception of their identity.

And let it be observed, that both in the conscious self and the recollected, we have the self perceived by us as operating in a great number of ways, with thoughts and emotions in infinite variety. We come too to discover (in a way which will come under our notice below) that there are other beings besides ourselves, who have the same personality and identity, and the like incalculable number and diversity of ideas, wishes, and feelings. As we begin to reflect on all this, and as we would speak about it, and make ourselves intelligible, we find it convenient to have a word to denote that which abideth in us, and is the same in us and in others. We have such a word in Substance, and we say that 'mind is a substance.' In saying so, we mean nothing more than this, that in us and in others there is (1.) *an existing thing;* (2.) *operating;* (3.) *with a permanence.* But in saying this, we say much, that is, we make a statement full of meaning. By multiplying words of description or explanation we should only confuse and perplex the subject, which may be clearly discerned if only we look steadily at it, and weigh the several parts which make up the indissoluble whole.

And here I feel myself called on to state that no doctrine of modern philosophy, not even the ideal theory, or theory of representative ideas, so condemned by Reid and exposed by Hamilton, has wrought such mischief in speculation as that of Locke in regard to substance. His statements on this subject are unsatisfactory throughout, and when they were attacked by Stillingfleet he defended them by a sparring and fencing unworthy of such a lover of truth; he employed himself in repelling the objections of his opponent, instead of seeking to make his own views clearer. "So that if any one will examine " himself concerning the notion of pure substance in " general, he will find he has no other idea of it at " all, but only a supposition of he knows not what " support of such qualities, as are capable of producing " simple ideas in us" (*Essay*, B. II. c. xxiii. § 2). In the controversy he affirms and re-affirms that he does not deny the existence of substance, or that we have an idea of it, and is very indignant with Stillingfleet for saying that he does. But he makes it to be " the support," but " unknown " support of qualities. As the support was something unknown, Berkeley in the next age did a good service to philosophy by discarding it altogether, so far as matter is concerned. But in the succeeding age the avenger came, and Hume took away the unknown substratum from mind, as Berkeley had done from body. Reid rushed in to save fundamental truth; but he did not show his usual shrewdness and wisdom when he retained Locke's " substratum," and argued so tenaciously that the known quality intuitively *suggests* an unknown substance. We should have been saved a world of confused and confusing controversy if Reid, when abandoning Locke's " idea," had also rejected his

" unknown support of qualities." Kant met the Scottish
sceptic in a still more unsatisfactory manner, when he
allowed that by the outward senses and by the internal
consciousness we perceive only the *phenomenon,* and then
referred us to some *noumenon* beyond. In the schools
which have ramified from Kant, the question has ever
since been, Is there merely a phenomenon, or is there a
noumenon also ? Sir William Hamilton in this, as in
so many other topics, has endeavoured to combine Reid
and Kant. He identifies the *phenomenon* of the German,
with the *quality* of the British, philosophy ; he argues
that the quality implies the substance, and the phenomenon the noumenon, but makes the substratum or
noumenon unknowable. Mr. Mill takes much directly
or indirectly from Hume ; he favours in Kant all that
is destructive ; he allows to Hamilton all his negative
positions : and so we find him building on the miserably
defective views which they have given of substance.
" As our conception of body is that of an unknown
" exciting cause of sensations, so our conception of mind
" is that of an unknown recipient or percipient of
" them, and not of them alone, but of all our other
" feelings. As body is the mysterious something which
" excites the mind to feel, so mind is the mysterious
" something which feels and thinks " (*Logic,* B. I. c. iii.
§ 8). He finds no great difficulty, as Hume had done
before him, in putting aside this unknown and mysterious something. And it is high time, I think, that
those metaphysicians who defend radical truth should
abandon this unknown and unknowable substratum or

noumenon, which has ever been found a foundation of ice, to those who would build upon it. Sir William Hamilton having handed over this unknown thing to faith, Mr. Herbert Spencer has come after him, and consigned religion to it as to its grave,—and there, it may safely be said, it will disturb no one, not even by sending out a ghost from its gloomy chambers.

We never know quality without knowing substance, just as we cannot know substance without knowing quality. Both are known in one concrete act. We may, however, separate them in thought. In contemplating any given object, such as the thinking self, we may distinguish between the 'thinking' which changes, and the 'existence' which abideth. As both are known in the concrete, so both may be said to have an existence, not an independent existence, but an existence in, or in connexion with, each other. The one always implies the other, that is, the thinking always implies a thinking existence, and the thinking existence is always exercised in some thought. Mr. Mill gets a momentary glimpse of this doctrine, but does not follow it out. "We " can no more imagine a substance without attributes, " than we can imagine attributes without a substance" (*Logic*, B. I. c. iii. § 6). Taking this view, we cannot without protest allow persons to speak of substance as being something unknown, mysterious, lying far down in a depth below all human inspection. The substance is known, quite as much as the quality. True, the substance is never known alone, or apart from the quality, but as little is the quality known alone, or apart from a substance. Each should have its place, its proper place, neither less nor more, in every system of the human mind.

Much the same may be said of 'phenomenon' and 'noumenon,' which, however, have a still more mysterious meaning than 'quality' and 'substance.' Phenomenon means an appearance, but appearance is an abstract from a concrete; we never see an appearance apart from a thing appearing. It is the object appearing to the subject seeing it. If the phrase is to be retained in philosophy, let us understand what is meant by it. Let us not as we employ it deceive ourselves by imagining that we have, or can have, an appearance apart from a thing appearing. A phenomenon is a thing manifesting itself to us, as a quality is a thing in action or exercise. As to the 'noumenon,' it is not so easy to determine what can be meant by it. If it signifies the thing perceived by the mind, this is neither less nor more than the phenomenon. If it means a thing perceived by no mind, I allow that there are certainly things existing not perceived by the human mind, but then these things may be perceived by other minds,—I suppose must certainly be perceived by the Divine Mind. But if the noumenon means something acting as the ground of the thing manifesting itself, or behind it as a support, I declare that we have no evidence of there being such a thing, and I can see no purpose, philosophical or practical, to be served by it in the way of hypothesis or otherwise. Here Mr. Mill seems to me altogether right: " This unknown something is a supposition without evi-

dence." But I abandon it, because we have a known
something; in the case of mind a thing existing, acting,
and permanent.

But then it is said we do not know *the thing in itself*
(*Ding an sich*). It is high time to insist on knowing
what is meant by this phrase, taken from Kant, and
with which of late years so many metaphysicians have
been conjuring. It cannot be allowed to play a part
any longer till it explains itself. It seems full of mean
ing, and yet I believe that if we prick it, it will be
found to be emptiness. I understand what is meant
by the *thing;* it is the object existing. But what is
meant by *in itself?* I acknowledge no *itself* beside, or
besides, or beyond the thing. I confess to be so stupid,
as not to be able to form any distinct idea of what is
meant by the thing *in* itself. If it mean that the thing,
the whole thing, is within the thing, I have about as
clear a notion of what is signified as I have of the whale
that swallowed itself. If it mean that there is a thing,
in addition to the thing as it manifests itself, and as it
exercises property, I allow that, for aught I know, there
may be many such things. My knowledge of the thing,
of all things, nay, of any one thing, is confessedly
limited. As to what may be beyond the phenomenon,
the thing as it appears to me, and to others who may
report to me, I venture to say nothing, as I can know
nothing about it. But believing that no other man
knows anything about it any more than I do, I pro
test against its being represented as being a support
of the thing known, or in any way essential to it.

Though I were to get new faculties and know that great unknown, I am not sure that it would make the thing known the least clearer, in any way more mysterious or less mysterious than it now is. As it is confessedly unknown, I can trace no relation of dependence, or of anything else between it and the known. Lying as it does in the region of darkness which compasses the land of light, I think it best to leave it there.

We are thus brought to the doctrine which commends itself to our first thoughts, that we know self immediately as existing, as in active operation, and with a permanence. This primitive knowledge furnishes a nucleus round which we may gather other information by experience and by reasoning, till we come at last to clothe mind with qualities so many and varied that it is difficult to classify them. I confess I grudge the school of Comte the epithet ' Positive.' It is a title which they have no right to appropriate to their crude system, which observes only the more superficial facts in these two wondrous worlds of mind and matter. I have in these two last chapters stated what I believe to be the true positive doctrine in regard to mind, that is, the expression of the facts without addition or omission or hypothesis.

CHAPTER VI.

BODY.

WE have now to face a more perplexing subject, the idea and conviction which we have in regard to an external world, the way in which we reach these, and the objective reality involved in them. In this border country there has been a war for ages in the past, and there is likely to be a war for ages in the future. There are real difficulties in the inquiry arising from the circumstance that conscious mind and unconscious matter are so different—while yet they have an evident mutual relation, and also from the apparent deception of the senses ; and speculators have gathered an accumulation of imaginary ones by their refined and elaborate speculations, so that now there are not only the original obstacles in the way, but a host of traditional feuds. I cling to the conviction that there is a doctrine of natural realism, which, if only we could seize and express it, will be found encompassed with fewer difficulties than any far-fetched or artificial system.

Sir William Hamilton has given us a very elaborate classification of the theories of sense-perception. It is

not needful to follow him in this treatise. But in order
to correct errors and prepare the way for a fair discussion, it may serve some good purposes to look at the
account given, of the steps involved, by the three British
metaphysicians who have given the greatest attention
to the subject. To begin with Dr. Thomas Reid. According to him, there is, first, an action or affection of the
organism ; there is, next, a sensation in the mind ; thirdly,
this sensation as a sign, suggests intuitively an external
object. The two points on which he dwells chiefly are,
first, that there is no idea between the external object
and the mind perceiving ; and secondly, that we reach
a belief in the external world intuitively, and not by
any process of reasoning. " This conviction is not only
" irresistible, but it is immediate ; that is, it is not by
" a train of reasoning and argumentation that we come
" to be convinced of the existence of what we perceive"
Works, p. 259). I believe that he has established his
two points successfully, and in doing so he has rendered
immense service to philosophy. Dr. Thomas Brown
gives a different account of the operation. There is
first, as in the other theory—indeed in all theories, an
affection of the bodily frame ; secondly, a sensation in
the mind ; and thirdly, a reference of that to an external
object as the cause. He calls in two general mental
laws to give us the reference. The first is an intuitive law of cause and effect, which impels us when we
discover an effect to look for a cause. We have a sensation of resistance, of which we discover no cause within the mind, and therefore we look for it beyond the

mind. The second law, of which he makes large use, is that of suggestion, which connects sensations, so that one becomes representative of others.

Sir William Hamilton and Mr. Mill are for ever criticis ing these two doctrines, but it may be doubted whether either has given a clear and correct exposition of them. Hamilton, when he commenced his edition of Reid, thought that philosopher's views were the same as his own (we shall see wherein they differ immediately) ; as he advances, he sees that this is not the case ; and he nowhere gives us a precise account of Reid's theory, which, whether well founded or not, is consistent and easily understood. As to Brown, Hamilton is for ever carping at him, as if he had a cherished determination to remove his system out of the way, as one that opposed the reception of his own. The circumstance that neither Reid's theory nor Brown's theory would quite fit into his compartments, is a proof that Hamilton's classifica tion of theories, though distinguished by great logical power, is not equal to the diversities of human concep- tion and speculation. He clearly does injustice to Brown, by insisting on making him an idealist—he makes him a cosmothetic idealist. Now there is no idea in Brown's system, as there was in the older theories. He made great use of sensation, and was in great difficulties when he attempted to show how, from this sensation, we could infer an external world ; but the sensation is an existing, and not an imaginary thing like the idea ; and the sensation was held by him to be an effect, but not at all a representative, of an external and extended object. Mr. Mill, in criticising Hamilton's criticism, would make Reid an idealist (p. 177). This is obviously a mistake. Reid did call in a sensation as a sign, but it was not supposed to be representative, that is, to bear any resemblance or analogy like the old idea to the external object. All that is asserted of it is that we are conscious of it, which we are not of the idea, and that it *suggests* a belief in an external object intuitively, and by the appointment of Him who gave us our constitution. Mill represents Reid and Brown as holding substantially the same doctrine : " The dif-" ference between them is extremely small, and, I will " add, unimportant" (p. 175). Reid held that we never could *reason* from the sensation within to the extended object without. Brown labours to show that the whole process is one of ordinary inference, proceeding always on the intuitive law of cause and effect, aided by the asso ciation of ideas. But Mr. Mill tells us that " Brown also " thinks that we have, on the occasion of certain sensa " tions, an instantaneous conviction of an outward object" (p. 164). I am surprised at such a statement from one who has imbibed so much from Brown, who so clearly represents the process as involving inference. We find everywhere such passages as the following : " Percep-" tion, then, even in that class of feelings by which " we learn to consider ourselves as surrounded by sub-" stance, extended and resisting, is only another name, as " I have said, for the result of certain associations and " inferences that flow from other more general principles " of the mind" (*Lectures*, xxvi.) I call the theory of Brown (which is taken from the Sensational School of France) the Inferential, as distinguished from the Ideal theory on the one hand, and the Intuitive theory on the other.

Hamilton's doctrine differs both from that of Reid and Brown. It is, that there is first an action of the organism, and secondly, a simultaneous sensation and perception. He labours particularly to show that sense-perception being evoked, there is nothing between it and the object, no sensation, no idea; but that we gaze at once on the object, in fact are conscious of it, conscious at one and the same time of the *ego* and the *non ego*. Between this and Brown's doctrine there is an irreconcilable difference. Brown . makes the process one of inference, implying, no doubt, an intuition, but an intuition of a general character bearing on all other mental operations. Hamilton makes the perception primitive, and original, and immediate. Hamilton also differs from Reid, but the point is not so important. Reid makes the sensation precede the perception; whereas Hamilton, in accordance, I think, with the revelations of consciousness, makes them contemporaneous. Both make the operation intuitive and not inferential. This doctrine of Hamilton is not without its difficulties. It leaves many points unexplained— perhaps they are ultimate and cannot be explained —possibly they are so simple that they do not need explanation. It does not profess to show *how* the preceding organic affection is connected with the mental perception. Perhaps the human faculties cannot clear up the subject. Possibly the question itself may be unmeaning, for there may be no *how* to ask about, no *connexion* except this, that the cognitive mind is so constituted as to know the bodily frame with which it is so intimately connected. This doctrine, as it is the most simple, seems to me to be upon the whole the most truth-like, that has yet been propounded. It does not profess to clear up all mysteries, but it embraces the acknowledged facts, and it starts no hypotheses. I regret the dogmatism which the author displays in asserting it. I do not agree with him in thinking that it can be established at once by an appeal to consciousness. But embracing as it does only facts, I am inclined to adhere to it, till some facts not contained in it be ascertained by physiology or psychology, or the two combined. I am certainly not disposed to abandon it for so hypothetical a doctrine as that adopted by Mr. Mill and elaborated by Professor Bain.

In the mature man we find certain ideas, beliefs, and, I would add, judgments. I readily allow all of these to be subjected to an analysis. Mr. Mill is quite justified in declaring that " we are not at liberty to " assume that every mental process which is now as un- " hesitating and rapid as intuition was intuition at its " outset " (p. 144). At present we have to look at the ideas and convictions which we entertain in regard to the external world. I allow at once that " we have no " means of now ascertaining by direct evidence, whether " we were conscious of outward and extended objects " when we first opened our eyes to the light " (p. 147). I am willing, therefore, to consider Mr. Mill's theory of the genesis of our apprehension and belief. His theory seems to be, that we can get them by means of sensations and associations of sensation. " All we know of " objects is the sensations they give us, and the order of " the occurrence of these sensations." "Of the outward " world we know and can know absolutely nothing, ex- " cept the sensations we experience from it" (*Logic*, B. I. c. iii. § 7). The result reached by him is, that " matter may be defined a permanent possibility of sensation" (p. 198). He does not commit himself, but he is not averse to the idea that " the *non ego* altogether may be but a mode in which the mind represents to itself the possible modifications of the *ego*" (p. 189).

In the discussion which is forced upon us by this doctrine, which at first sight seems so strange, there are two points to be specially attended to : First, is Mr. Mill's account of the ideas and convictions which we have concerning body correct ? Under this head our appeal must be to consciousness. I believe that it de- clares that Mr. Mill, in his analysis, commonly leaves out the main element. A second question has to be answered, Does Mr. Mill's hypothesis explain all that is in our apprehension and belief ? In answering this question we must be careful not to allow him to do, what Mr. Crosse and M. Pouchet are suspected of having done in professing to establish the doctrine of spontaneous generation by experiment. Mr. Crosse is alleged to have had the germs of the *acari* produced by him in his carelessly cleaned vessels ; and M. Pouchet to have had the germs from which he derived animals

in the putrescent matter. Certain it is, that when other
persons performed the same experiments as Mr. Crosse,
taking care to exclude all organized bodies, no animals
were produced ; and M. Pasteur maintains that, if you
allow him to destroy the germs in the putrescent fluid,
no life will appear. Now, we must keep a strict watch
on Mr. Mill, lest he be guilty of a like oversight in deriving all our ideas and convictions from so few germs.
As we do so, we shall find that in order to prop up the
theory, which he professes to rear on so narrow a basis,
he is obliged to add buttress after buttress in the shape
of new ideas and implied faculties. In particular, we
shall find him guilty of a very grave logical mistake :
he is ever assuming, without perceiving it, the idea
which he professes to explain. In admitting the veracity of memory, he himself lays down a most important
principle, that we should *assume* the belief " for which
" no reason can be given which does not presuppose the
" belief, and assume it to be well-grounded." We shall
find that in unfolding his theory of the genesis of our
ideas of body he neglects this rule, and without being
aware of it, assumes the ideas of Externality, and
Resisting Force, and Extension, which he is seeking to
generate and explain by a circuitous process. Let us
look at these ideas in the order now mentioned.

(1.) *What is implied in Externality ?* Mr. Mill says
we are aware of ourselves as a series. If I were in
clined to adopt this representation, I would say that by
externality we mean a something without and beyond
the series. But I have objected to this account as

inadequate. I have endeavoured to show that in all
mental action, even in sensation, there is a perception
of self as existing, that in memory there is a remembrance of self, and that we proclaim the present self
and the remembered self identical. Now, by an external object I mean a thing existing but not this self, a
thing different from this permanent and identical self.
I believe that our first perceptions of externality are
derived from things apprehended as extended, as having
a direction and stretching away in space. But as this
involves extension, the consideration of it falls under
next head. For the present we must look at externality
simply as denoting an existing thing, different from,
and not part of, the *ego* known by self-consciousness.
Mr. Mill admits that every man comes to entertain
some such apprehension. " I consider them (the sen-
" sations) to be produced by something not only existing
" independently of my will, but external to my bodily
" organs and my mind" (*Logic*, B. I. c. iii. § 7). I am
here to examine his account of the generation and the
nature of this idea and conviction. I have found great
difficulty in handling the subject, owing to the gossamer
character of the theory, which is far too subtle and ingenious to be solid or true.

In conducting this whole discussion, we must be on
our guard against being misled by an ambiguity in the
use of the phrase 'outward world.' It may mean the
world out of the conscious mind—this I venture to call
the *extra-mental* world ; or it may mean the world beyond the body— this, for distinction's sake, I call the

extra-organic world. I am not sure that Mr. Mill, or Mr. Bain who helps him to develop his system, have escaped the perplexities thus arising. I insist that they are not at liberty to assume the existence of the bodily frame, and then and thus account for the idea of a world beyond. Assuming only a series of sensations aware of itself, they must thence generate something exterior.

Mr. Mill thus gets the idea of externality :—" I see a " piece of white paper on a table. I go into another " room, and though I have ceased to see it, I am persuaded " the paper is still there. I no longer have the sensations " which it gave me ; but I believe that when I again " place myself in the circumstances in which I had " those sensations, that is, when I go into the room, I " shall again have them ; and further, that there has " been no intervening moment at which this would not " have been the case. Owing to this law of my mind, " my conception of the world at any given instant con - " sists, in only a small proportion, of present sensations. " The conception I form of the world existing at any " moment comprises, along with the sensations I am " feeling, a countless variety of possibilities of sensation" (p. 192). I wish Mr. Mill would employ language consistent with his theory, and we should then be in a posi tion to judge whether he is building it up fairly. As yet we know nothing of " white paper," " a room," " another room ;" least of all can we be aware of being placed in " circumstances :" all which certainly imply the very ex ternality he is seeking to gender. We may believe that

Mr. Mill does not forget, but it is necessary to warn his
readers against forgetting, that we have yet only one
sensation succeeding another. He refers to "a law of
mind." The law he postulates is, "that the human
"mind is capable of Expectation. In other words, that
"after having had actual sensations, we are capable of
"forming the conception of possible sensations" (p. 190).
It is one of the many postulates he is ever making.
His assumptions are far from being the fewest and the
simplest fitted to explain the phenomena. If he had
postulated that in every act of sense-perception we apprehend a something external, the facts would have
been explained much more satisfactorily. But let us
go on with his explication. He calls attention to the
circumstance. that "the sensations are joined in groups,"
so that "we should have, not some *one* sensation, but a
"great and even an indefinite number and variety of
"sensations, generally belonging to different senses,
"but so linked together that the presence of one
"announces the possible presence, at the same instant.
"of any or all the rest" (p. 194). But let it be observed
that we do not yet know that the sensations belong to
different senses, or come from different parts of the
body, and the groups of sensations can no more give us
externality than the individual sensations. But then
"we also recognise a fixed order in our sensations."
We have not yet cause and effect, but we have "an
"order of succession which, when ascertained by obser-
"vation. gives rise to the ideas of cause and effect."
"Whether we are asleep or awake the fire goes out, and

" puts an end to one particular possibility of warmth
" and light. Whether we are present or absent, the
" corn ripens and brings a new possibility of food." I
have again to remind Mr. Mill's readers that we do not
yet know that we have bodies to sleep or wake; the
sleeping and waking, the fire and the corn, are all in us
as sensations. The " present" and the " absent" slip
in very dexterously; but as yet we know no place at
which we are present, or from which we may be absent.
The incipient cause and effect are as yet mere antecedence and consequence within the mind.

" When this point has been reached, the Permanent
" Possibilities in question have assumed such unlikeness
" of aspect, and such difference of position relatively to
" us, from any sensations, that it would be contrary to
" all we know of the constitution of human nature
" that they should not be conceived as, and believed to
" be, at least as different from sensations as sensations
" are from one another" (p. 196). Still, all is within the
thread of consciousness. But then it is said there is
something in our " constitution" that makes us believe
the possibilities to be different from sensations. I am
glad of an appeal to our constitution, in which there is
more, I believe, than Mr. Mill has unfolded. Yet I fear
that the actual appeal is in no way complimentary.
Our constitution makes us believe this " possibility"
of sensations to be different from the sensations. But
Mr. Mill does not say, and would not say, that our
constitution is right in all this, or that there is any
reality corresponding to the belief. I am not quite

sure to what law of our constitution he refers. If it be
his favourite principle of association of sensations, it is
clear that it cannot help him, for the associated sensations are all in the mind ; and if a train of sensations
could give us (which, I believe, it cannot) what is not
in the ideas, it must be in virtue of some power in
the train which is not unfolded. If he mean the tendency, on which he dwells so much elsewhere, to give
an external reality to things within, I admit that there
is such a tendency in loose thinking ; but then it is in
minds that have already reached a knowledge of something outward, and it is for Mr. Mill to show, which
would be difficult, that it could exist in a mind that as
yet had no idea of externality. I cannot see that by
either process Mr. Mill has got the conception of an
outward world, and I am sure that neither process would
justify our belief in the reality of such a world. A belief generated by an accidental or fatalistic association
might be error quite as readily as truth, and the disposition to give an external embodiment to internal
feelings is avowedly illusory. Already we see those
flaws in the foundation which render the whole structure insecure, and make it impossible for man to be
certain that he can reach any truth beyond the consciousness of the present sensation.

Our author now crosses at one leap the widest gulf
of all. "We find that they (possibilities of sensation)
" belong as much to other human or sentient beings as
" ourselves." "The world of possible sensations, succeed-
" ing one another according to laws, is as much in other

" beings as in me, it has therefore an existence outside
" me ; it is an external world." But where in the pro-
cession of internal feelings which has passed before us
can other human beings come in ? " I conclude that
" other human beings have feelings like me ; because,
" first, they have bodies like me, which I know in my
" own case to be the antecedent condition of feelings ;
" and because, secondly, they exhibit the acts and other
" outward signs which in my own case I know by ex-
" perience to be caused by feelings." Doubtless, if we
had got our bodily frames as out of ourselves, the argument might have been conclusive. He tells us that we
observe bodies which do not call up sensations in our
consciousness ; and since they do not do so in my consciousness, I infer that they do it out of my consciousness. The inference might be legitimate, provided we
had otherwise got an apprehension of things out of and
beyond the consciousness. All reasoning is usually said
to be from what we know ; but in this inference we
have in the conclusion what is not in the premisses.
Or, if we take Mr. Mill's theory of reasoning, that it is
from particulars to particulars, by some sort of registered
observation, the argument is seen to be equally fallacious ; for we have no register of objects out of ourselves
to authorize us to infer that these possibilities constitute
an external world. I am not at all sure that Mr. Mill
(p. 207) has cause to condemn Reid, when he maintains that a like position taken by Hume lands us in a
system of solitary egoism, or, as Mr. Mill expresses it,
that " the *non ego* altogether may be but a mode in

" which the mind represents to itself the possible modi-
" fications of the *ego*." I am convinced that it is not by
such a process, that babies come to believe in the existence of those who nurse them and are round about
them. So far as I can see, Mr. Mill has never logically
got out of the shell of the *ego ;* nor can I see how any
one can get out of it, except by means of an original
impulse. I suspect that in Mr. Mill's belief of the existence of his fellow-men, for whose benefit he has written
so many able volumes, there is involved a spontaneous
step more convincing than his reflex logic.

The conclusion reached is : " Matter may be defined,
a permanent possibility of sensation" (p. 198). We
shall not be in circumstances thoroughly to examine
this definition till we have fully unfolded, in the next
two heads, the nature of our perceptions of Resistance
and Extension, which enter essentially into our apprehension of Matter. Considered as an account even of
Externality it is defective. I believe, indeed, that it is
the only result which Mr. Mill can reach from his induction or his premisses. It should be observed that
he does not, as some would expect him, define matter
the *Cause* of sensations. Mr. Mill says what he means,
and means what he says, when he describes Matter as
the *Possibility*, not the cause of sensations. Dr. Brown,
by help of ingenuity and twisting, could reach a cause,
for he called in an intuitive conviction, which impels
us when we discover a phenomenon to look for a cause ;
and when, as in the case of certain sensations, we can
not get a cause within, we are driven to seek it without.

His theory, however, was after all defective, for it makes matter, as a cause, unknown, whereas we know matter, as we shall see forthwith, as resisting our effort, and as extended. But Mr. Mill cannot be sure, and does not profess to be sure, that he has reached matter even as an unknown cause. For our sensations have no discoverable causes within the mind ; and as we have no sensitive experience of sensations having causes, and no original conviction constraining us to seek for a cause, it is quite conceivable that they have no causes. But do these ' possibilities ' amount to the idea, which we have, of an outward world ? So far as we have gone, we do not seem to be beyond the ' series of feelings,' for the idea we have got is simply of possibilities of sensation. Mr. Mill thinks that " both philosophers and the world at large, when they " think of matter, conceive it really as a Permanent Pos- " sibility of Sensation" (p. 200).[1] The ' permanence ' is really an important element, presupposing the idea of time, and of the past and the future ; all of which carry us into a region high above sensation, and imply mental faculties with an extensive capacity and wide

---

[1] Mr. Mill (p. 200) admits that the majority of philosophers fancy that matter is something more, and that the world at large, if asked the question, would undoubtedly agree with the philosophers. But then he accounts for this " imaginary conception," as he calls it, by two tendencies of the mind,—one derived from our observation of differences, the other from our observation that every experience has a cause ; it is thus that we are led to suppose that things have a substantive reality. As I do not stand up for a substance different from the thing known, I do not require to examine this theory. In future chapters his defective view of the comparative power of the mind and of causation will be subjected to criticism.

range. But not even with this addition does the description come up to the reality, I mean mental reality. Mr. Mill says that these "Permanent Possibilities" are now "conceived as, and believed to be, as different from "sensations as sensations are from one another" (p. 196). It should be observed that the sensations thus discovered to be different, are all sensations in the "series of feelings" or "thread of consciousness." But our apprehension of an outward world is of something, not only differing from the sensations as one sensation differs from another, but different from the *self*, which, as we have found in last chapter, we know as sentient. We apprehend the material object as an existing thing—quite as much as the self, but distinct from the self.[1] It never has been shown how the *ego*,

---

[1] Professor Bain reaches the conclusion : " It is quite true that the " object of consciousness, which we call Externality, is still a mode of " self in the most comprehensive sense, but not in the usual restricted " sense of ' self' and ' mind,' which are names for the subject to the ex-" clusion of the object" (*Senses and Intellect*, p. 381). We are accustomed to say that " light exists as independent fact, with or without any " eyes to see it. But if we consider the case fairly, we shall see that " this assertion errs not simply in being beyond any evidence that we can " have, but also in being a self-contradiction. We are affirming that to " have an existence out of our minds which we cannot know but as in " our minds. In words, we assert independent existence, while in the " very act of doing so we contradict ourselves " (p. 385). Again, " we " are incapable of discussing the existence of an independent material " world : the very act is a contradiction " (p. 379). At this point extreme sensationalism and extreme idealism, Mr. Bain and Mr. Ferrier, meet and are one ; it would be a contradiction to speak of the one as independent of the other ; they are joined in this philosophy of identity, which transcends that of Hegel himself ! But joking aside, it is easy to represent the doctrine which affirms the existence of independent objects out of the mind so as to make it contradictory ; but there is no contradiction in the doctrine when correctly stated. Of course, knowledge is in a mind, but it may be of an existence " out of our minds."

by reasoning or any other logical process, can give the *non ego*. I must therefore look on the *ego* as having a capacity of discovering the *non ego*, directly or indirectly. Mr. Mill has utterly failed to rear up the actual mental idea and conviction from the postulated materials. Till such time as a *mean* can be pointed out by which we can reach the outward world as an existence, I cling to the belief that the self is endowed with a capacity of immediately knowing not only the self, but the not-self.

But it will be necessary to review Mr. Mill's theory of the genesis of our idea of Matter more carefully. We shall find it throughout a series of assumptions, no one of which admits of proof, and some of which can be disproven. Often do I wish, as I examine it, that Sir William Hamilton had been still alive to brush away by his sweeping logic the ingenuities which are employed to support it. " Our conception of Matter," says Mr. Mill, " comes ultimately to consist of Resistance, Exten- " sion, and Figure, together with miscellaneous powers " of exciting other sensations" (p. 219). There is a palpable omission here, for it omits those powers (specially mentioned by Locke, *Essay*, B. II. c. ii. § 23) by which one body operates upon another; " thus the sun has a power to make wax white, and fire to make lead fluid." It is enough for us here to examine Mr. Mill's theory of the production of the idea of Resistance and of Extension.

(2.) *We have certainly an idea of* RESISTANCE *and a belief in it.* In the mature man it becomes a perception, and a conviction of an object out of the body, or in the body, resisting an effort to move a member of the body. In next chapter I will give some account of the sense which reveals the resisting object; for the present we are examining Mr. Mill's theory (see pp. 219-21). " Re-" sistance is only another name for a sensation of our muscular frame, combined with one of touch." It should be remarked that this language is not meant to imply that we have a muscle, or that we have skin ; the resistance and the touch must yet be considered as sensations in the mind. " When we contract the muscles " of our arm, either by an exertion of will or by an " involuntary discharge of our spontaneous nervous ac-" tivity, the contraction is accompanied by a state of sen-" sation, which is different according as the locomotion. " consequent on the muscular contraction, continues " freely or meets with an impediment. In the former case " the sensation is that of motion through empty space." We shall see that we seem to have no sensation of motion in empty space. When our muscular effort is not opposed by anything without the body, what we have is a feeling of tension, or of one muscle resisting another. But let this pass, as having no special connexion with our present discussion. He goes on to say, that if we will to exert our muscular force, and the exertion is accompanied by the usual muscular sensation, but the expected sensation of locomotion does not follow, we have what is called the feeling of resistance, or, in other words, of muscular motion, and that feeling is the fundamental element in the notion of matter. He shows how " skin sensations of simple contact in-

" variably accompany the muscular sensations of resist-
" ance ;" how our sensations of touch " become *represen-*
" *tative* of the sensations of resistance with which they
" habitually coexist ;" and " our idea of matter as a re-
" sisting cause of miscellaneous sensations is now consti-
" tuted." Every one knows that the muscular sense and
touch combine, to give us the knowledge of matter as
a resisting object. But does Mr. Mill's account come
fully up to the facts falling under the eye of consciousness? Does his theory explain the facts? Both
questions must be answered in the negative. In touch,
as we shall see in next chapter, we localize, I believe
intuitively, our sensations in a given direction, and at
a given point in the surface of the body. Again, in
the exercise of the locomotive energy, accompanied by
muscular sensation, we have a sense of a member of our
body which we will to move, of which member we
must have some idea, otherwise we could not form a
volition regarding it ; and we have a perception of this
member in motion, resisted by a body out of our frame.
Mr. Mill's theory does not yield all of these,—I rather
think not even any one of these thoroughly. It takes
no notice of the volition which moves the member, for
this would introduce an element above sensations. It
is not consistent with that idea of a member of the
body, which is necessary to the volition ; for the theory
to be consistent must presuppose that we have yet no
knowledge of our bodily frame. There can yet be no
apprehension of motion in space, for as yet we have no
idea of space. The idea is not even of resistance, pro-

perly speaking, for we have no idea of a resisting object. So far as we have gone we have only sensations differing from each other in feeling or in intensity, and sensations coexisting, and sensations succeeding each other, and sensations the signs of other sensations.

(3.) *The mature man has also an idea of Extension and a belief in Extended objects.* We have an apprehension and a conviction of our bodies as extended, and of other bodies as extended, that is, as occupying space, as being contained in space, as being of a certain spatial form, and as being movable in space. Can the sensation and association theory account for the generation of this mental phenomenon? I believe it breaks down both psychologically and physiologically.

At this point Mr. Mill hands us over to his friend Professor Bain, who, in *The Senses and the Intellect,* has elaborated into a minute system the general statements scattered throughout Mr. Mill's *Logic.* Beginning with Feelings he goes on to Thought, making its fundamental attributes to be Consciousness of Difference, Consciousness of Agreement, and Retentiveness; and he builds up his system mainly out of Feelings by means of the laws of Association by Contiguity and Resemblance. I cannot in a work like this, devoted to a different individual, review Mr. Bain's theories. But I beg to ask whether we ever have Feeling without some perception of an object, say self, as feeling? Feelings, even such as joy or pain, are mere abstracts separated from our consciousness of self, as rejoicing or in distress. A proper psychological system should begin with the concrete

perception, and not with a quality separated from it.
So much for his foundation.   And as to his mode of
building, it will be shown to be altogether unsatisfactory, in the strictures we have to offer on such subjects
as Association of Ideas, Comparison, and Relativity of
Knowledge, as treated by Mr. Mill.   Mr. Bain has
received great praise for combining physiology with
psychology.   It is true that in his introduction, and in
various parts of his work, he has given an account of
the anatomy and physiology of the brain and nerves
and organs of movement.   But there is a mighty gap,
which he can scarcely be said to have tried to fill
up, between these unconscious parts and the conscious
thoughts and feelings of mind proper.   The most valuable part of his work is that in which he describes, more
minutely than had ever been done before, the feelings
excited by muscular and nervous action, accounting, I
think, so far successfully, for many of our spontaneous
and supposed instinctive movements.   But he is out of
his proper region when he comes to deal with the peculiar operations and the higher ideas of the mind.   With
a fine capacity for observing bodily affections, and an
undoubted vigour and tenacity of intellect in dealing
with material facts, he seems to be unfitted for realiz-
ing fully pure mental or spiritual phenomena, as falling
simply under the eye of consciousness.   He makes as
much use of nerve-forces as Hartley did of vibrations,
and seems to identify conscious feelings with them,
making the current and the consciousness two sides
of one thing.   Even when he is professedly treating of

Emotions, Thoughts, and Volitions, he has great difficulty in rising above nerve affections; and when he
does make the attempt, it is immediately to fall back
to his old level of sensations. He is to be constantly
watched when he would draw our higher ideas of necessary truth, of beauty and of moral good from sensitive
affections variously associated. It could be shown, that
in treating of our intellectual and moral and voluntary
operations, while apparently proceeding in so matter of
fact a manner, he is continually passing, without seeing
it, from unconscious to conscious action, from bodily
sensations to mental ideas, and advancing hypotheses as
to the influence of nervous and muscular action, which
could be shown to be true only by their explaining all
the mental facts revealed by consciousness; and this he
cannot be said to have attempted, as consciousness is
seldom consulted, even formally or professedly. There
is proof of all this in his theory of what constitutes our
idea of extension and its mode of growth.

In the earlier editions of his *Logic* (B. I. c. iii. § 7),
Mr. Mill had described Brown as showing clearly that
the notions of extension and figure are derived " from
" sensations of touch, combined with sensations of a class
" previously too little adverted to by metaphysicians
" —those which have their seat in the muscular frame."
He adds, characteristically, " Whoever wishes to be
" more particularly acquainted with this admirable
" specimen of metaphysical analysis, may consult the
" first volume of Brown's *Lectures* or Mill's *Analysis of*
" *the Mind.*" The thought has germinated, and in his

later editions he is able to refer to Mr. Alexander Bain and Mr. Herbert Spencer as following out the investigation. Mr. Bain has certainly taken up the idea, and ridden it to exhaustion, I should say to death.

" We may accede," says Professor Bain, as quoted by Mr. Mill (p. 226), " to the assertion sometimes made, " that the properties of space might be conceived or felt " in the absence of an external world, or any other " matter than that composing the body of the percipient " being; for the body's own movements in empty space " would suffice to make the very same impressions on " the mind as the movements excited by outward objects. " A perception of length, or height, or speed, is the " mental impression or state of consciousness accompany- " ing some mode of muscular movement, and this move- " ment may be generated from within as well as from " without." In criticising this theory, so cloudy in its outline, we are placed in difficulties, in consequence of its not being clear whether Mr. Mill and Mr. Bain assume the existence of the bodily frame as a material object, in the common acceptation, as implying objective existence and extension, or, even in their own sense, as "the mere possibility of sensations." Are they accounting for the extra-mental world, including the bodily frame? or simply for the extra-organic world? In most places Mr. Bain seems to posit the body as a reality. In the passage quoted, he speaks of the matter composing "the body of the percipient being," as if he needed it to explain our idea of "the properties of space." He talks of a movement being "generated from within," which cannot mean within the mind, which is a mere series of feelings ; it must mean within the body, which is quietly assumed. The whole plausibility, I had almost said intelligibility, certainly the expressibility, of the theory lies in its being supposed that there is a body, and even an extended body. He derives all from nerve-currents which imply space, and motion in space and he constructs the idea of extension by a *sweep* of the hand, or a *sweep* of the eye, or a *volume* of feeling, which, if taken metaphorically, explain nothing, and if taken literally, that is, as actualities, imply space and motion in space. But if the body is assumed as known immediately, then there is admitted a vast body of intuition, of which he should have measured the amount, and acknowledged the significance. Or if it be said that the bodily frame is assumed as an hypothesis, the answer is obvious. If it explains, as he thinks (I do not), the whole facts, then the hypothesis is rendered probable, and he must adhere to it ; for the author of an hypothesis cannot be allowed to employ it to reach a conclusion and then abandon it ; on the contrary, he must keep by it and all its logical consequences. On whatever ground assumed, it is clear that when assumed there is little left to call for explanation. After we have got our own bodies, with " matter " composing them, capable of taking a " sweep," and of having " a movement generated within," it can be no difficult matter to conceive of other bodies being extended, and in motion, and resisting our movement.

But in this discussion I must in all fairness suppose

that he does not assume the existence of the bodily frame.[1] His business is to show, on his theory, how our conception in regard to body is generated. As he attempts to do so, I am entitled, after this statement, to take care that he does not assume surreptitiously what he professes to produce by a process. He has as yet got nothing but a series of feelings, with a possibility of sensations coming no one can tell from what quarter. I cannot allow him, in order that he may ingeniously get more, to employ a supposed body with a " sweep " and " contractions."

" When a muscle," says Mr. Bain, as quoted by Mr. Mill (see pp. 222-24), " begins to contract, or a limb to " bend, we have a distinct sense how far the contraction " and the bending are carried ; there is something in " the special sensibility that makes one mode of feeling

[1] Since writing the above, I find Mr. Herbert Spencer saying of Mr. Mill : " If, knowing more than his own states of consciousness, he declines " to acknowledge anything beyond consciousness until it is proved, he " may go on reasoning for ever without getting any further ; since the " perpetual elaboration of states of consciousness out of states of con- " sciousness can never produce anything more than states of conscious- " ness. If, contrariwise, he postulates external existence, and considers " it as merely postulated, then the whole fabric of his argument, standing " upon this postulate, has no greater validity than the postulate gives it, " *minus* the possible invalidity of the argument itself. The case must not " be confounded with those cases in which an hypothesis or provisional " assumption is eventually proved true by its agreement with facts ; for " in these cases the facts with which it is found to agree are facts known " in some other way than through the hypothesis : a calculated eclipse of " the moon serves as a verification of the hypothesis of gravitation, because " its occurrence is observable without taking for granted the hypothesis " of gravitation. But when the external world is postulated, and it is " supposed that the validity of the postulate may be shown by the ex- " planation of mental phenomena which it furnishes, the vice is that the " process of verification is itself possible only by assuming the thing to be " proved."—Art., Mill *v.* Hamilton, in *The Fortnightly Review.* No. V.

" for half contraction, another for three-fourths, and an-
" other for total contraction." " If the sense of degrees of
" range be thus admitted as a genuine muscular deter-
" mination, its functions in outward perception are very
" important. The attributes of extension and space fall
" under its scope. In the first place, it gives the feel-
" ing of *linear extension*, inasmuch as this is measured
" by the sweep of a limb or other organ moved by the
" muscles. The difference between six inches and
" eighteen inches is expressed to us by the different
" degrees of contraction of some one group of muscles ;
" those, for example, that flex the arm, or, in walking,
" those that flex or extend the lower limb. The in-
" ward impression corresponding to the outward fact of
" six inches in length, is an impression arising from the
" continued shortening of a muscle—a true muscular
" sensibility. It is the impression of a muscular effort
" having a certain continuance ; a greater length pro-
" duces a greater continuance (or a more rapid move-
" ment), and, in consequence, an increased feeling of
" expended power. The discrimination of length in
" any one direction includes *extension* in any direc-
" tion." This reads very like assuming an extended
bodily arm taking a sweep, and thus giving us the idea
of extension. Of course we understand, on reflection,
that the sweep is only a sensation in the " series of
feelings," but when we understand this, we see how far
we are from having the idea of extension produced.

In explanation of the theory, Mr. Mill says, " Mr.
" Bain recognises two principal kinds or modes of dis-

" criminative sensibility in the muscular sense : the
" one corresponding to the degree of intensity of the
" muscular effort—the amount of energy put forth ;
" the other corresponding to the duration—the longer
" or shorter continuance of the same effort. The first
" makes us acquainted with degrees of resistance,
" which we estimate by the intensity of the muscular
" energy required to overcome it. To the second we
" owe, in Mr. Bain's opinion, our idea of extension."
I have already commented on the defects in Mr. Mill's
account of our apprehension of resistance. We have
here to consider the theory of the genesis of the idea of
extension. It is referred to the continuance of a sensation.

And here it is proper to state, that some deny the
existence of such a sensation as arising when the arm
sweeps through empty space. E. H. Weber had come,
in 1852, to the conclusion :—" Of the voluntary motion
" of our limbs we know originally nothing. We do not
" perceive the motion of our muscles by their own
" sensations, but attain a knowledge of them only
" when perceived by another sense. The muscles most
" under our control are those of the eye and the voice,
" which perform motions microscopically small, yet
" we have no consciousness of the motion. We move
" the diaphragm voluntarily against the heavy pres-
" sure of the liver, etc., yet with as little consciousness
" of the motion. It follows that the motions of our
" limbs must be observed by sight or touch in order
" to learn that they move, and in what direction."

Mr. Abbot quotes this passage in his *Sight and Touch* (p. 71), and he adds, " The more recent researches of " Aubert and Kammler not only confirm this result, but " tend further to prove that there is not in the muscles " any sense whatever of their contraction." " Accord- " ingly, they remark that the friction of our clothing is a " considerable aid in judging of our motions, especially " if it is close fitting. When wearing boots, etc., with " which we are not familiar, we are less certain of our " judgments, and this is the more noticeable in riding, " as the eye does not then control our judgment." The question is for physiologists to settle. I am not satisfied that the Germans referred to can have established their point. But until there is a more thorough determination of the exact function of the nerves attached to the muscles, it is preposterous to found a huge metaphysical theory on our muscular sensations when the arm moves in empty space.

My opinion on such a subject is of no value, but I am disposed to think that we have a sense of the contraction of at least some of our muscles, and of its continuance.[1] On the supposition that we have a sense of resistance, which seems established, the muscles of our arm, being always in a state of more or less tension, must feel the resistance offered by one muscle to another.

---

[1] Mr. H. Lewes thinks he has demonstrated the existence of the Muscular Sense. He skinned a frog, and thus made it insensible to external impressions, and found it " to manifest all those phenomena usually attributed to the muscular sense " (*Brit. Assoc.*, 1859). We require a more thorough investigation of the relations, and differences, of the precise functions of the nerves of touch-proper and the muscular sense.

Dr. Kirkes says that the muscles "possess sensibility
" by means of the sensitive nerve-fibres distributed in
" them.   The amount of common sensibility in muscles
" is not great."   "But they have a peculiar sensibility,
" or at least a peculiar modification of common sensi-
" bility, which is shown in that their nerves can com-
" municate to the mind an accurate knowledge of their
" states and position when in action" (*Phys.*, p. 530,
5th ed.)   We may, therefore, know the contractions.
But let us take along with us the full facts.   The sense
of touch-proper, as we shall see in next chapter, always
refers the sensations to the points in the skin at which
the nerves terminate ; and the muscular sense merely
intimates that one organ is resisting another.   In that
" sweep of the arm," of which Mr. Bain makes so much,
there is implied, first, a direction of the points of sensation in the skin, secondly, a muscular resistance, and,
I rather think, thirdly, an experience to enable us to
combine the two.   There is, I suspect, a further element.
In whatever way it may begin, the continuance of the
experimental bending of the arm, which Mr. Bain employs, must be done by the will.   But a vague direc-
tionless effort will not move a limb, still less continue
to move it in a certain way.   The volition to continue
the sweep of the arm implies a contemplated end, or
some idea of the arm, and a belief in its existence, and,
I should think, in its extension.   It thus appears that
it is to reverse the proper order of things, to make the
continuance of "the sweep of the arm" constitute or
give us the idea of extension.   In the very movement

we have an idea of an extended arm by touch-proper or feeling; as we move the arm, we become acquainted with the resistance of one felt member by another; and in order to the continuance of the voluntary sweep, there must be some apprehension, more or less vague, of the limb which we continue to move.

There are many serious physiological difficulties in the way of accepting this muscular theory. The extent of a sweep of the arm does not depend merely on the amount of force put forth; nor does it depend solely on the continuance of the effort: it depends also on the proportionate length of the two arms of the lever on which the muscle operates. For instance, the biceps muscle of the arm is inserted an inch below the elbow-joint, whilst the distance from the point of insertion to the end of the limb may be sixteen inches. When the muscle contracts to a certain extent, the rapidity of the movement at the extremity will be sixteen times as great as it would have been if the insertion had been at the extremity; and, on the other hand, the force employed by the muscle has been sixteen times as great as would have been required if the insertion had been at the extremity. A large amount of force is thus expended in order to secure the great advantage of rapidity of movement. It is clear, therefore, that neither the intensity nor the extent of contraction can give us the amount of motion in the part on which the muscle operates; and, that while the muscular sense may inform us of the intensity, and extent of the intensity, and extent of the contraction of the fibres of a muscle, it can give us no information of the extent of the movement of our limbs, till after long experience applied to each limb. " It is doubtful," says Dr. Kirkes (*Phys.*, p. 646), " how far the extent of muscular movement is obtained " from sensations in the muscles themselves. The sen- " sation of movement attending the motions of the hand " is very slight ; and persons who do not know that the " action of particular muscles is necessary for the pro- " duction of given movements, do not suspect that the " movement of the fingers, for example, depends on " action in the forearm." Mr. Abbot has pressed some of the difficulties (*Sight and Touch*, p. 70) : " Let us " suppose a blind man trying to get the notion of dis " tance from the motion of his hand. He finds a cer- " tain sweep of the hand brings it into contact with a " desk ; the distance of which, therefore, is represented " by that effort. But it requires a greater effort to " reach the eyes or the nose ; and distance being " = locomotive effort, it is demonstrated that the nose " extends beyond the desk. The top of the head must " be conceived as more remote, and the back farthest " of all. In general, when we refer distances to the " eye, as we habitually do, objects four inches from the " eye must appear farther from us than those at twelve. " This is another novelty. But again, since the hand " moves in curves, and cannot without considerable " effort be made to move in a straight line, it is also " demonstrated that an epicycloid is shorter than a " right line between the same points."

But, after all, the question is to be decided by psycho-

logical rather than physiological considerations. The
phenomenon to be explained is our idea of extension,
and consciousness will require to be consulted. The
theory was started by Brown, and Hamilton had thus
examined it (Append., Reid's *Works*, p. 869) : " The
" notion of Time or succession being supposed, that
" of longitudinal extension is given in the succession of
" feelings which accompanies the gradual contraction
" of a muscle : the notion of this succession constitutes
" *ipso facto* the notion of a certain length ; and the
" notion of this length" (he quietly takes for granted
" is the notion of longitudinal extension sought. The
" paralogism here is transparent. Length is an ambi-
" guous term ; and it is length in space, extensive length.
" and not length in time protensive, whose notion it
" is the problem to solve." Mr. Mill (p. 227) quotes
this language, and tries to avoid the argument by urging
that the " assertion of Brown, and of all who hold
" the Psychological theory, is that the notion of length
" in space, not being in our consciousness originally,
" is constructed by the mind's laws out of the notion of
" length in time. The argument is not, as Sir William
" Hamilton fancied, a fallacious confusion between two
" different meanings of the word length, but an idea-
" tification of them as one." This statement is certainly sufficiently clear, but it crowns the absurdity.
" When we say that there is a space between *A* and *B*.
" we mean that some amount of these muscular sensa-
" tions must intervene ; and when we say the space is
" greater or less, we mean that the series of sensation

" (amount of muscular effort being given) is longer or
" shorter." " Now this, which is unquestionably the
" mode in which we become *aware* of sensation, is con-
" sidered by the psychologists in question to *be* exten-
" sion." I need not repeat that what is here represented
as *unquestionable,* has been questioned physiologically.
But we are now discussing the psychological question.

We have here three different phenomena—consciousness being the witness. We have—(1.) Series of
Muscular Sensations; (2.) Length of Time; (3.) Length
of Space. These three may have relations one to another, but they are surely diverse from one another.
Mr. Mill explains that he does not draw the one from
the other, which would be preposterous enough, but he
declares them identical, which is absurd in the extreme.
It matches the doctrine of Hegel, justly regarded as the
reductio ad absurdum of his whole philosophy, that all
things are one. Hegel lessened the absurdity of this
statement by another, that all things are different; but
Mr Mill has no such explanation to offer, for he declares muscular sensations, time, and space to be identical, without a difference. Mr. Mill gives a scanty
enough account of the faculties of the mind, but he
acknowledges that we possess a power of discerning
differences. If we can trust our capacities at all, they
declare that the three things under consideration are as
different as any one thing can be from any other.

A series of *muscular sensations* and *length of time* are
surely different. They are different in themselves, and
we can conceive an animated being, say a lobster, to

have a succession of sensations, and yet no idea of time. Again, *series of muscular sensations* and *extension* are not the same. The series of feelings excited as I pass my hand over a table is not the same as the yard square which is the size of the table. Curious consequences would seem to follow from this doctrine of identity. If, in the next attempt with the same series of sensations, my hand passed over a table two yards long, the theory would identify the time with two yards, as before it did with one ; and as Mr. Mill admits the law of identity (see *ω*.), or, that things which are identical with the same thing are identical with one another, it would make one yard, which is the same with a series of sensations, identical with two yards, which is identical with the same series of sensations. To represent this otherwise. The length of time taken by us to travel between London and Paris does not merely help us (as every one admits) to estimate the length of way when we have an idea of the rate at which we are travelling (as the thermometer measures heat for us), but is the very same with the length of the way ; and as we travel it in a longer or shorter time, or with more or fewer sensations, so is the length of way actually longer or shorter at different times. If we draw back from such consequences by appealing to a different measure, would not this show that we had unfortunately taken the wrong rule ? But, after all, I will not positively affirm that such consequences follow, for the doctrine is one that baffles all reasoning, because it sets aside the first premisses of reasoning. Mr. Abbot says very properly

" Indeed the obvious differences between the two ideas
" are so great, that a philosopher who has neglected
" them can scarcely be convinced by more abstruse
" considerations. Thus, muscular effort has degrees, its
" parts are not equal; extension does not admit of
" degrees, its parts are equal. Extension has three
" dimensions, muscular effort only one. The parts of
" extension are co-existent, those of muscular effort are
" successive." Finally, *length of time* and *length of space*
are not the same. As well might we identify colours
with smells, sounds with shapes, sweet with sour, light
with darkness, love with hatred, virtue with vice, Mr.
Mill with Sir William Hamilton, as identify extension
with duration.

Mr. Mill's attempt to get support to his hypothesis
from the sense of sight is, if possible, still more unsuc-
cessful. He is obliged to suppose that in vision we
have originally only a sensation of colour, and that the
idea of an extended surface is given by, or rather is
identical with, the time occupied by the muscular sensations as we move the eye. Sir William Hamilton, in
reviewing Berkeley, had noticed the doctrine that the
eye gives us only colour, and his criticism has commonly
been regarded as amounting almost to a demonstration:
" All parties are, of course, at one in regard to the fact
" that we see colour. Those who hold that we see ex-
" tension, admit that we see it only as coloured: and
" those who deny us any vision of extension make colour
" the exclusive object of sight. In regard to this first
" position all are therefore agreed. Nor are they less

" harmonious in reference to the second ; that the power
" of perceiving colour involves the power of perceiving
" the differences of colours.   By sight we, therefore, per-
" ceive colour, and discriminate one colour, that is, one
" coloured body,—one sensation of colour, from another.
" This is admitted.   A third position will also be denied
" by none, that the colours discriminated in vision are,
" or may be, placed side by side in immediate juxta-
" position ; or one may limit another by being super-
" induced partially over it.   A fourth position is equally
" indisputable ; that the contrasted colours, thus bound-
" ing each other, will form by their meeting a visible
" line, and that, if the superinduced colour be sur-
" rounded by the other, this line will return upon itself,
" and thus constitute the outline of a visible figure.
" These four positions command a peremptory assent :
" they are all self-evident.   But their admission at once
" explodes the paradox under discussion"—(that extension cannot be cognised by sight alone).   " And thus :
" A line is extension in one dimension—length ; a figure
" is extension in two—length and breadth.   Therefore
" the vision of a line is a vision of extension in length ;
" the vision of a figure, the vision of extension in length
" and breadth" (*Metaph.* vol. ii. p. 167).

Mr. Mill acknowledges " I cannot make the answer
to this argument as thorough and conclusive as I could
wish" (p. 239).   His attempts to lessen its force are
exceedingly weak and palpably insufficient.   He calls
attention to the circumstance that the eye " does not
" cognise visible figure by means of colour alone, but

" by all those motions and modifications of the muscles
" connected with the eye, which have so great a share
" in giving us our acquired perceptions of sight." Be it
so, the demonstration remains untouched, that we take
in figure when we take in colour. He says, that an eye
immovably fixed "gives a full and clear vision of but a
small portion of space." The admission is sufficient for
our purpose. He throws us once more on Mr. Bain, who
tells us, " When we look at a circle, say one-tenth
" of an inch in diameter, the eye can take in the whole
" of it without movement." The tenth of an inch is as
good as a whole inch, or a foot, or a yard. In the tenth
of an inch is extension with a boundary, and may be a
measure to aid us in ascertaining the extent we can
take in by the sweep of the eyes. Mr. Mill admits " a
" rudimentary conception must be allowed ; for it is evi-
" dent that even without moving the eye we are capable
" of having two sensations of colour at once, and that
" the boundary which separates the colours must give
" some specific affection of sight.' He would lessen the
significance of this admission in a very unworthy manner : " But to confer on these discriminative impres-
" sions the name which denotes our matured and per-
" fected cognition of extension, or even to assume that
" they have anything in common with it, seems to be
" going beyond evidence." No one maintains that our
primary vision of a surface by the eye comes up to our
perfected cognition of extension ; still it is a surface,
and it has a boundary, and therefore it has something
in common with it. Mr. Bain tells us, " We may still,

" however, see very strong grounds for maintaining the
" presence of a muscular element, even in this instance."
Be it so, the demonstration of Hamilton holds good,
that in the two colours in this space, whether with or
without the aid of the muscles, we have lines and
spaces. But he adds, " In the second place, the essential
" *import* of visible form is something not attainable
" without the experience of moving the eye. If we
" looked at a little round spot, we should know an
" optical difference between it and a triangular spot ;
" and we should recognise it as identical with another
" round spot." And then, subjecting the fact to his theory,
instead of forming his theory from the facts, he tells us,
" We mean by a round form something which would
take a given sweep of the eye to comprehend it." I
suppose this is what he means by the *import* of form,
that it is the time spent in muscular action (!), which I
rather think might be the same for a square, or a triangle,
or an oval, of a certain size, as for a circle. I really
cannot understand how we should optically know the
difference of the figures, unless we perceived them as
figures. In spite of all these perverted attempts at the
resolution of them into something else, there still remains the surface and the boundary perceived by the eye.

Failing utterly in the psychological analysis, Mr.
Bain and Mr. Mill (p. 232) fall back on a statement of
Platner, which Sir William Hamilton had copied into
his Lectures without knowing what to make of it. " In
" regard to the visionless representation of space or
" extension, the attentive observation of a person born

" blind, which I formerly instituted in the year 1785,
" and again in relation to the point in question, have
" continued for three whole weeks—this observation, I
" say, has convinced me that the sense of touch by
" itself is altogether incompetent to afford us the repre-
" sentation of extension and space, and is not even
" cognisant of local exteriority ; in a word, that a man
" deprived of sight has absolutely no perception of an
" outer world beyond the existence of something effec-
" tive, different from his own feeling of passivity, and in
" general only of the numerical diversity,—shall I say
" of impressions or of things ?   In fact, to those born
" blind, *time serves instead of space.*   Vicinity and dis-
" tance means in their mouths nothing more than the
" shorter or longer time, the smaller or greater number
" of feelings which they find necessary to attain from
" some one feeling to another.   That a person blind
" from birth employs the language of vision—that may
" occasion considerable error ; and did, indeed, at the
" commencement of my observations, lead me wrong ;
" but, in point of fact, he knows nothing of things as
" existing out of each other ; and (this in particular I
" have very clearly remarked) if objects, and the parts
" of his body touched by them, did not make different
" *kinds* of impressions on his nerves of sensation, he
" would take everything external for one and the same.
" In his own body he absolutely did not discriminate
" head and foot at all by their distance, but merely by
" the difference of the feelings (and his perceptions of
" such differences was incredibly fine) which he ex-

" perienced from the one and from the other, and,
" moreover, through time. In like manner, in external
" bodies, he distinguished their figure merely by the
" varieties of impressed feelings ; inasmuch, for example,
" as the cube by its angles affected his feelings differently
" from the sphere."

Let it be observed of this account, that it is largely
theoretical, by one who believed with Kant, that there
were *a priori* forms of space and time in the mind,
and that these were brought forth empirically only by
the sense of sight. Platner does not give us the facts
to enable us to judge for ourselves ; he favours us only
with his conclusions. His observations carry us as far
back as 1785, when the distinction between touch-
proper and the muscular sense was not established.
Later physiological research has shown that, in the case
of the blind, as in all others, touch-proper makes us
localize the affections of our bodily frame, and that the
muscular sense gives us " something effective, different
from our feeling of passivity :" we may add, different
from our felt bodily frame. It has been proven by
later and fully detailed researches, that those born blind
know their own body as extended by the common sensations of feeling, and know extra-organic objects by
the resistance offered to their muscular efforts. Even
Mr. Mill is obliged to modify and explain Platner's
statement (p. 233) :—" But Platner, though uninten-
" tionally, puts a false colour on the matter when he
" says that his patient had no perception of extension :
" he had conceptions of extension after his own man-

" ner ;" in fact, " all that is meant by persons who see."
Without this explanation the statement of Platner would
be fatal to the theory of Mill, who makes us get our
knowledge of extension from the muscular feelings,
and not as Platner, whose avowed aim is to get it from
sight. With this explanation it can help neither side,
for it puts those who see in the same position as the
blind, and those who see will be admitted by all to
have " a perception of an outer world" by the sense of
touch. I believe that Platner may be right when he
says that " local exteriority," that is, objects out of the
body, may not be given by touch-proper or feeling ; but
this is certainly given by the muscular sense in the case
of the blind, as in that of the seeing. When he speaks
of time serving instead of space to those born blind, and
that vicinity and distance means only shorter or longer
time, or the smaller or greater number of feelings which
they find necessary to attain from some one feeling to
another, I believe he was led astray by not distinguishing between our apprehension of space and the
measure of space. The idea of members of the body
localized is given most probably by all the senses.
But the actual measurement of space is always a subsequent process, implying comparison and a standard.
I believe that in all of us the succession of our feelings,
of our muscular feelings, but also of our mental ideas
and feelings as well, is one means of helping us to
measure (not only time, but) space ; we measure it in a
loose way, by the feelings we have experienced in passing over it in travelling, or by a member of our body.

Those born blind must be specially dependent on such a measure. Those who see have a natural measure provided in the surface which falls under the perception of the eye. Those born blind have such a measure in the surface of the body given by touch, and in the effort of the locomotive energy reported by the muscular sense. We shall see in next chapter that a very different account from that of Platner is given by later German physiologists.[1]

As the result of these discussions, it appears that we have ideas and convictions of externality, of resistance to the energy of self, and of extension, that cannot be resolved into any elements which do not imply them. But do these subjective apprehensions and beliefs imply corresponding objective realities? This is the old

[1] In order to be able to form an intelligent opinion on these subjects, I put myself in communication with the Rev. J. Kinghan, who for twenty years has been connected with the Institution for the Blind in Belfast, first as assistant, and now as Principal. He declares that he has never found anything, in all his teaching of the blind, or intercourse with them, to confirm Platner's statement. Those born blind cannot have the visual idea of space, but they have, he says, a very clear notion of figure and distance got directly from the sense of touch. With his aid I have experimented with very young children born blind. I put two small pieces of wood, one triangular and the other square, under the palm of the hand, and without being allowed to move the hand over it, they at once told us the shape of each. When their head, and their legs, and their arms were pricked exactly alike, they at once showed us the seat of sensation, and knew the points to be out of each other. I moved their hand first over a book seven inches long, and then over a desk fourteen inches long, occupying the same time with each process, and they at once declared that the latter was much longer than the former. We allowed a boy to feel round a room with which he was unacquainted, and he at once declared its shape. One of these children was a girl of the age of eight, just entered the Institution, so ignorant that she did not know the meaning of angle or corner or point, calling the corners of the figures " little heads." She said the square had two little heads and two little heads, but was not sure that two and two make four.

question of metaphysics. To treat it historically, logically, and critically, would require a separate volume. Fortunately it is not necessary here to enter upon the wide question. Mr. Mill grants that there is an assurance which is " a test to which we may bring all our convictions" (see κ.), and that " we may be sure of what we see as well as what we feel" (see μ.) Following these admitted principles, I do not see that Mr. Mill can object to the reality of an extended world, provided always that it be shown that our ideas as to externality and extension cannot be resolved into simpler elements. The conviction we entertain as to an external world is of the nature of a primitive perception, and not a derivative idea. We perceive objects out of ourselves resisting us and extended. This perception, like that of consciousness, is self evident : we seem to look at once on the object. It is also necessary : no doubt we can imagine it to be otherwise, but we cannot be made to judge or believe that our hand is not an extended object. It is universal : all men entertain it and act upon it. Ingenious objections may be urged against all this, but they are such as are advanced not only against all truth, but against all inquiry, and proceed upon a universal scepticism, which Mr. Mill, who professes to be a lover of truth, does not avow.

These same considerations justify us in looking upon body as a substance. It will be remembered that I do not stand up for an unknown *substratum* beneath the known thing. Whatever is known as existing, as acting, and having permanence, I regard as a substance.

Mind is a substance, as it can be so characterized. But we have seen that we know body as an existence, in operation, and with, as Mr. Mill allows, a permanence; it is therefore a substance. It is vastly more than a "possibility;" it is an actuality. It is more than a possibility of "sensations;" it has an existence even as the sensations have; and a body is known not only as giving sensations, but as capable of acting on other bodies in a variety of ways, which it is the office of physical science to classify and to reduce to laws. By adhering to these simple principles we are made to feel that we are out of the region of phantoms and in the land of realities.

CHAPTER VII.

THE PHYSIOLOGY OF THE SENSES.

THERE is an impression among many that Mr.
Mill's theory has the support of physiology, and this is
strengthened by the anatomical and physiological de-
tails which constitute so large a portion of Mr. Bain's
work. But I cannot discover that either has found
a basis, or even a starting-point, for their general theory
of the mind, or for their particular theory of the manner in which we reach the idea of an extended world,
in any ascertained phenomena of our bodily frame.
Their speculations receive no aid from physiology, and
must stand or fall by their psychological merits or
demerits. The physiology of the senses is still in a
very uncertain condition, and, whatever it may do in
ages to come, can as yet throw little light on strictly
mental action, except, indeed, in the way of correcting
premature hypotheses. It may be profitable to look at
some of the later researches into the senses conducted
by eminent physiologists, especially in Germany. We
shall find that they give no sanction to the hypothesis
of Mr. Mill and Mr. Bain, and seem to favour a theory

of a very different character. In the sketch that follows, I have made free use of the great works on physiology which have been published in our country, and still more particularly of the admirable historical, critical, and expository summary by Wundt, in his *Beiträge zur Theorie der Sinneswahrnehmung.*

TOUCH.

The scientific investigation of this sense may be said to have commenced with the researches of J. Müller and E. H. Weber. The general result reached by Müller is, that "every point in which a nerve-fibre ends is represented in the sensorium as a space-particle" (Wundt, *Theor. Sinneswahr.*) There are disputes as to how the general law should be stated, but we have a fact here which has not been and cannot be set aside. The nerves of touch proper, setting out from the base of the brain, tend towards the periphery of the body. They reach the skin each at a determined point : there is a special aggregation of these points in the mid-finger and the tip of the tongue. Now, wherever the nerve termi nates, there the sensation is felt : thus, if we prick a nerve which reaches the mid-finger, the pain is localized at the point where the nerve terminates. If we stretch or pinch the ulnar nerve, by pushing it from side to side, or compressing it with the fingers, the shock is felt in the parts to which its ultimate branchlets are distributed, namely, in the palm and back of the hand, and in the fourth and fifth fingers. "According as the pressure

" is varied the pricking sensation is felt by turns in the
" fourth finger, in the fifth, in the palm of the hand, or
" in the back of the hand ; and both on the palm and
" on the back of the hand the situation of the pricking
" sensation is different, according as the pressure on the
" nerve is varied ; that is to say, according as different
" fibres or fasciculi of fibres are more pressed upon than
" others. The same will be found to be the case in
" irritating the nerve in the upper arm" (Müller's *Physiology*, by Baly, p. 740). So strong is this tendency to
localize the sensation at the extremities of the nerves,
that when an arm or leg is amputated the person has
still the feeling of the lost limb. Müller has collected
a number of such cases (*Ib.*, pp. 746, 747). " A student,
" named Schmidts, from Aix, had his arm amputated
" above the elbow thirteen years ago ; he has never
" ceased to have sensations as if in the fingers. I
" applied pressure to the nerves in the stump ; and M.
" Schmidts immediately felt the whole arm, even the
" fingers, as if asleep." " A toll-keeper in the neigh-
" bourhood of Halle, whose right arm had been shattered
" by a cannon-ball in battle, above the elbow, twenty
" years ago, and afterwards amputated, has still, in
" 1833, at the time of changes of the weather, distinct
" rheumatic pains, which seem to him to exist in the
" whole arm ; and though removed long ago, the lost
" part is at those times felt as if sensible to draughts of
" air. This man also completely confirmed our state-
" ment, that the sense of the integrity of the limb was
" never lost." When there is a change made artifi-

cially in the peripheral extremities of nerves, the sensations are still felt as if in the original spots. "When, " in the restoration of a nose, a flap of skin is turned " down from the forehead and made to unite with the " stump of the nose, the new nose thus formed has, as " long as the isthmus of skin by which it maintains its " original connexions remains undivided, the same sensations as if it were still on the forehead; in other " words, when the nose is touched, the patient feels the " impression in the forehead. This is a fact well known " to surgeons, and was first observed by Lisfranc" (*Ib.*, p. 748).

No doubt it is possible to ascribe all this to experience and the association of ideas. We first, it is said, find by observation that a certain sensation originates in a particular part of the body, and the same sensation ever after suggests the part. But the facts, as a whole, will not submit to this explanation. It is difficult to see how the phenomena quoted can be thus accounted for. For surely an experience of thirteen or twenty years might have been sufficient to change the associations acquired at an earlier date, and to place the persons under the influence of new ones, provided always that the original ones had not been instinctive or native. In the case of the transference of the flap of skin, Müller says, "When the communication of the nervous fibres " of the new nose with those of the forehead is cut off " by division of the isthmus of skin, the sensations are " of course no longer referred to the forehead; the sensibility of the nose is at first absent, but is gradually

" developed." This language implies that the old reference to the forehead ceased in spite of the old association when the isthmus was cut; and that the new
reference to the nose was occasioned by the sensibility
of the nerve, according to the physiological law, which
makes us ascribe the sensation to the extremity of the
nerve. It is not easy to see how experience could give
us the ready localization of the sensation, more particularly when the feeling is within the body, and in a
part which has never fallen under the senses of touch
or sight. It is hard to believe that the instantaneous
voluntary drawing back of a limb when wounded, and
the shrinking of the frame when boiling liquid is poured
down the throat, can proceed from an application of an
observed law as to the seat of sensations. From a very
early age, and long before they give any evidence of
knowing distance beyond their bodies, or having any
other acquired perceptions, children will indicate that
they know at least vaguely the seat of the pain felt by
them,—if a child is wounded in the arm, it will not
hold out its foot. But the question seems to be set at
rest by a physiological fact, thus stated by Dr. Baly :—
" Professor Valentin (*Repertor. für Anat. und Physiol.*,
" 1836, p. 330) has observed, that individuals who are
" the subjects of congenital imperfection, or absence of
" the extremities, have, nevertheless, the internal sensa-
" tions of such limbs in their perfect state. A girl aged
" nineteen years, in whom the metacarpal bones of the
" left hand were very short, and all the bones of the
" phalanges absent—a row of imperfectly organized

" wart-like projections representing the fingers, assured
" M. Valentin that she had constantly the internal sen-
" sation of a palm of the hand, and five fingers on the
" left side as perfect as on the right. When a ligature
" was placed round the stump, she had the sensation of
" 'formication' in the hand and fingers ; and pressure
" on the ulnar nerve gave rise to the ordinary feeling
" of the third, fourth, and fifth fingers being asleep,
" although these fingers did not exist. The examina-
" tion of three other individuals gave the same results"
(*Ib.*, p. 747).[1]

Müller maintains, that in this way we get a knowledge of the greater number of the parts of our body,
and in all the dimensions of space ; and that when our
body comes into collision with another body, if the shock
be sufficiently strong, the sensation of our body to a
certain depth is awakened, and there arises a sensation
of the contusion in the whole dimensions of the cube.
He thus makes the knowledge not only of the third
dimension of space, but of our own body, to depend on
an original disposition (*Anlage*). He carries this doctrine so far as to hold that as the nerves of all the senses
are extended over the frame, so there is a representation
of space given not only by touch and sight, but also by
taste and smell—the sense of hearing alone not giving
us a perception of space, because it does not perceive

---

[1] Mr. Mill refers (p. 246) to a case given him by Hamilton from Maine
de Biran, of a person who had lost the power of the motor nerves, but who,
though still alive to the sense of pain, was unable to localize the feeling.
The case is valueless, as evidently the functions of the nervous apparatus
were deranged.

its special extension. " The first idea of a body having
" extension, and occupying space, arises in our mind
" from the sensation of our own corporeal extension.
" This consciousness of our own corporeal existence is
" the standard by which we estimate in our sense of
" touch the extension of all resisting bodies" (*Physiology*,
p. 1081). Wundt says (p. 2), " These views, if they are
" not always carried out with such consistency, are in
" their essential fundamental positions still acknow-
" ledged at this day by most physiologists."

It is interesting to notice that a like doctrine was
held on independent grounds by two of the greatest
psychologists of this century,—by M. Saisset in France,
and Sir William Hamilton in this country. The former
dwells on the localization of our sensations in their
various organic seats (see Art. " Sens " in *Dict. des Sciences
Philos.*) The latter says that " an extension is appre-
" hended in the apprehension of the reciprocal exter-
" nality of all sensations," and that " in the conscious-
" ness of sensations relatively localized and reciprocally
" external, we have a veritable apprehension, and con-
" sequently an immediate perception of the affected
" organism, as extended, divided, figured," etc. (App.,
Reid's *Works*, pp. 884, 885.)[1]   I confess that I have a
great partiality for this doctrine. Even the sense of
hearing, if it does not yield the extension of our frame,
may give a direction to the sound heard in the ear. The
conclusion is the result of accurate physiological research,

[1] It is interesting to find D. Stewart saying, " It is characteristical of
" all sensations of *touch*, that they are accompanied with a perception of
" the *local situation* of their exciting causes " (*Elem.*, vol. iii. p. 310).

and it seems to me to clear up most of the psychological difficulties connected with the senses, and to favour a metaphysical realism which enables us to stand up for the veracity of our original sense-perceptions, which are mainly of the body as affected. It supposes that when the soul is roused into consciousness by an affection of the nerves, it gives a direction and a localization to its sensations, and as it feels simultaneously a number of sensations from different members of the body, it feels them to be out of each other, and related in respect of direction; and as sensations accumulate and succeed each other, it gives a sensation, or rather perception, of our capacity of being affected at very different points of the periphery, and consequently of a volume. When in a tepid bath we have not only a pleasant sensation (which is all that Mr. Bain allows), we have a feeling of the frame as affected over the whole surface. But let not this statement be misunderstood. No one means to affirm that we have as yet a representation or image in the mind of the external configuration of the body, and of its several parts, such as we reach when we come to feel them with the hand or see them in a mirror. This is a subsequent attainment made by a gathered experience through the combination of various senses; and we are often in perplexity from the difficulty of uniting the intuitive with the acquired knowledge, as when we know that the pain in toothache is in a certain direction, and yet are in doubts as to what tooth corresponds externally to the internal localization. But as the ground of the whole, we have a localized perception of points, and of different points and directions, in our bodily frame, which, I may add, is felt to be ours by the command which our efforts have over it, and the sensations of which it is felt to be the seat. Some parts of this general view seem to me to be established by physiological arguments, and the theory as a whole is vastly better fitted to meet and account for our idea of extension than the baseless hypothesis sanctioned by Mr. Mill.

The curious experimental researches of Weber seem to confirm the general doctrine that Touch Proper or Feeling is very specially, as the Germans represent it, a space-giving organ. His experiments were conducted by means of a pair of compasses sheathed with cork, with which he touched the skin while the eyes were closed, in order to determine how close the points of the compasses might be brought to each and still be felt as two bodies. The distance between the points necessary to indicate different sensations was found to vary in different parts of the body, from one-half Parisian line on the tip of the tongue to thirty Parisian lines on the back of the body, thus showing the sensitiveness of the one part to be sixty times finer than that of the other part. The capability of discerning the difference of sensation is somewhat different in different individuals, but it is said that their relative proportion in different parts of the body remains tolerably constant in the same individual. The researches seem to imply that the sense of touch indicates to us, in a way which cannot be the result of a gathered experience, both points

of space and intervals of space, always within and not
beyond the bodily frame. The points must be per
ceived immediately, and an interval or line between is
either perceived immediately, or is necessitated in
mathematical thought by the comparison of the different points.

Weber regards the skin as a sort of mosaic of circles
or compartments, which in different positions have
different magnitudes and shapes, and that each has its
own capacity of sensation. The theory suggested by
Fick is thus stated by Dr. Carpenter: " Each nerve-
" fibril breaks up into a pencil of fine filaments at the
" periphery, which are distributed over a certain space,
" perhaps on the average about 1·25 of an inch in
" diameter. An impression made upon any one of these
" filaments conveys the same sensation to the sensorium,
" providing no other nerve be distributed to the same
" space ; but this hardly ever occurs, and hence com-
" pound sensations arise by which our perception of the
" precise spot of the skin touched by a point is accurately
" determined. It is obvious that the closer these
" ' sensory circles' are, and the more intimately the
" branches of different nerves are intercalated with one
" another, the greater will be the sense of locality of
" that part ; or, in other words, the greater will be
" the facility with which minute differences in the pre-
" cise spot touched will be appreciated" (*Hum. Phys.*,
p. 611). The subject has been keenly discussed in Germany. According to George, movement is the source
of all objective consciousness. If by objective con-

sciousness is meant not that of our bodily frame, but of something beyond, I believe the doctrine is correct. We discover extra-organic objects by the resistance offered to our movement. Fortlage ascribes our intuition of body to the restraint laid on our impulse (*Triebhemmung*). It is thus, no doubt, we know the existence of objects beyond our bodies, but already in touch we have an apprehension of our frames as extended. Lotze has observed much, and speculated more on this whole subject. He says that when two object-points come into perception through two excitations of the nerves, the consciousness of their spatial nearness to one another is not given ; and he starts the hypothesis that this is furnished by a third nerve-process, which he calls " place indicators." Meissner has sought to bring Lotze's hypothesis into unison with physiological and anatomical researches. He thinks he has discovered "touch-corpuscles," which he represents as the actual touch-organs. These are found specially in the hand and the foot, and they at once give us bodies without us as objects, apart from the sensation of pressure. These researches and discussions all proceed on the idea that our knowledge of an extended world is obtained not exclusively by a sweep of the hand, but by some special provision in the sense of touch proper or feeling.

The admitted conclusions are thus stated by Wundt (pp. 64, 65) : " With every single sensation (*Empfind-* " *ung*) is connected involuntarily the representation " of the place at which it occurs. As soon as there

" are two contemporaneous sensations in the percep-
" tion (*Wahrnchmung*), there is thence given a dim re-
" presentation of the extent of the skin which the
" impressions embrace, whereby the impressions are
" immediately conceived as spatially separated. But
" about the magnitude of their separation in space
" nothing determinate can yet be declared, as that re-
" presentation is for this purpose altogether indistinct.
" It is usually only when one is first led through an
" internal or external impulse to resolve upon an esti-
" mation by measure, that there is raised a clear image
" of the entire parts of the body and of the points
" touched, and thereby is first given the determinate
" representation of the interspace which lies between
" the impressions." He then explains, that, in regard to
the distance which is to be found between two impressions, the soul, in that it perceives two different sensations of place (*Ortscmpfindungen*), is compelled to put
an interspace between them, and to represent this out
of the like experience through sight or the muscular
sense.

MUSCULAR SENSE.

Sir Charles Bell established the great truth, that the
nerves of sensation differ from those of motion. From
his physiological researches, and the ingenious psychological speculations of his contemporary, Dr. Thomas
Brown, has proceeded the very general acknowledgment
in this country of the existence of a Muscular Sense to
be distinguished from Touch Proper. Physiologically

the Muscular Sense consists of a Motor nerve, under the control of the will, going out from the brain and moving the muscle attached to it, and of a Sensor nerve going back to the brain and giving intimation of the motion. Psychologically this sense serves as important purposes as either touch proper or sight. It may be doubted whether, apart from this endowment, we should have a sense or knowledge of any object beyond our bodily frame. Feeling, or the skin-sense as it has been called, seems to give us merely the periphery of our bodies; and when we become cognizant of an extra-organic object, as when on pressing the palm of the hand on a table we feel a surface, I believe there is a combination of the two senses of touch proper giving us a sense of the surface of the hand, and of the muscular sense giving a knowledge of an outward object resisting this surface. "If we lay our hand upon a table, we be-"come conscious, on a little reflection, that we do not "feel the table, but merely that part of our skin which "the table touches" (Müller, p. 1081). Even as to the coloured surface falling under the eye, it is doubtful whether we should place it certainly out and beyond our organism without the concurrence of the muscular sense and a gathered experience. The boy born blind, whose eye was couched by Cheselden, said that objects at first seemed "to touch his eyes as what he felt did his skin." In a like case operated upon, and recorded by Home, objects seemed at first to touch the eye. The expressions are somewhat vague, but it is clear that the objects were felt as having a close relationship to the

eye, and were not known as being at a distance. It is
certain that it is mainly and most effectually (if not
exclusively) by the muscular sense that we obtain an
apprehension, or rather knowledge, of an object beyond
our bodily frame, and independent of it. Dr. Carpenter,
with his usual sound judgment, declares that it is
probably on the sensations communicated through this
sense that " the idea of the material world, as some-
" thing external to ourselves, chiefly rests ; but that this
" idea is by no means a logical deduction from our ex-
" perience of these sensations, being rather an instinc-
" tive or intuitive perception directly excited by them "
(*Hum. Phys.*, p. 612).

I cannot do better than quote once more from Wundt,
who gives us the result of German research (p. 427).
" The first acts of sense-perception are grounded on the
" operation of the Muscular Sense [that is, so far as
" objects beyond the body are concerned]. When we
" move our members we come upon external resist
" ances. We observe that these resistances some-
" times give way before our pressure ; but we find
" at the same time that this takes place with very
" different degrees of facility, and that in order to put
" different bodies in motion we must apply very different
" degrees of muscular force ; but to every single degree
" of the contraction-force there corresponds a determi
" nate degree in intensity of the muscular sensations.
" With these muscular sensations, the sensations of the
" skin which cover our members of touch so continually
" mingle, that the intensity of these touch-sensations

" goes parallel to the intensity of the accompanying
" muscular sensations. We succeed in this way in con-
" necting the degree of intensity of the muscular sen-
" sations in a necessary manner with the nature of the
" resistances which set themselves against our move-
" ment."

VISION.

The eye is a more complicated structure than any of
the other organs of sense, and there are more disputes
as to the functions and operations of its parts than in
regard to those of any of the other senses. On some
points, however, there is a pretty general agreement
among the scientific physiologists in Germany, who have
devoted so much attention to the subject; and these are
sufficient for our purpose, being opposed to the hypothesis supported by Mr. Mill and Mr. Bain.

It seems to be admitted on all hands, that by the eye
we have immediately a perception of space in two
dimensions, or of a surface. In stating the views of
Müller, Wundt says (p. 95), " We can perceive spatial
" extension and the relation in position of outward objects
" only so far as we have a spatial sensation of our own
" retina and the relative position of its single points.
" As the retina spreads itself in a surface, the images of
" objects obtain upon it only two dimensions. But this
" disadvantage, under which sight labours as compared
" with feeling, is compensated by the body's own move-
" ments, by means of which we can view successively the
" one object from different stand-points. As regards

" the sense of sight, the perception (*Anschauung*) of the
" third dimension is through a judgment, and so Müller
" calls it a representation (*Vorstellung*), while he desig-
" nates the intuition of surface as a sensation." " The
" grand principle of the theory of Müller, that the
" perception of a surface is a sensation, and that the
" perception of depth on the other hand is a represen-
" tation formed through judgment, is to this day the
" universally received one, and the researches remain
" settled, although this department since that time has
" been enriched by a great many new facts, and although
" this principle, so far as certain matters of fact are
" concerned, does not seem to be sufficient." The in-
sufficiency does not relate to the original discernment
of a surface by the eye, which seems to be acknowledged on all hands, but to the provision in the eye
itself for discovering the three dimensions of space.
" The perception of superficial space, which goes before
" all representations of space, and makes the same
" possible, is bound up in the sense of sight so inti-
" mately with the pure sensation, that there is nowhere
" in the consciousness any act lying in the middle be-
" tween the sensation and its perception in the form
" of space " (p. 145). It should be added that Waitz
and Lotze are opposed as to whether the chief importance should be attached to the sensible or motor
factors : Waitz ascribing the greater value to the sensation ; and Lotze, to the motor element. Wundt (p. 104)
says that all observation shows that both exercise an
influence at the same time.

L.

So much for our perception of a superficies by the eye. But there is a provision in the organ of sight for giving us space in three dimensions, and for discovering the distance of objects. This can be done even by the single eye, not immediately with every perception, as may be done by the two eyes, but by a succession of perceptions. This is accomplished in the case of a single eye by its power of accommodating itself to different distances. Much attention has been given of late years to the nature of the accommodation-mechanism by Helmholtz and others. The accommodation seems originally to be involuntary and unconscious, but is brought under our notice by the attached muscular feeling. So far as this means is concerned, the determination of distance by one eye is confined within very narrow limits ; but there is a great help to it in the movement of the ball of the eye, of which intimation is given by the attached muscles. But by far the most important provision in the visual organ for discovering the third dimension of space is to be found in binocular vision, that is, in the convergence of the axis, according as the objects are near, and in the different aspect of the object falling under each eye. Wundt again supplies us with an excellent summary : " The measurements which " we are able to bring out by means of our senses which " give us the intuition of space show this remarkable " difference between the two, that the eye as the sense " operating in the distance measures space according to " all the four dimensions; whereas sensations by the skin, " which are effected only by the immediate contact of

" the outward object with the surface of the skin, are all
" disposed only over one surface. The perception of the
" third dimension of space through the sense of sight is,
" however, so far as can be proven by experience, a
" mediate one derived from the movements of the
" muscles of the eye (partly of the external, which move
" the apple of the eye ; partly of the internal, which
" regulate the accommodation - mechanism). These
" measurements of distance depend on nothing but
" the estimation of the muscular sensations accom-
" panying the movements, and therefore the percep-
" tion is accomplished only by means of a lengthened
" experience and practice, and hence arise the great
" uncertainty and incompleteness of all measurements
" of that kind. Originally all spatial sense-intuitions
" are of surfaces; depth for the eye comes forth gradually
" out of the surface ; the sense ever penetrates deeper
" and deeper into boundless space, its circle of vision
" widening as the visual circle of its experience ex-
" tends" (p. 29).

That the eye is immediately cognizant of direction
and superficial figure, is proven by the reported cases of
persons born blind, but who acquired eye-sight by
means of a surgical operation. The best reported case
is that of Dr. Franz of Leipzig (*Phil. Trans. of Roy. Soc.*
1841), and I shall quote from it at considerable length.
The youth had been born blind, and was seventeen years
of age when the experiment was wrought which gave him
the use of one eye. When the eye was sufficiently
restored to bear the light, " a sheet of paper on which

" two strong black lines had been drawn, the one hori-
" zontal, the other vertical, was placed before him at
" the distance of about three feet. He was now allowed
" to open the eye, and after attentive examination he
" called the lines by their right denominations." " The
" outline in black of a square, six inches in diameter,
" within which a circle had been drawn, and within the
" latter a triangle, was, after careful examination, recog-
" nised and correctly described by him." " At the dis-
" tance of three feet, and on a level with the eye, a solid
" *cube* and a *sphere*, each of four inches diameter, were
" placed before him." " After attentively examining
" these bodies, he said he saw a *quadrangular* and a
" *circular* figure, and after some consideration he pro-
" nounced the one a *square* and the other a *disc*. His
" eye being then closed, the cube was taken away and
" a disc of equal size substituted and placed next to the
" sphere. On again opening his eye he observed no
" difference in these objects, but regarded them both as
" discs. The solid cube was now placed in a somewhat
" oblique position before the eye, and close beside it a
" figure cut out of pasteboard, representing a plane out-
" line prospect of the cube when in this position. Both
" objects he took to be something like flat quadrates. A
" pyramid placed before him with one of its sides to-
" wards his eye he saw as a plain triangle. This object
" was now turned a little so as to present two of its
" sides to view, but rather more of one side than of the
" other : after considering and examining it for a long
" time, he said that this was a very extraordinary figure ;

" it was neither a triangle, nor a quadrangle, nor a
" circle ; he had no idea of it, and could not describe it;
" ' in fact,' said he, ' I must give it up.' On the con-
" clusion of these experiments, I asked him to describe
" the sensations the objects had produced, whereupon
" he said, that immediately on opening his eye he had
" discovered a difference in the two objects, the cube
" and the sphere, placed before him, and perceived that
" they were not drawings ; but that he had not been
" able to form from them the idea of a square and a
" disc until he perceived a sensation of what he saw in
" the points of his fingers, as if he really touched the
" objects. When I gave the three bodies (the sphere,
" cube, and pyramid) into his hand, he was much sur-
" prised he had not recognised them as such by sight,
" as he was well acquainted with mathematical figures
" by his touch." These observations show that the eye
takes in surface and superficial figure at once, but cannot immediately discern solidity. If the persons have
the use of both eyes, they would observe the difference
between a disc and a solid, but they would not be able to
say, till they feel it, that the latter is a solid. It re
quires to be added, that persons who have their sight
thus given them require observation and thought to recon-
cile the information they had got from touch with that
which they are now receiving from sight—just as persons
who have learned two languages, say German and French,
require practice to enable them readily to translate the
one into the other. In the case reported by Cheselden,
the boy, " upon being told what things were whose form

" he before knew from feeling, said he would carefully ob-
" serve that he might know them again." Dr. Carpenter
tells us of a boy of four years old, upon whom the operation for congenital cataract had been very successfully
performed, that " he continued to find his way about
" his father's house rather by feeling with his hands, as
" he had been formerly accustomed to do, than by his
" newly acquired sense of sight, being evidently per-
" plexed rather than assisted by the sensations which
" he had derived through it. But when learning a new
" locality, he employed his sight, and evidently perceived
" the increase of facility which he derived from it "
(*Man. of Phys.*, p. 593).

All the recorded cases show that there is also a process of reasoning and experience in the discovery of distance. Mr. Abbot (p. 150) gives the following account of
the observations of Trinchinetti :—" He operated at the
" same time on two patients (brother and sister), eleven
" and ten years old respectively. The same day, having
" caused the boy to examine an orange, he placed it
" about one metre from him, and bade him try to take it.
" The boy brought his hand close to his eye (*quasi a*
" *contatto del suo occhio*), and closing his fist, found it
" empty, to his great surprise. He then tried again a
" few inches from his eye, and at last, in this tentative
" way, succeeded in taking the orange. When the same
" experiment was tried with the girl, she also at first
" attempted to grasp the orange with her hand very
" near the eye (*colla mano assai ricina all' occhio*),
" then, perceiving her error, stretched out her forefinger

" and pushed it in a straight line slowly until she
" reached the object." Other patients have been observed
(by Janin and Duval) to move their hands in search of
objects in straight lines from the eye. Trinchinetti
" regards these observations as indicating a belief that
" visible objects were in actual contact with the eye."
It is clear that the eye gives direction to the object, but
does not apprehend distance immediately. Franz says
of his patient, that " if he wished to form an estimate of
" the distance of objects from his own person, or of two
" objects from each other, without moving from his
" place, he examined the objects from different points of
" view by turning his head to the right and to the left."

The German physiologists have paid great attention
to the case of persons born blind, and the conclusions
reached do not correspond with those of Platner. " As
" respects persons born blind," says Wundt (p. 60),
" who are not supported by the accompanying and pre-
" ceding experience of the sense of sight, the perception
" of the sensation of place takes place after a much
" more tedious and laborious manner. The blind man
" receives the representation of his body wholly through
" his own touch. While he touches with the finger or
" hand different parts of his body, there arise in the
" muscles of the arm just as many different muscular
" feelings. These become to him a measure of different
" distances. Thus he receives from the mutual spatial
" position of single points a representation of his skin-
" surface, and while at the same time, at every point,
" the *Quale* of the sensation corresponding to the same

" imprints itself, he is placed in a position also to de-
" clare the place where are to be found the impressions
" which work from without."

This is more fully explained (p. 31) : " The represen-
" tation of the third dimension can also be awakened
" in the person born blind, but this only through a long
" series of conclusions, in which the changing impres-
" sions of the sense of feeling, and the muscular sensa-
" tions of the entire self-moving body, work together.
" As the person seeing remains in his place, and lets
" the objects in a manner come towards him, while
" he, at his will, opens his eyes to the far or the near ;
" so must the blind person, when he would discover
" the outer world, go and seek out the objects which
" remain to him in unchangeable rest."   " The person
" seeing accommodates only his eye, the blind man his
" whole body, to the objects."

It does not concern us in this discussion to inquire
what truth there is in the Berkeleyan theory of vision.
If the above conclusions be trustworthy, as I believe
they are, they show it can be accepted only with important modifications.   Berkeley was positively mistaken
in arguing that the eye is percipient only of colour,
and not of extension.   He was further guilty of an
oversight in not attending to the very special provision
in the organs of vision for enabling us, always by experience, to discover the third dimension of space, and
distance.   It is firmly established that a surface is ever
presented to the eye, and is perceived immediately ; and
this surface supplies a measure to us in all our other

visual perceptions. It is now proven that there is a beautiful teleological apparatus in each eye, and still more in the relative position of the two eyes, whereby we can discover the solidity and estimate the distances of bodies.[1]

As the result of this criticism, conducted on the Psychological Method, we find ourselves entitled to adhere to a certain body of intuitive truth respecting both mind and matter. Instead of looking on mind as a mere "series of feelings," we apprehend it as an abiding existence, with various properties which evolve themselves from day to day in our experience. Instead of regarding matter as a "possibility," we contemplate it as having a permanent being, with diverse forms of activity, which are ever manifesting themselves to our senses. On this intuitive truth we build others by a gathered observation, and as we do so we feel that they are laid on a foundation which cannot be shaken.

Some object to this realistic doctrine, whether as held by the world at large or by professed metaphysicians, that it is contradicted by the established truths of modern physical science, which shows that light and heat are not substances, but vibrations in an ether, and that all the other physical forces are correlated with them. But these discoveries of recent science are all consistent with a doctrine of natural realism, when the same is properly expounded. Our senses afford us primarily a knowledge of the affections of our bodily frame, these affections being always localized. Such

---

[1] Thus far there is truth in Abbot's *Sight and Touch.*

information is given us by touch, by sight, and probably also by smell, taste, and hearing. Then, by the muscular sense, we come to know objects resisting the movement of our localized organs, and external to these organs. In these operations, and especially in muscular resistance, we know motion and force, that is, we are sensible of a limb moving in consequence of an effort, and being stayed by an extended object with a resisting force. This is all we know primarily of matter by the senses, and it has not been set aside by any doctrine of modern physical science.

I have no partiality for the distinction between the Primary and Secondary Qualities of bodies. In fact, as has often been acknowledged, the secondary qualities, such as heat and smell, are not so much properties of matter as felt affections of our organism, which may indeed imply an external cause, but with which they are not to be identified. We can, however, specify the qualities of body which are primarily or intuitively known. These seem to be Externality, Resisting Force, and Extension, together, I think, with Motion in Space. All besides, such as temperature, odours, tastes, and sounds, are mere affections of our organism, giving notice of changes in our bodily frame. Lotze says that our sense of pressure and of temperature is not an object, but a condition which the incitement in the parts of the skin brings forth. Meissner, following out the same doctrines, says that they are not sensations (*Empfindungen*), but feelings, in so far as they do not stand in relation directly and immediately to an object, but are a condition of the subject, our own selves. Even colour itself, though more objective, is felt merely, as in the seen surface, standing in relation to our eye, and we can say nothing more of it than that it affects us in a particular manner.

Taking this view of matter, we see that we have first an original or intuitive knowledge. To this we are ever adding by observation, by generalization, and by deduction. But then, in the rapidity of thought and the hurry of life, our observations are often loose, our generalizations too wide, and our reasonings hasty. Hence the errors into which we are led, which, however, are not to be charged on our senses, but upon the judgments we have superinduced upon the information which they furnish. It cannot be shown that our intuitive perceptions, being those that have the sanction of Him who made us, ever do deceive us, or that they are contradicted by any established truth of science.[1]

Adopting these views of our original perceptions, we see how we have a confirmation of their trustworthiness in the circumstance that the different senses yield the same testimony. I am persuaded, indeed, that our conviction rests primarily, and all along most firmly, on the assurance we have as to the veracity of each sense (see μ.) Still it is possible to get verifications even of our intuitions and demonstrations,—thus land measur-

[1] I have endeavoured to show that the difficulties connected with the apparent deception of the senses can be removed by attending to three distinctions :—(1.) That between our Original and Acquired Perceptions ; (2.) That between Sensation and Perception ; (3.) That between the Objects Intuitively Perceived : all of them being *extra-mental*, but some of them also *extra-organic.*—(*Intuitions*, Pt. II. B. II. c. i. § 3.)

ing and astronomy corroborate our geometrical deductions. It is certainly satisfactory to find that, in their
original depositions, the senses, which are so far independent witnesses, thoroughly concur. Thus both
touch and sight give us surfaces, which a little experience enables us to discover to be identical. It is probable that all the senses give us direction outward. It
is certain that they all give us information directly or
indirectly of external objects: and thus each in its own
way prepares us for looking out upon and estimating a
world which, beginning at self as a centre, extends as
far into space as the eye, aided by the telescope, can
penetrate.

CHAPTER VIII.

MEMORY, ASSOCIATION OF IDEAS, BELIEF, AND UNCONSCIOUS
MENTAL OPERATIONS.

THE faculty of Memory has not received any very
special consideration in the writings of Mr. Mill. When
we turn to the account given by his predecessors in the
school, we find it defective, in fact, as is usual with
them, overlooking the main element. Our recollections
are represented as 'revived sensations.' The statement
might be allowed to pass in common conversation, or
in loose literature, but cannot be accepted from a metaphysician. There may be a revival not merely of our
sensations, but of our mental operations generally, of
our thoughts, our emotions,—of our very recollections.
And in every exercise of memory there is more than a
revival of our experience. As the new and the essential
element, there is a *belief* that *we have had the experience*,
and that the *event* has been before us, *in time past*. All
this being matter of constant consciousness, we seldom
notice it, just as we pay no attention to the bodies
which we ever see falling to the ground. But as it was
the falling apple. which ordinary men thought beneath
their regard, which seemed to Newton (if the common

story is to be credited) the phenomenon to be weighed, and which actually furnished the key to the explanation of the path of the moon and planets in their orbits ; so it is in the familiar facts of our consciousness that the psychologist finds the means of clearing up the more complex laws of our mental nature. In particular, every one who would dive into the deeper mysteries of mind must specially estimate what is involved in memory, which is quite as important a faculty as even sensation in our mental constitution.

In memory, let it be observed, we are beyond the territory of immediate knowledge, with the object before us : we are now in the region of *Faith*. We believe in the existence of an object not now present ; in that, say, of a departed friend never again to be met with in this world. We believe that this friend lived, and that we had frequent intercourse with him, in time past. I call this the Recognitive Power of Memory, to distinguish it from the mere reproductive, the recalling and imaging power. What we thus experience, what we are conscious of, cannot be called ' a revived sensation ' without giving the *revival* much that was not in the *sensation*. We have now not only Faith in its rudiments, we have *Time* in all its significance. No doubt it appears first in the concrete mixed up with other things ; but so do all our ideas, so do our very sensations. It comes in the form of an event believed to have happened in time past. But it is there in the mind, consciousness being witness ; and we have only to abstract the time from the event to have the abstract idea of time,—just as we have the idea of sensation by separating in thought the sentient from the self-sentient. Time thus reached has quite as real an existence as the very sensation which may have been conjoined with our original perception of the event.

Mr. Mill, in language already quoted (*supra*, pp. 59, 85), admits the existence of the belief involved in memory, and asserts its veracity and ultimate veracity. Our memories and expectations are present feelings, but " each of them involves a belief in more than its own existence." A remembrance involves " the belief that " a sensation, of which it is a copy or representation, " actually existed in the past ;" and an expectation involves the belief, " that a sensation or other feeling to which it directly refers will exist in the future ;" and the belief the two include is, " that I myself formerly " had, or that I myself and no other shall hereafter " have, the sensations remembered or expected." He is fond, as we shall immediately see, of ascribing most of our convictions, beliefs, and judgments to association of ideas. Mr. James Mill had declared broadly, " that " wherever the name Belief is applied, there is a case of " the indissoluble association of ideas ;" and that " no " instance can be adduced in which any thing besides " an indissoluble association can be shown in belief" (*Analysis*, p. 281). But his son has been obliged to modify this doctrine, and to allow that there is an " ultimate " belief prior to association, and independent of it. I am sure that he is right in calling in such a belief. But I am also sure that he should have called in other beliefs equally independent of association ; and we shall have to supply his deficiencies as we advance by showing how wide is the domain of faith. Meanwhile let us observe how much is involved in the faith of memory and expectation. We have seen in last chapter that the senses directly or indirectly open to us the distant and the remote, till our minds are lost in the immensity of space. Now we see time stretching away into the past and the future, till it goes out into eternity. And it is interesting to notice, that while these ultimate beliefs, like the senses, carry with them their own evidence, they are ever meeting with corroborations. We remember a field, a dell, a cottage which we once visited ; we have not seen it for many years, but as we now go back to it, we find it as we have been picturing it in our minds. These confirmations of our lower faiths help us to put a more implicit trust in our higher natural beliefs, which may not admit of any confirmation by sense. Already, in this belief of memory and expectation, we have the beginnings and the rudiments of that faith in the unseen, which in its higher flights carries us so far beyond ourselves, and lifts us as on wings high above this world.

The subject of Association of Ideas, which is intimately connected with Memory, has long engaged the attention of British metaphysicians. It is referred to by Hobbes, who was evidently aware of what Aristotle had written. It was employed by Locke to explain certain anomalies and eccentricities of mind and character. Its importance in accounting for ordinary mental action was first brought out fully by Francis Hutcheson, who showed in particular how it helped to create secondary affections. Some of its properties had a prominence given them by Hume, who used it to help his sceptical purposes by explaining by it many of the beliefs usually ascribed to reason. A fuller and a juster account of it than any previously published was given by Turnbull (the preceptor of Reid) in his *Moral Philosophy*. Hartley speculated upon it in an empirical and peculiarly Anglican manner, identifying association with vibrations in the nerves. All the Scottish metaphysicians, including Reid, Beattie, and Stewart, discoursed upon it with greater or less fulness. But as universal attention was called to it, its power and significance came to be greatly exaggerated. This was certainly done by Alison when, passing far beyond the more sober views entertained on the same subject by Hutcheson and Beattie, he sought to account by this one principle for all the phenomena of beauty. Brown drew back from so extreme a position, and maintained that there was excited by beautiful objects a class of feelings which could not be resolved into association of ideas nor anything else. But in his mental physiology suggestion plays a very important, I would say the principal, part. He treats of our intellectual operations under the heads of Simple and Relative Suggestion, and indulges in an excess of ingenuity in making these two faculties manufacture so many of our ideas. Mr. James Mill followed, and carrying out a hint thrown out by Brown, that all our associate feelings could be reduced to " a fine species of proximity" (Lecture xxxv.), resolved all suggestion into the one law of contiguity; and abandoning Brown, who stood up for intuitive beliefs, and adhering to Hume, accounted for our very beliefs and judgments by association. The time for a reaction had now come. Artists never favoured Alison's reduction of beauty to association. New and profound ideas were introduced into English metaphysics by Coleridge, and through the taste stimulated by him and others for German speculation. But the recoil was actually called forth by Sir James Mackintosh's *Dissertation on Ethical Science*, which at once created the opposition of our higher moralists to the attempt made by him to manufacture our idea of moral good by means of association. Sir W. Hamilton, who belongs to this period, devoted his penetrating intellect to the more thorough expression of the laws of the reproduction of our ideas, and has thrown not a little light on the subject, at the same time keeping the principle in its own place. Some of us had hoped that this tendency to exaggerate the power and importance of association had enjoyed its day, and was now past for ever. But the wheel of speculative opinion seems to have come round to the position it had an age ago; and we find association of ideas occupying in the writings of the younger Mill and Mr. Bain as high a place as it ever had in the works of Alison and Brown, of Mackintosh and the older Mill,— or, we may add, as it had two ages earlier still in the philosophy of Hume and of Hartley. There is evidently clear room for a new discussion of the whole subject.

Of late it has been taken up by the German metaphysicians generally; and the School of Herbart, in particular, has been seeking to give a mathematical expression to the laws of the succession of our ideas. I should like to see the results of the investigations of the British School—especially of Hamilton, and of the later German metaphysicians, wrought out into a consistent system.

Mr. Mill can scarcely be said to have added much to our knowledge of the laws of association. He specially dwells on two points, and he exaggerates and distorts both. The first is what he calls the Law of Inseparable Association. " Associations produced by " contiguity become more certain and rapid by repeti-" tion. When two phenomena have been very often " experienced in conjunction, and have not in any " single instance occurred separately, either in experi-" ence or in thought, there is produced between them " what has been called Inseparable Association; by " which is not meant that the association must inevi-" tably last to the end of life, that no subsequent ex-" perience or process of thought can possibly avail to " dissolve it, but only that, as long as no such experience " or process of thought has taken place, the association " is irresistible, it is impossible for us to think the one " thing disjoined from the other " (p. 191). We have here an important truth, which was much dwelt upon by our author's father. It can scarcely be raised to the dignity of a law : it results from higher laws. According to the frequency with which two ideas have been together, so will be the tendency of the one to recall the other.

When they have often been associated, the one will bring up the other, not only without an act of will on our part, but it may be in opposition to our utmost efforts. Thus there are painful recollections which we would fain be rid of, but they cleave to us with horrid pertinacity, because conjoined with objects which are for ever pressing themselves on our notice. The only way of dissolving such a combination is by forming a new one,—as in chemistry we dissolve a compound by bringing to bear upon it another substance, which having a strong affinity to one of the elements, draws it away from that with which it is now united. It is thus we break up an old set of associations by forming new ones, say by a change of scene or society.

So far we have a well-known operation, according to a well-known law. But let us understand precisely what is involved. We shall find that Mr. Mill has so stretched the law as to make it embrace an entirely different phenomenon. It is implied that two ideas having been together, the one will never cast up without the other tending to follow. But this does not require that we judge or decide that there is, and still less that there must be, some relation between them in the nature of things, or discerned by the mind. On the contrary, we may see them to be utterly discrepant, and wish that we could only break the links that join them in the chain of association. Thus there is a lovely spot where we once saw a foul act committed, and ever since, as we pass it, the whole scene rushes into our mind; but we never think or conclude that there is any necessary or even natural connexion between the place and the deed. Mr. Mill has slipped in a word very dexterously, when he says, "It is impossible for us ever to think the one disjoined from the other." This is true only when by 'think' we understand 'having the idea of.' It is a fact that the one idea recalls the other, but we do not therefore *think* the one to be joined to the other, either in the nature of things, or according to the laws of thought.

We have here come to one of the gravest errors into which Mr. Mill has fallen in his theory of the operations of the mind. It is that of making the association of ideas usurp the province of judgment, which declares that two ideas or objects have a relation. I admit that the two, suggestion and judgment or comparison, often coincide and co-operate, and accomplish most important ends as they do so. Things that have a natural connexion are often presented to us together, they are thus brought under the law of association, and they are henceforth often recalled at the same time. In this way the association of ideas may lead to a hasty belief, not founded on a careful comparison of facts. I believe that much of what is usually reckoned understanding or judgment, contains little else than an association of ideas. The so-called 'thought' of the lower animals, of children, and even of men of mature years, consists mainly in ideas succeeding each other in a train determined by outward circumstances or by habit. It has to be added, that association of ideas often essentially aids us in forming a mature judgment, by bringing

things that have a positive relation into juxtaposition,
whereby we are enabled to discover the connexion.
As the association helps the judgment, so the judgment,
when it once connects the two things, creates an association of ideas, whereby the one tends to bring up the
other, and thereby we may be led to discover further
relations, real or imaginary. But the actual comparison
of two ideas or objects, and the predication of their
agreement or disagreement, is always an operation different from, and should be regarded as higher than, the
mere alliance of them by an accidental association in
our minds. The psychologist, instead of confounding,
should be careful to distinguish them. Philosophy
should aim at delivering us as much as possible from
the power of accidental conjunctions, and bringing us
under the habitual influence of a judicial temper of
mind, which looks to the nature of things. Mr. Mill
has done as much as within him lies to degrade human
intelligence, by grounding beliefs on association, when
he should have led us to seek for a deeper foundation
in the mind's capacity of discerning realities and their
relations. This is a subject which will come more fully
before us when we consider Comparison.

Mr. Mill makes great use of another peculiarity of
association, which had been much dwelt on by Brown.
" When impressions have been so often experienced in
" conjunction, that each of them calls up readily and in-
" stantaneously the ideas of the whole group, these ideas
" sometimes melt and coalesce into one another, and
" appear not several ideas but one" (*Logic*, B. VI. c. iv. § 3).

Thus far we have a correct statement. When ideas have often been in company, they flow together so spontaneously, and in the end so rapidly, that we cannot stay or even watch them in their course. As thus having no attention bestowed on them, some, or perhaps the whole, pass away into oblivion, according to a law to be immediately unfolded. Possibly we do not declare them to be one—I rather think we make no declaration about them at all ; but we do not, we cannot, distinguish them one from another. And when high feeling mingles with them, there may be produced upon our nervous organism a combined result of a peculiar, perhaps of an intense, kind, which may abide when the mental ideas and emotions are gone.

But Mr. Mill goes much further than this. " When " many impressions or ideas are operating in the mind " together, there sometimes takes place a process of a " similar kind to chemical combination" (*Logic*, B. vi. c. iv. § 3). This he explains, " The effect of concurring " causes is not always precisely the sum of the effects " of those causes when separate, nor even always an " effect of the same kind with them ;" thus water, the product, differs in its qualities from its two elements, oxygen and hydrogen. We must be very careful here to ascertain the precise facts, to guard against exaggerating them, or allowing them to be turned to illegitimate purposes. Let it be observed, that in chemical action we have always two substances, each with many properties known and unknown : we bring them into a certain relation to each other ; an action takes place very much of an unknown character, but implying the operation of electricity, or of one of the correlated forces of the universe; the result is the formation of water, which possesses properties different from the oxygen, and the hydrogen, and the energy exerted in producing the changes, but which is always capable of being resolved into the same old elements with the same measure of energy. Now the question is, is there an analogous operation produced by the association of ideas? I have admitted that, as the result of long and repeated conjunction, ideas, each, it may be, with its own peculiar feeling, succeed each other with incalculable rapidity, so that we cannot distinguish between them; and that they may coalesce in a result. Show the mother a plaything which belonged to a deceased child, and what a rush of remembrances and attached emotions will spring up, which she is not only not inclined, but not able, to analyse. But is there anything in all this like chemical action? There is a mighty torrent, but it appears to me that in the confluence there is nothing after all but the individual ideas with their corresponding feelings. There may be new associations, but there does not seem to be a new idea. Some of the ideas may pass away on the instant never to be recalled, whereas others may bulk largely before the mind, and leave their observed or abiding consequences. But in the agglomeration there seems to be nothing but the ideas, the feelings, and their appropriate impressions, coalescing; there is no new generation, no generation of an idea not in the separate parts of the collection.

In particular, it is altogether unwarrantable out of mere associated sensations to draw those lofty ideas which the mind can form as to substance and quality, cause and effect, moral good and moral obligation. Let us observe with care what is implied in the production of a new body by chemical composition. There is one element with its properties, and another element with its properties, a mutual action in which there is potential energy expended, and a new product with its properties. And this mutual action we reckon a wonderful action of bodies ; we distinguish it from mechanical action ; we call it by the name of chemical affinity, and we seek to determine its laws. But let us suppose that instead of two elementary bodies we have two sensations, say of two colours, or two smells, or two sounds, and that these have been often together, so that the one always comes up immediately after the other ; I ask, whether we have any ground to believe that these would of themselves generate a third thing different from the two ? If they do, it must be by some causal power in the sensations, or out of the sensations, in the mind or out of the mind : and it is the business of the psychologist not to overlook this power, not to confound it with the mere association of old ideas, but to separate it from them carefully, diligently to observe it, and endeavour to discover its laws—as the chemist seeks to find the law of elementary affinity. I can discover no evidence that two sensations succeeding each other will ever be anything else than two sensations, or that two remembered sensations will ever be anything else than two remembered sensations. When a further product appears, such as the idea of power, or the idea of the good, it cannot be the effect of a mere sensation, except in the sense above explained (p. 76), of an occasion, implying a co-operative capacity in the mind, such as a judgment or a power of discerning moral good,—which capacity should be noted as carefully as the sensations. In short, the laws of association are the mere laws of the succession of our ideas and attached feelings, and can generate no new idea, without a special inlet from without or capacity within. Association cannot give a man born blind the least idea of colour, and as little can it produce any other idea. By mixing the colours of yellow and blue the hand could produce green; but give a person the idea of yellow and the idea of blue, and from the two he could not manufacture the idea of green; still less could he from these sensations, or any others, form such ideas as those of time or potency.

There are two points in regard to the association of ideas which require to be cleared up. The first is the precise and ultimate expression of the law, that things which are related, in particular, that things which are like suggest each other. This law, under one form or other, has appeared in nearly every classification of the laws of the succession of our mental states from the time of Aristotle downwards. Mr. Mill puts the law in the form, "Similar phenomena tend to be thought of together" (p. 190). I believe that other related things do also suggest each other; but let this pass. The unsettled question is, must the relation be seen by the mind before the law operates? I see a portrait, and it at once suggests the original. I have never seen the two together; I see the portrait for the first time, the original is not present, and yet it is immediately called up. It can scarcely be alleged in such a case that I first discover the resemblance, and then have the idea of the original, for until the idea of the original springs up I cannot discover the resemblance. Is the law then to take this form, that like suggests like before the likeness is observed? This is a topic on which Hamilton often pondered, and he has advanced some subtle considerations which are perhaps not sufficiently reduced to a consistent system. Mr. Mill severely criticises Hamilton, but has not himself sounded the depths of the subject, which requires to be further cleared up before we have an ultimate expression of the laws of association. In endeavouring to explicate it, we must ever keep a firm hold of the distinction between the observation of relations, which is an act of comparison, and the mere suggestion of one thing by another. We shall see that the school of Mr. Mill has perseveringly confounded them.

The other point requiring further elucidation relates to the Secondary Laws of Suggestion, as they have been called by Brown, or the Law of Preference, as it has been called by Hamilton. To explain what this means: suppose that the idea now before the mind has been associated with a great number of others, according to the laws of contiguity and correlation; the question arises, why among these ideas does it go after one rather than another? I met with a dozen people at a dinner: what makes me think of some one of them rather than the others? Many references had been previously made to the facts bearing on this subject, but the first enumeration of Secondary Laws, as different from the Primary, was made by Brown, whose arrangement though clear was defective in logical reduction. I am sure there are two Laws of Preference which have a powerful influence. One of these is the law of native taste and talent. We go after the ideas which have the deepest interest to our natural faculties. Some, for instance, have a great tendency to observe resemblances, and among possible associations they will find likenesses, analogies, and affinities coming up most strongly and frequently. Some have constitutionally certain strong appetencies or passions, and their thoughts will tend towards the corresponding objects. The mother with a strong love of offspring will find every topic started and event occurring, suggesting possible perils or enjoyments to her children. I need not dwell on this, as it has no special reference to our present discussion. which certainly the other has.

I call it the Law of Mental Energy. Those ideas are brought up most readily and frequently on which we have bestowed the greatest amount of mental force. Every mind seems to be endowed with a certain amount of power, and, according to the power expended on an idea, so is it remembered for a greater length of time, and so is it suggested more easily and frequently. It may be an energy of sensation, as when the idea has

been very pleasurable or very painful. It may be an
energy of intelligence, as when we have devoted one or
several of our faculties, eagerly or for a length of time,
to a given object. It may be an energy of emotion, as
when a lively hope or an anxious fear has collected
round a particular event. Or it may be an energy of
will, as when we have given earnest attention to a subject. Of course, the ideas, when they appear, always
come up according to such Primary Laws as those
of contiguity and correlation; but the Law of Energy
shows why, among a variety of objects which it might
follow, the mind takes one rather than another. It is
thus we explain that Law of Inseparable Association
on which Mr. Mill dwells so much : the ideas have
been together, and much energy having been expended
on them in their frequent combination, they come up
together, and they come up often. Much the same
effects as are produced by frequent occurrence follow
from a very strong energy being exerted only for a brief
period, only, may be, for a few minutes or moments.
A strong sensation, as that of an avalanche, heard, it
may be, only once in our lives, may leave a life-long
impression of itself. We can never forget the moment
when, after long search and toil in some branch of research, a glorious thought burst on our view like the
sun, and threw a flood of light on all surrounding
objects. A terrible convulsion of fear will imprint itself on our souls for life, and be renewed by every correlated circumstance. An acute sorrow will burn itself
into the soul, and leave a wound which a thousand cir-

cumstances will tend to open,—thus the widow can never pass the spot where her husband was thrown out of a carriage and killed in her presence, without having the whole scene with its nervous agitations revived.

This train of thought and observation opens to us what I regard as a very deep and fundamental law of memory in its recalling power. I believe we are momentarily conscious of every sensation, idea, thought, or emotion of the mind. But it is mercifully provided that many of our mental states are never reproduced : they are happily allowed to pass away into forgetfulness, at least they cannot be brought up in ordinary circumstances,—though there are curious recorded instances of their reappearing in extraordinary positions. We should certainly be in a pitiable condition if every tick of the clock in the room in which we sit, if every act of will put forth in moving our limbs, if every passing thought in our day dreams or our night dreams, came up as readily as our more important cogitations, which have engaged and engrossed much thought and attention. While we are conscious (so it appears to me) of every mental operation, it seems to be necessary that a certain amount of mental force should be expended in order to our having the capacity to recall it. Very possibly this mental law may be connected with a physiological one, with what has been called by Dr. Carpenter "unconscious cerebration." I am inclined to think that our conscious mental affections tend to produce an unconscious brain affection, and that the concurrence of the brain thus affected is necessary in order to memory, or the reproduction of an idea. Now, a certain amount of mental force may be necessary to produce the cerebration, without which there can be no recollection. Whether from purely mental or cerebral causes, or as I think from the two combined, it looks as if the recalling of ideas requires that they should first have been in the consciousness with a certain amount of force or vividness. Many ideas which have been in the mind never reappear, and those which do, come forth, according to the power or prerogative we have imparted to them—like the stars, which do not all show themselves,—for otherwise the sky would be one blazing concave, but which, when they do appear, come out according to their nearness to us and their magnitude.

It is by this broader and deeper principle that I account for what Mr. Mill chooses to call the Law of Obliviscence. I agree with Sir William Hamilton in thinking that there may be more than one object before the mind at one time. Suppose that there are five objects before the eye, I believe that we could notice all of them. But our apprehension of all and each is so spread and dissipated, is so faint and vague, that the chance is, that no one of them ever presents itself to the mind at any future time. But let one of them be of a very brilliant colour, or let it have a large amount of attention centred upon it for a special end, or suppose that it had created an interest in itself in time past so that it now awakens lively feeling, that object will be found to have so imprinted itself on the mind, that it will remain when others pass into obliviscence.

" After reading," says Mr. Mill (p. 260), "a chapter of
" a book, when we lay down the volume do we remem-
" ber to have been individually conscious of the printed
" letters and syllables which have passed before us ?
" Could we recall, by any effort of mind, the visible
" aspect presented by them, unless some unusual cir-
" cumstance has fixed our attention upon it during the
" perusal ? Yet each of these letters and syllables must
" have been present to us as a sensation for at least a
" passing moment, or the sense could not have been
" conveyed to us. But the sense being the only thing
" in which we were interested—or, in exceptional cases,
" the sense and a few of the words or sentences—
" we retain no impression of the separate letters and
" syllables." By the same principle, we account for the
facts which of late years have been commonly ascribed
to Unconscious Mental Action.

Mr. Mill has done essential service to philosophy by
opposing the tide which, both in Germany and in Britain,
has been flowing too strongly in favour of this theory.
And yet I am not sure that he has apprehended all that
is in the facts supposed to favour the doctrine.

(1.) I hold that the soul, from the very first, is endowed with certain powers or tendencies. Even matter
has capacities which lead to action, and to changes of
state when the needful conditions are fulfilled ; and
much more must the soul have original properties,
which come forth in operation according to the law imposed on them. But in these primary endowments
there is no action, conscious or unconscious ; there is

simply a capacity of action. Some of the German philosophers who support the theory confound these *a priori* powers or regulative principles of the mind, of which we are certainly not conscious, with the actions that proceed from them, and of which we are conscious.

(2.) The mind by action is ever acquiring and laying up power, capacity, tendency. We have something analogous in physical nature. In the geological ages, the plants by drinking in the sunbeams acquired a stock of power, which went down with them into the earth as they sank into it, which abides in the coal which they helped to form, and is now ready to burst out in heat and flame in our fires, and supply mechanical power to our steam-engines. There seems to be a like laying up of power in the mind; of intellectual, and, I may add, of moral or immoral power—the result of continued mental action. When we have done an act, we have a greater capacity, along with a tendency to do it again. Thus it is that we are, all our lives long, and on every day of them, acquiring powers, tendencies, dispositions, habits, inclinations, which are to abide with us for years —perhaps for ever. This is one of the regulating principles in the reproduction of our mental states generally, and particularly in the association of ideas. What is done, and especially what is done repeatedly, leaves its trace on the soul, and may appear in deeds long long after. Ideas which have been together simultaneously or in immediate succession, have the property and the tendency to come up together, and this in proportion to

N

the mental energy which has been expended in producing them, and under this to the frequency with which
they have been together. This is one of the elements
which gives its beneficent and its awful power to habit.
But let it be carefully observed, that in all this we have
not come in sight of unconscious mental action. We
were conscious of every step of the actual operations of
the mind, and we were responsible for them throughout.
Those who support the theory mistake the unconscious
acquired power for unconscious acts.

(3.) The mind by action may affect the structure of
the brain, or the forces—mechanical, chemical, vital—
operating in it, and in the nervous system. Material-
istic physiologists represent high mental capacity as
resulting from a large or finely constructed brain. The
more probable theory is, that a nicely adapted and a
finely strung cerebral structure results from high mental
capacity and activity. It is not the casket which forms
the jewel, but it is the jewel that determines the size
and shape of the casket ; or, to use a better illustration
in such a connexion, it is the kernel that determines
the form of the husk. The finely organized brain thus
produced may, in man and the lower animals, tend to
go down by the ordinary laws of transmission from
parent to offspring. It is thus, that in certain of the
West India Islands, by examining the heads of the
negroes on a plantation, a hatter can tell at what age
their forefathers were transplanted from Africa,—the
brain being larger in those families whose ancestors
have been longest in contact with civilized men. It is

thus, that in our own country, the average size of the heads of the educated classes is larger than that of the uneducated. But in this, the actual action of the mind is conscious throughout. It is only the organic product of which we are unconscious.

This is not the place to work out these principles to their results. They imply important and far-ranging consequences—mental and organic. But these are not the doctrines defended by those whose opinions I am here reviewing. Not satisfied with native endowments, and acquired powers, and bodily effects, which are un-conscious, they insist on the existence of actual opera-tions which are unaccompanied with consciousness. They are not agreed among themselves as to what is the nature of this action. The theory was introduced into modern speculation by Leibnitz, who connected it with the essential activity of his monads. It was eagerly seized by certain of the pantheistic speculators of Ger-many, who maintained that the Divine Idea awakes to consciousness according to certain laws. As held in the present day, it takes two different, I should say incon sistent, forms. According to a numerous school in Germany, which may be held as represented by the younger Fichte, the unconscious mental action is thought, and thought of the highest kind : the thought which in the bee constructs the cells on mathematical principles ; which bursts out in the highest products of genius, artistic, literary, and philosophic, and gives birth even to inspiration. The theory under this form seems to me to be fanciful in the highest degree. As to ani mal instincts, they are clearly to be traced to original or inherited properties, obeying laws not yet determined. And as to genius, it is to be explained by far different principles. We account for it by high mental endow ment, often stimulated into intense action by a peculiar nervous temperament. We have no evidence that, prior to Bacon composing the *Novum Organum*, or Shakspeare writing *Hamlet*, there was any mental operation below consciousness. There were lofty gifts in both, and also a training and experience which left their permanent effects ; but when these came forth into action, I apprehend that the illustrious authors were quite conscious of them, though they might not have been able or disposed to furnish a metaphysical analysis of them.

The theory of Hamilton is of a more sober character, but seems to be equally devoid of evidence to support it. The class of facts on which he rests his opinion are misapprehended. " When we hear the distant murmur " of the sea, what are the constituents of the total per-" ception of which we are conscious?" (*Metaph.*, vol. i. p. 351.) He answers that the murmur is a sum made up of parts, and that if the noise of each wave made no impression in our sense, the noise of the sea, as the result of these impressions, could not be realized. " But the noise of each several wave at the distance, " we suppose, is inaudible ; we must, however, admit " that they produce a certain modification beyond con-" sciousness on the percipient object." He speaks of our perception of a forest as made up of impressions

left by each leaf, which impressions are below consciousness. There is an entire misapprehension of the
facts in these statements, and this, according to Hamil
ton's own theory of the object intuitively perceived.
The mind is not immediately cognizant of the sound
of the sea, or of its several waves,—nor of the trees of
the forest and their several leaves. All that it knows
intuitively is an affection of the organism. The im
pression made by the distant object is on the organism ;
and when the action is sufficiently strong, the mind is
called into exercise, and, from the perceived affections,
argues or infers the peculiar nature of the distant cause.
In this class of phenomena there is no proof of a mental
operation of which we are unconscious.

Hamilton explains, by supposed unconscious acts, a
class of mental phenomena with which we are all familiar. We walk in a " brown study" from a friend's house
to our home : there must have been many mental acts
performed on the way, but they cannot be recalled.
The question is, were they ever before the consciousness ? Dugald Stewart maintains that they were for
the time, but that we cannot recollect them. Notwithstanding the acute remarks of Hamilton, I adhere to
the explanation of Stewart. I do so on the general
principle, that in propounding an hypothesis to explain
a phenomenon, we should never call in a class of facts,
of whose existence we have no other proof, when we
can account for the whole by facts known on indepen
dent evidence. Hamilton tells us, " When suddenly

" awakened during sleep (and to ascertain the fact, I
" have caused myself to be roused at different seasons
" of the night) I have always been able to observe that
" I was in the middle of a dream ;" but, he adds, that
he was often scarcely certain of more than the fact that
he was not awakened from an unconscious state, and
that we are often not able to recollect our dreams.   He
represents it as a peculiarity of somnambulism, that
we have no recollection when we awake of what has
occurred during its continuance (vol. i. pp. 320-322).
Every one will admit that we are often conscious of
states at the time, which we either do not remember at
all, or more probably cannot remember, except for a very
brief period after we have experienced them.   We have
thus an established order of facts sufficient to explain
the whole phenomena, and do not require to resort to
alleged facts of which we have and can have no direct
evidence.   We walk home of an evening from a place
at a distance conversing as we go along with a friend.
In order to our reaching our dwelling, there must have
been a number of mental acts to enable us to thread our
way, along possibly a very perplexed road.   Next morn-
ing we remember the topics gone over in the conversation, but have entirely and for ever forgot the acts of
will implied in guiding our steps.   But I venture to
affirm that at the time we were conscious of both, that
we were conscious even of the volitions that brought
us safely to our home, and that we should have seen
this and acknowledged it, and remembered it, had

there been anything to call our attention to it at the
time. The reason why the one is remembered while the
other is forgotten, is to be found in the circumstance,
that the conversation excited our interest, whereas the
walk, as being the result of long acquired habit, called
forth no feeling, and so passed into oblivion.

CHAPTER IX.

JUDGMENT OR COMPARISON.

In this chapter I have to point out, first, a grave defect, and then a still graver error.

There is no part of the psychology of the school to which Mr. Mill belongs in which their defects are so evident as in their account of the Judging, Comparative, or Correlative capacity. They may have been misled in part by Brown, who joined in one suggestion and relation, under a faculty which he called Relative Suggestion, whose function it is at once to discover relations and suggest objects according to relations. Brown was wrong, I think, in allowing two such diverse functions to one power; but it is justice to him to say that he has given a comprehensive view of the relations which the mind of man can discover. He has a generic and a specific division. He has first a grand twofold division into Co-existence and Succession. Under the first he embraces Position, Resemblance or Difference, Proportion, Degree, Comprehension; and under the second, Causal and Casual Priority. The later members of the school, such as Mr. James Mill, Mr. J. S. Mill, and

Mr. Bain, have been lessening the number, and lowering the importance of the relations which can be discovered by our faculties, and thus narrowing our mental powers, so as to enable them the more readily to account for the phenomena of the mind by sensations and association. Mr. James Mill does speak of Relative Terms, but contrives to get them without calling in a special faculty of Comparison. Mr. J. S. Mill, after specifying 1st, Feelings, 2d, Minds, and 3d, Bodies, as included among nameable things, mentions, " 4th and last, the " Successions and Co-existences, the Likenesses and " Unlikenesses between feelings or states of conscious- " ness." In explanation, he tells us, " Those relations, " when considered as subsisting between other things, " exist in reality only between the states of conscious " ness which those things, if bodies, excite, if minds, " either excite or experience " (*Logic*, B. I. c. iii. § 15). This statement is quite in accordance with his general theory as he has now developed it. As we know originally only feelings or states of consciousness, so the relations we discover can only be between feelings and possibilities of feeling. No doubt most people imagine that in comparing Julius Cæsar, Charlemagne, and Napoleon Buonaparte ; and in comparing or contrasting Louis Napoleon with Augustus, Comte with Hobbes, and Mill with Hume, we are comparing things out of our states of consciousness : but the new philosophy corrects this vulgar error, and in doing so is consistent with itself—whether it be consistent with our intuitive assurances or no. To complete the simplicity of the reduction, Mr. Bain tells us, in reviewing Grote's *Plato* (*Macmillan's Magazine*, July 1865), "These two facts, " Cognisance of Difference and Cognisance of Agree- " ment, can be shown to exhaust the essence of know- " ledge, and both are requisites. All that we can " know of a gold ring is summed up in its agreement " with certain things, round things, small things, gold " things, etc., and its differences from others, squares, " oblong, silver, iron," etc.

I maintain that this account of man's power of cor- relation is far too narrow,—consciousness being the witness and arbiter. Profound thinkers have given a much wider sweep to the intellect. I have quoted the enumeration by Brown, and I have presented below the classifications of such thinkers as Locke, Hume, and Kant.[1] I ask the reader to look at them, and to decide for himself whether they can all be reduced to agree- ment and disagreement. Mr. Mill gives a place to co- existences and successions. In this he is surely right : for when I say that Shakspeare and Cervantes died the same year, and that the ancient epic poets, Homer and Virgil, lived before the modern ones, Dante and Milton, I indicate more than an agreement in the former case and a disagreement in the latter,—I intimate the point of

---

[1] Locke specifies Cause and Effect, Time, Place, Identity and Diversity, Proportion and Moral Relations (*Essay*, B. II. c. xxxvii.) Hume mentions Resemblance, Identity, Space and Time, Quantity, Degree, Contrariety, Cause and Effect. Kant's categories are,—I. Quantity, containing Unity, Plurality, Totality. II. Quality, containing Reality, Negation, Limita- tion. III. Relation, containing Inherence and Subsistence, Causality and Dependence, Community of Agent and Patient. IV. Modality, containing Possibility and Impossibility, Existence and Non-Existence, Necessity and Contingence.

relation, which is that of Time,—a relation, I may add, the significance of which has not been estimated by Mr. Mill. When I say that one figure before my eyes is a disc, and another a solid, I declare more than a difference or co-existence, I declare that the two differ in respect of their occupation of space. Again, when I affirm that oxygen is one of the elements of water, I predicate a relation of part and whole, and imply one of composition, which is surely more than agreement, or co-existence, or succession. The same may be said of other relations, such as that of quantity, when I maintain that Chimborazo is higher than Mont Blanc : and of active property, when I declare that the sun attracts the earth, and that oxygen combines with hydrogen to form water.[1]

We are now in a position to discover and expose what is perhaps the most fatal error in the whole theory : it consists in ascribing to association the functions of judgment. Mr. James Mill thus sums up a statement : " We have now then explored those states " of Consciousness which we call Belief in existences : " Belief in present existences; Belief in past existences; " and Belief in future existences. We have seen that, in " the most simple cases, Belief consists in sensation alone, " or ideas alone ; in the more complicated cases, in sen - " sation, ideas, and association, combined; and in no " case of belief has any other ingredient been found."

[1] I have arranged the Relations as those of Identity and Difference, Whole and Parts, Space, Time, Quantity, Resemblance, Active Property, and Cause and Effect.—*Intuitions.* P. II. B. III. c. i.

As to Propositions, he says they are either of general
names or particular names.   Of the former he says,
" They are all merely verbal ; and the Belief is nothing
" more than recognition of the coincidence, entire or
" partial, of two general names."   As to the latter, he
says, " Propositions relating to individuals may be ex-
" pressions either of past or future events.   Belief in
" past events, upon our own experience, is memory ;
" upon other men's experience, is Belief in testimony ;
" both of them resolved into association.   Belief in
" future events is the inseparable association of like
" consequents with like antecedents" (*Analysis*, pp. 290,
307, 308).   I am not sure whether the son would adopt
the whole of this statement : he has been obliged to
admit that memory yields an ultimate belief, which is
not the result of association.   But his theory in the
main coincides with that of the father.   It is admitted
that there is an original consciousness of sensations,
and that there is a memory of sensations, which cannot
be resolved into anything simpler.   It is further postulated that there is an association of sensations according
to contiguity and agreement, and that there is an expectation of sensations.   Out of these, as I understand,
spring our judgments (if indeed we have the power of
judging) and our beliefs, which imply, and can imply
nothing more than contiguity or agreement in the sensations.   I charge this doctrine with stripping man of
the capacity of judging of the actual relations of things ;
and making all our beliefs, except those involved in sensations, and the memory of them, to be the creation of

circumstances, and capable of being changed only by circumstances with their conjunctions and correspondencies, which, for anything we can ever know, may be altogether fortuitous or fatalistic.

The defects of the theory commence in the account given of the matter with which the mind starts : this is supposed to be merely sensations. But the fatal consequences do not become evident till we see what must be the explanation rendered of the mind's capacity of Judgment. I have endeavoured in this treatise to meet and stop the error at its inlet, that so we may be preserved from the issues. I have shown that the mind starts with an original stock of knowledge and belief. In sense-perception it knows objects, with an existence, external to self, extended, and capable of resistance and of motion. In self-consciousness it knows self as an existing thing, sentient, or knowing, or remembering, or believing, or judging, or resolving, or entertaining moral or other sentiments. In memory we remember ourselves and the event in the past, and thus have a continuous and identical self, with the important element of time. And now we can compare all these, and discover relations among them. By this further faculty the domain of our knowledge is indefinitely extended : in fact our acquaintance with an object is very vague and very limited till we have detected its connexions with other things. But what I wish specially noticed is, that the comparison is not between mere " feelings or states of consciousness," but between *things*, without us as well as within us. I compare self in one state, say under sensation, with self in another state, say re-collecting or resolving. I compare one extended object with another, and declare the one to be larger than the other. I compare events remembered, and declare that they happened at different times. I compare my very comparisons, and discover further, it may be more recondite, proportions and harmonies, till we link all nature within and without us in a series of uniformities. And let it be observed, that our judgments throughout are judgments as to realities. As being cognizant of extended objects in perception by the senses, on noticing two extended objects, say St. Paul's and its door, we declare the one to be greater than the other; and our judgment is about things, and not about sensations, or the mere possibilities of sensation. On seeing two persons on our right hand and two persons on our left hand, we declare them to be four, as soon as we understand what 'two' and what 'four' mean. We remember our school days and our college days, and we declare the one to be prior to the other. Our comparisons in such cases are of things, and our judgments upon things, and not on mere feelings, or mere possibilities of feeling. Circumstances have not produced the judgments, nor can circumstances change or modify them. In all circumstances I decide that the house is larger than its door; that two and two make four; and that an event which occurred when we were ten years old must be prior to one which happened when we were twenty.

I admit that association tends to produce action, in-dependent of judgment upon a comparison of the things.

When things have often been together in the mind, we
go spontaneously from the one to the other; and if action
be needed to secure the second, we will be disposed to
exert it. As Mr. Bain, in unfolding the nature of our
Beliefs, expresses it (*Emot. and Will*, p. 579),[1] " An
" animal sees the water that it drinks, and thereby
" couples in its mind the property of quenching thirst
" with the visible aspect. After this association has
" acquired a certain degree of tenacity, the sight of
" water at a distance suggests the other fact, so that,
" from the prospect, the animal realizes to some degree
" the satisfying of that craving. The sight of water to
" the thirsty animal, then, inspires the movements
" preparatory to actual drinking; the voluntary organs
" of locomotion are urged by the same energetic spur
" on the mere distant sight, as the organs of lapping
" and swallowing under the feeling of relief already
" commenced. This is the state of mature conviction
" as to the union of the two natural properties of water."
I reckon this as a case mainly of association, and not of
judgment. I do allow that association tends to make
us form judgments. When two objects have been often
brought together, we are led to discover a resemblance,
real or imaginary, between them. But admitting all
this freely, I maintain that the mind has a power of
judgment, upon the bare contemplation of objects, and
apart altogether from the association of instances. On
the simple consideration of two straight lines, I am sure

[1] Mr. Bain admits Intuitive Beliefs. but then they deceive us. " The
inborn energy of the brain gives faith, and experience scepticism," p. 582.

they cannot enclose a space. I have only to hear of a case of ingratitude for favours to declare it to be bad and blameworthy.

While the two, association and comparison, often help each other, yet they are never the same. The one may exist without the other; and the one does not increase nor decrease with the other. In many cases there is a strong and inseparable association without the judgment perceiving any relation, nay, where it would declare that there is no connexion in the nature of things. Thus the letter A naturally suggests the letter B, because they have come so often together in our repetition of the alphabet; yet no one thinks that the two have in themselves any bonds of union. It so happens that, when the name St. Patrick is brought up, I always associate with it the legend I heard in my youth about the saint swimming from Donaghadee to Portpatrick, with his head in his teeth; yet the frequency of the conjunction has not been able to convince me of the possibility of the act. Often have the numbers 17 and 20 been together in my mind, from the accident of their having been printed together on a card on which I had frequent occasion to look; but it has never occurred to me that the two must have a necessary connexion. It thus appears that frequency of association cannot of itself generate a judgment with its attached belief. On the other hand, a judgment declaring that there is a connexion does not imply that there has been a frequent association. Comparatively seldom have $17 + 20$ been conjoined in my mind with

37—certainly not so frequently as 17 has been associated with 20,—and yet, on the bare contemplation of 17 + 20, I declare them to be equal to 37, and cannot be made to decide otherwise. If I hear that Peter Jones robbed his master John Smith who trusted him, I declare that Peter Jones deserves punishment, and this though I never heard of Peter Jones before.

Mr. Mill is prepared to carry out his principles to consequences, which seem to me a *reductio ad absurdum* of the principles. He tells us (p. 69) that " the reverse " of the most familiar principles of geometry might have " been made conceivable, even to our present faculties, " if these faculties had co-existed with a totally different " constitution of external nature," and quotes at length, in proof of this, from *Essays by a Barrister*, in which it is said,—" There is a world in which, whenever two " pairs of things are either placed in proximity or are " contemplated together, a fifth thing is immediately " created and brought within the contemplation of the " mind engaged in putting two and two together. This " is surely neither inconceivable, for we can readily " conceive the result by thinking of common puzzle " tricks, nor can it be said to be beyond the power of " Omnipotence. Yet in such a world surely two and " two would make five." This certainly would be the result on Mr. Mill's theory. But such consequences can be admitted only by those who deny the mind all power of knowing the nature of things. Those of us who stand up for a power of independent judgment, that is, a judgment founded on the perception of things, cannot allow such conclusions. Were we placed in a world in which two pairs of things were always followed by a fifth thing, we might be disposed to believe that the pairs caused the fifth thing, or that there was some prearranged disposition of things producing them together; but we could not be made to judge that $2 + 2 = 5$, or that the fifth thing is not a different thing from the two and the two. On the other supposition put, of the two pairs always suggesting a fifth, we should explain their recurrence by some law of association, but we would not confound the 5 with the $2 + 2$, or think that the two pairs could make five.

The same ingenious gentleman supports the theory by another illustration, and receives the sanction of Mr. Mill. " It would also be possible to put a case of a " world in which two lines would be universally sup- " posed to include a space. Imagine a man who had " never had any experience of straight lines through the " medium of any sense whatever, suddenly placed upon " a railway stretching out on a perfectly straight line " to an indefinite distance in each direction. He would " see the rails, which would be the first straight lines " he had ever seen, apparently meeting, or at least " tending to meet, at each horizon; and he would thus " infer, in the absence of all other experience, that they " actually did enclose a space when produced far enough." Now I allow that this person, as he looked one way, would see a figure presented to the eye of two straight lines approaching nearer each other; and that as he looked the other way he would see a like figure. But I deny that in combining the two views he would ever decide that the four lines seen, the two seen first and the two seen second, make only two straight lines. In uniting the two perceptions in thought he would certainly place a bend or a turn somewhere, possibly at the spot from which he took the two views. He would continue to do so till he realized that the lines seen on either side did not in fact approach nearer each other. Or to state the whole phenomenon with more scientific accuracy: Intuitively, and to a person who had not acquired the knowledge of distance by experience, the two views would appear to be each of two lines approaching nearer another; but without his being at all cognisant of the relation of the two views, or of one part of the lines being farther removed from him than another (see *supra*, pp. 160-168). As experience told him that the lines receded from him on each side, he would contrive some means of combining his observations probably in the way above indicated; but he never could make two straight lines enclose a space.

The same remarks apply, *mutatis mutandis,* to a third case advanced by the Barrister. Thomas Reid, who was a man of humour and addicted to mathematics, amused himself and relieved a dry discussion by drawing out a " Geometry of Visibles " (*Works,* p. 147), in which he exhibits the conclusions which could be deduced from the supposed perceptions of sight. He proceeds upon the Berkeleyan doctrine of vision, and supposes that by

sight we could have " no conception of a third dimension " of space ; and that a person with sight, but without touch, would see length and breadth, but could
have no idea of thickness, or of the distinction of figures
into planes and curves. Such a one, he thinks, might
be driven by geometry to the conclusion that " every
" right line being produced will at last return into
" itself ;" that " any two right lines being produced will
" meet in two points ;" and that " two or more bodies
" may exist in the same place." But these inferences
can be deduced only by denying to vision functions which
belong to it, and ascribing to it others which are not
intuitive or original. We have seen that the eye takes
in intuitively a coloured surface, and if there be two
colours on the surface, divided by a curve line, we at
once have the perception of a curve. Again, by binocular vision we have, if not intuitively, at least by an
easy process of experience and inference, space in the
third dimension. It is further to be borne in mind, that
in our acquired perceptions we lay down rules which
may help us in common cases, but which, not being
absolutely correct, may lead into error when improperly
applied to other cases ; as when we argue from the
crooked image presented to the eye that there is a
crooked stick corresponding to it in the water. Proceeding on such assumptions as these, it is possible to
show that we are landed in the consequences so graphi-
cally pointed out by Reid. But the consequences are
not legitimate, because they are drawn from a misapprehension of the precise nature of our intuitive

perceptions in vision. There is and can be no evidence
that a person with the sense of sight, but without the
sense of touch, would draw them. I hold that the very
vision of two straight lines would prevent us from
being led to declare that they could meet at two
points. Upon the bare contemplation of the lines,
whether made known by sight or touch, we at once
reject all such conclusions, however ingeniously constructed from premisses which have not the sanction of
our constitution.

When such consequences are allowed and defended,
we see how ominous is this conjunction in the philo
sophic firmament of the School of Comte with that of
Hume. The philosophy thus generated places truth,
that is, a knowledge of the nature of things, beyond the
reach of the human faculties ; which commence with
they know not what, and close, after a laborious process,
with results which may have as little reality as a succession of dissolving views. Stripping us of a power of
independent judgment, it leaves us the servants, I should
rather say the slaves, of circumstances, with their conjunctions and correspondences, which may all be the
issue of blind chance or dead mechanism,—certainly
without our being able to say that they are not. Along
with independence, I fear there is also taken away all
responsibility, of judgment and belief, -except, indeed,
such accountability as we may require of a horse or a dog
when we associate its vices with a lash, simply to prevent the animal from doing the deed again. I am per-

suaded that such a creed must exercise, whether the persons are or are not aware of it, whether they do or do not confess it, a deadening influence on those who actually believe it and come under its sway; and if ever it should be accepted in its results (I say *results*, for its processes are too subtle to be grasped by the rough hands of the common people), and its appropriate sentiments diffused, in a community, the consequences would be as fatal as those which flowed in the end of last century in France, from the prevalence of the Sensational Philosophy, when it gave a wrong direction to the great political upheaval, and helped to degrade the national character.

We can avoid these issues only by maintaining that man is so constituted as to know originally something of the reality of things, and to be capable of rising to an acquaintance with their relations. Association may help us to form a reasonable judgment—and it is a happy circumstance when it does so; but whether we are or are not so aided, we should be taught that it is our duty to found our beliefs on a previous judgment, in which we look to the nature of things as the same can be discovered by us. One end, no doubt, of a good training is to encompass us with profitable associations in the family, in the social circle, and in the community; with associations originating in the highest sentiments, and sanctioned by the common conscience and the universal reason of the men of former ages. But it is a still higher end of the highest education to raise us above all hereditary and casual association of times or circumstances, and to constrain us to base our beliefs on an inspection of realities and actualities. Every youth should be taught that he is endowed with an inherent power of discernment, which he is not at liberty to lay aside in any circumstances, and for the proper use of which he is responsible.

CHAPTER X.

WHEN Professor Ferrier propounded the theory that one's self mixes as an integral and essential part with our knowledge of every object, and Sir William Hamilton unfolded his doctrine of the relativity of knowledge, I felt constrained to declare that there were views prevalent in metaphysical speculation which were working as much mischief as the ideal theory had done in the days of Berkeley; and I ventured to affirm that if Professor Ferrier's speculations were not regarded as a *reductio ad absurdum* of the whole style of thinking, " the next phenomenon appearing in the philosophic " firmament must be a Hume or a Fichte" (*Meth. of Dir. Govern.*, 4th Edit. App. pp. 536-539). In now holding that this fear has been realized, it is not needful to maintain that Mr. Mill is in every respect like either the great Scottish sceptic or the great German idealist, any more than to assert that these two are like each other. Mr. Mill is not so original a thinker as Hume, nor does he like him profess scepticism. He does not possess the speculative genius of Fichte, and he defends his system in a much more sober manner. But it can be shown that his philosophy comes very nearly to the positions taken up by Hume, when Hume is properly understood ; and in maintaining that mind is a series of feelings aware of itself, and that matter is a possibility of sensations, he has reached conclusions quite as visionary as those of Fichte. As Hume brought out fully the results lying in the philosophy of Berkeley —as one of the offshoots of the philosophy of Locke, and as Fichte carried to their logical consequences certain of the fundamental principles of Kant, so Mr. Mill, and we may add Mr. Herbert Spencer, are pursuing to their proper issues the doctrine floating in nearly all our later metaphysics, that we can know nothing of the nature of things.

Mr. Bain speaks complacently of " the great doctrine " called the Relativity of Knowledge, which has risen " by slow degrees to its present high position in philo- " sophy." But unfortunately—I should rather say for- tunately—no two defenders of the doctrine have agreed as to the sense in which they hold it ; in fact I can see no point in which they meet except the Comtian posi- tion, that the knowledge of the actual nature of things is beyond the reach of man. Mr. Mill remarks very properly (p. 5), that the phrase "relativity of knowledge " admits of a great variety of meanings, and that when a philosopher lays great stress upon the doctrine, " it is " necessary to cross-examine his writings, and compel " them to disclose in which of its many degrees of " meaning he understands the phrase."

There is a doctrine sometimes passing by this name, which will recommend itself to all sober thinkers : who will admit—(1.) that we can know objects only so far as we have faculties of knowledge ; (2.) that we can know objects only under the aspects presented to the faculties ; and (3.) that our faculties are limited in number and in range, so that not only do we not know all objects, we do not know all about any one object.   These posi-tions have been disputed by none except some of the Alexandrian Neo-Platonists in ancient times, and a few German defenders of the Absolute Philosophy in modern times.   A doctrine embracing these positions has been known and acknowledged under such designations as that of " the limited knowledge of man," and should not be expressed by so ambiguous a phrase as " the relativity of knowledge," which is applied to a very different theory.   That theory has of late years assumed four different forms.

I. There is the form given to it by Sir W. Hamilton. He thus unfolds it (*Metaph*. i. 148) : " Our knowledge is " relative,—1*st*, because existence is not cognisable ab-" solutely and in itself, but only in special modes ; 2*d*, " because these modes can be known only if they stand " in a certain relation to our faculties."   Mr. Mill thus comments : " Whoever can find anything more in these " statements than that we do not know all about a " thing, but only so much as we are capable of knowing, " is more ingenious or more fortunate than myself." But surely it is desirable to have even this much al-lowed and clearly enunciated ; only I think it unfortunate that two such inexplicable phrases as 'absolutely' and 'in itself' should have been introduced. Sir William gives a third reason, and here the error appears. " 3*d*, " Because the modes, thus relative to our faculties, are " presented to, and known by the mind only under modi- " fications determined by these faculties themselves." This doctrine is thoroughly Kantian in itself and in its logical consequences. It makes the mind look at things, but through a glass so cut and coloured that it gives a special shape and hue to every object. " Suppose that " the total object of consciousness in perception is $= 12$; " and suppose that the external reality contributes 6, " the material sense 3, and the mind 3,—this may enable " you to form some rude conjecture of the nature of " the object of perception "[1] (*Metaph.* ii. p. 129). This doctrine very much neutralizes that of natural realism, which Hamilton seems, after the manner of Reid, to be so strenuously defending. To suppose that in per- ception or cognition proper we mix elements derived from our subjective stores, is to unsettle our whole con- victions as to the reality of things; for if the mind adds three things, why not thirty things, why not three hundred, till we are landed in absolute idealism, or in the dreary flat into which those who would float in that empty space are sure in the end to fall, that is, absolute scepticism. By assuming this middle place between Reid

---

[1] Sir William Hamilton has used very unguarded language as to human nescience; but I have reason to believe that he thought himself misunder- stood, and I am inclined to think that he had some means of satisfying himself that he held by the reality of things. There is a point here on which it is hoped some of his pupils may be able to throw light.

and Kant, this last of the great Scottish metaphysicians has been exposed to the fire of the opposing camps of idealism and realism, and it will be impossible for the school to continue to hold the position of their master.

It required no great shrewdness to foresee the logical consequences that would be drawn, and so I take no credit for resolutely opposing the doctrine from the time of its publication. It should be allowed that sensations, feelings, impressions, associate themselves with our knowledge, but every man of sound sense easily separates them ; and it should not be difficult for the philosopher to distinguish between them, to distinguish between our intuition of a tooth and the pain of toothache, between the perception of a landscape and the æsthetic emotions which it calls up. Following the spontaneous convictions of assurance and certitude in the mind (see κ.), which all but the sceptic allow speculatively, and which even the sceptic must actually proceed upon in defending his scepticism, we should hold— (1.) that we know the very thing as appearing, and not a mere appearance without a thing to appear; and (2.) that our knowledge is correct so far as it goes, and is not modified by the subjective forms of the mind. I have been striving in these chapters to show that we immediately know a self and extended objects beyond. But we have the same grounds for affirming that our knowledge is correct as for asserting that we have knowledge. In the event of man's intuitive knowledge being mistaken or fallacious in any point, it is certain he could never discover it to be so with his present faculties. Our perceptions of sense, consciousness, and intuitive reason all combine in a consistent result, and we must receive the whole or reject the whole. Hamilton declares that " no attempt to show that the data of " consciousness are (either in themselves or in their " necessary consequences) mutually contradictory, has " yet succeeded." "An original, universal, dogmatic " subversion of knowledge has hitherto been found " impossible" (App. to Reid's *Works*, p. 746). That there should be such consistency in intuitive truth that the acutest human intellects have not been able to detect a contradiction, is not the primary proof, but is a confirmation of its truth. That there should be such consistency in total error, or in a mixture of truth and error, is scarcely believable : we could account for it only on the supposition that it was produced by a mischievous deity, who wished so to deceive us that we could never discover the deception, a supposition contradicted by the circumstance that the whole constitution of our minds and of things is fitted to impress us with the importance of veracity, showing that the Creator and Ruler of our world is a God of Truth.

II. Mr. Mill has enunciated the doctrine in a second form, and accepts it as expressing " a real and impor- " tant law of our mental nature. This is, that we only " know anything by knowing it as distinguished from " something else ; that all consciousness is of difference : " that two objects are the smallest number required to " constitute consciousness ; that a thing is only seen to " be what it is by contrast with what it is not" (p. 6.

He tells that the employment of the phrase to express this meaning is sanctioned by high authorities, and he mentions Mr. Bain, " who habitually uses the phrase ' relativity of knowledge' in this sense." It is quite true that the doctrine, that all knowledge consists in comparison, has appeared again and again in speculative philosophy ; but as destroying the simplicity of our mental operations, and reversing the order of nature, it has wrought only mischief.

The mind, as I apprehend, begins its intelligent acts with knowledge, and, we may add, with beliefs, and then it can go on to compare the things known and believed in, and thereby widens the domain both of knowledge and belief. It commences, we may suppose, with a perception—which is knowledge—of an external object, and a consciousness—which is knowledge—of self as perceiving the object. Then it remembers, and in doing so has a belief in the object which has been perceived. In all this there is no comparison, but having this, the mind can forthwith institute a comparison and pronounce a judgment. Thus, having a knowledge of body in the concrete, the mind can then, when a purpose is to be served by it, declare that body exists, and that it is extended ; and having a knowledge of self, it can assert that it exists, and that it is under grief or joy—as our experience may be at the time. Remembering an event as happening in time past, it can declare that the event is real, and the time real. But while such judgments are involved in our primary cognitions, I rather think that they come in later life : the child, I rather think, as knowing its own existence and never doubting it, is not at the trouble of asserting it. But the child on perceiving two objects successively, or it may be simultaneously, delights to discover a relation between them. Such judgments follow so immediately on the cognitions, that it is not necessary to distinguish them from one another except in scientific psychology. But if metaphysicians lay down an opposite doctrine, and draw consequences from it, it is absolutely necessary to correct the statement.

I suppose Mr. Mill would represent the mind as beginning with sensations. We have then a sensation. Is there comparison in this? I cannot discover that there is. No doubt, upon another sensation rising up, we may compare the one with the other and discover an agreement or difference. But in order to this comparison there is memory; and memory, in recalling the sensation, must bring it up prior to the comparison. But Mr. Mill may say that we have two sensations simultaneously,—say a sensation of resistance by one sense, and a sensation of colour by another, and we declare them at once to agree or to differ. But could we not have the sensation of resistance or the sensation of colour though each came alone? Even when they come simultaneously, we are able to compare them, because we know so much of each. We ever proceed on a supposed knowledge of the objects when we compare and decide. When I say that $2 + 2 = 4$, it is because I know what is meant by the terms. If I say Ben Nevis is a few feet higher than Ben Macdhui, it is because I know somewhat of the height of each mountain. If I say that Aristotle's Induction was not the same as Bacon's; that Comte's Positive Method differs essentially from Bacon's Inductive Method; that Locke was not a follower of Hobbes; that Condillac had no right to proclaim himself a disciple of Locke; that Reid met Hume in a more sagacious manner than Kant did; that Brown vainly endeavoured to combine the Sensational School of France with the British Association School and the School of Reid; and that a good Inductive Logic must combine certain principles of Whewell with those of Mill,—I do so because I think I know something of the philosophic systems of which I speak, and am thus able to compare or to contrast them.

But Mr. Mill may refer me to the philosophy of Hamilton, which declares that in the very first act of consciousness we discover the relation of the *ego* and the *non ego*. My readers, however, will have seen by this time that I am not bound to follow Hamilton, who, in fact, though without meaning it, prepared the way for a farther doctrine from which he would have turned away with the strongest aversion. I believe that in our conscious sense-perceptions we know both the self and the not-self in one concrete act; and of course we have in all this the materials for a judgment; but I doubt much whether the infant actually pronounces the judgment. But then it is said that our knowledge of the object is an apprehension of the relation of the object or sensation to the perceiving mind. Now I believe that a relation is formed in the very act of knowledge. But my knowledge does not consist in the perception of the relation; on the contrary, the relation may arise simply from the knowledge. I apprehend the President of the United States of America; as I do so, I have constituted a relation between myself and him; but there may have been no previous relation; and if I declare the relation, it is by a consequent and subsequent act. I strive to rise to a contemplation of the Divine Being; there is no doubt a relation of my mind to the object viewed; but the relation consists in my contemplation. When the Divine Being looks down on His works and pities those who suffer, it is not because the Creator in all this is dependent on His creatures; the viewing of them by Him with regard and commiseration constitutes the particular and interesting relation. It is high time to lay an arrest on that style of representation, so frequent in the present age, which would make us perceive a relation before perceiving the things related, and make the very Divine knowledge, so far as we can comprehend it, depend on creature relations.

I take exception, on like grounds, to another part of the same doctrine: " That a thing is only seen to be " what it is by contrast with what it is not." I admit that where we can discover contrasts, our notions are rendered more distinct and vivid. But I cannot allow that we should not have known a sensation, say the feeling of a lacerated limb, to be painful, unless we had contrasted it with a pleasurable one; on the contrary,

I maintain that in order to contrast the two we must have experienced them in succession. I cannot believe that we should never have known body as extended, unless we had previously known something as unextended; or that no one could know and appreciate moral good unless he had been acquainted with moral evil.

The doctrine I am expounding in this volume makes the relations to be in the things compared, and not the creation of the mind as it compares them. The opposite doctrine reverses the order of the mind's procedure, and, logically followed out, unsettles the foundation of knowledge. It makes us discover relations between things in themselves unknown, and it leaves us standing on a bridge of which we do not know that it has a support at either end. If we know a thing only in relation to another thing, and this only in relation to some other thing, as we thus ever chase the thing without catching it, we are made to feel as if we had only a a series of strings put into our hands, at which we have to pull for ever without their bringing anything but other strings.

Mr. Mill's theory obliges him to accept the special doctrine I am now examining in its very lowest form. The school of Kant, both in its German and British modifications, supposes that the mind has a rich furniture of forms and categories, out of which can be fashioned an ideal world of a very lofty character. But the school of Mill, admitting no *a priori* elements, and limiting the comparative capacities of the mind, can furnish no such glorious creation. Mr. Mill gives us the power of discovering only the relations of co-existence and succession, and of resemblance and difference. He says that " equality is but another word for the exact resem " blance, commonly called identity, considered as subsist- " ing between things in respect of their *quantity.*" And then, in explaining what is implied in quantity, " When " we say of two things that they differ in quantity, just " as when we say they differ in quality, the assertion " is always grounded upon a difference in the sensations " which they excite" (*Logic,* B. i. c. iii. § 11. 12) : thus making us know nothing of either quality or quantity or number, except as denoting agreements in the sensations forming the series which we call mind. Mr. Bain goes down to a still lower level, when he tells us, in a passage already quoted (p. 202), that cognisance of difference and cognisance of agreement exhaust the essence of knowledge; that all we can know of a ring is its agreement with certain things, and its differences from other things; which other things, of course, can be known only as they agree with, or differ from, yet other things. Knowledge can have no resting-place when driven from one thing to another in this shuttle-cock process. It falls through, by being placed between such instabili ties. The way to meet all this, and put knowledge on its proper basis, is by showing that we have an original knowledge of self, and of objects, such as a ring, beyond self; and that, proceeding on this, we are able to discover not only resemblances and differences, but various other important relations, which enable us to combine every one thing known with others as also known in a com pact structure, in which every one part binds all the others, and helps to support the whole.

III. Mr. Mill would especially apply the phrase, " relativity of knowledge," to a third doctrine, being, in fact, his own theory of the mind. " Our knowledge of " objects, and even our fancies about objects, consist of " nothing but the sensations they excite, or which we " imagine them exciting in ourselves." " This know- " ledge is merely phenomenal." " The object is known " to us only in one special relation, namely, as that " which produces, or is capable of producing, certain " impressions on our senses ; and all that we really " know is these impressions." " This is the Doctrine of " the Relativity of Knowledge to the knowing mind, in " the simplest, purest, and, as I think, the most proper " acceptation of the words " (pp. 7-14). I confess I can see no propriety in applying to such a theory a phrase which had been appropriated by Sir William Hamilton, or by some of us who had criticised him, to a different doctrine. I do not see that it has any right to claim the title of ' knowledge,' or that it can get ' relations,' when it has no things to bring into relation. The theory is simply that we know sensations, and possi- bilities of sensations, while we cannot be said to know what sensations are. But I have no interest in giving the phrase any one special application rather than another—I believe it to be vague and ambiguous—in fact, not used by any two philosophers, I rather think by no one philosopher, at different places, in one and the same sense ; and I think it should be altogether banished from speculation. And as to the doctrine to which Mr. Mill would specially apply it, I need not enter upon the consideration of it here, as I have been examining it all throughout this volume. But there is a fourth form of the general theory, defended by an illustrious member of the same school, which demands a notice.

IV. Mr. Grote, in his exposition of Plato's philosophy (Art. *Theætetus*), has developed a theory of relativity, which he ascribes to the Sophists, at least to Protagoras, and which he himself is prepared to accept. It is the doctrine of *Homo Mensura*, which, construed in its true meaning, is said to be, " Object is implicated with, " limited or measured by, Subject: a doctrine proclaiming " the relativeness of all objects perceived, conceived, " known or felt--and the omnipresent involution of the " perceiving, conceiving, knowing, or feeling, Subject : " the Object varying with the Subject. ' As things ap- " pear to me, so they are to me : as they appear to you, " so they are to you.' This theory is just and important " if rightly understood and explained" (vol. ii. p. 335). " So far as the doctrine asserts essential fusion and " implication between Subject and Object, with actual " multiplicity of distinct subjects—denying the reality " either of absolute and separate Subject, or of absolute " and separate Object-- I think it true and instructive " (p. 340). Proceeding on this general doctrine, he reaches another : " What is Truth to one man, is not truth, and " is often Falsehood, to another : that which governs the " mind as infallible authority in one part of the globe, is

" treated with indifference or contempt elsewhere. Each
" man's belief, though in part determined by the same
" causes as the belief of others, is in part also determined
" by causes peculiar to himself. When a man speaks
" of Truth, he means what he himself (along with others,
" or singly, as the case may be) believes to be Truth;
" unless he expressly superadds the indication of some
" other persons believing in it " (p. 360).

I have looked from time to time into the Platonic
and Aristotelian discussions on the subject, but I confess I have never been able to discover what was the
precise philosophy of the Sophists, or whether indeed
they had a philosophy, or whether they were anything
more than instructors of youth, professing to teach
wisdom—without knowing what wisdom is. So far as
any of them, such as Protagoras, had a philosophic
system, I think it probable that they meant it to be
that which has been elaborated by the British Section
of the school of Comte. But I have here to do not
with the Greek Sophists, but with Mr. Grote. I am
surprised to find him repeating the juggle, which has so
often been exposed, arising from the ambiguity of the
phrase ' Subject and Object.' No doubt, if you use the
terms as correlative, meaning by ' subject' the mind
contemplating an object, and by ' object' a thing contemplated, then the subject implies the object, and the
object the subject, as the husband implies the wife, and
the wife the husband. But as we cannot argue from the
husband implying the wife that every man has a wife,
or from the wife implying a husband that every woman

has a husband, so we cannot argue from the mere existence of a mind that there must be an external thing to think about, nor from the bare existence of an object or thing that there must be a mind to think about it. As to the allegation that the subjective mind necessarily mixes its own shapes and colours with the things known, I have already examined it when discussing the first form of the theory of relativeness. There is, there can be no proof advanced in its behalf—that is to show that the mirror does not correctly reflect the object presented to it. We have the same grounds for believing in the accuracy of our primitive knowledge as we have for believing in the existence either of the subject or the object.

But the fatal part of the doctrine lies in the assertion, that truth varies with the individual, and with the circumstances in which he may be placed : a tenet which, if held by the Sophists, deserves all the reprobation heaped upon it by Socrates, Plato, and Aristotle,—and, I may add, that the defence of it, in the further light we now enjoy, is worse than the original offence. By truth, I mean what philosophers in general have understood by it—the conformity of our ideas to things. There is no truth where there is no correspondence of our notions to realities. I admit that human knowledge never comes up to the extent of things. I allow that human knowledge is often partial, that is, is only partly correct, and may have error mixed up with it. But truth, so far as it is truth, is the agreement of thoughts with things. To illustrate this, I will not trouble the

school with transcendental or religious truth. I appeal
to judgments pronounced on more common and familiar
affairs. Were any one to affirm that there never had
been such a country as ancient Greece, such a man as
Socrates, or such a sect as the Sophists; that Queen
Victoria is incapable of cherishing the memory of departed friends, that Louis Napoleon is a man of guile-
less transparency and openness of character, or that
President Lincoln was a man given to crooked and dis-
honest policy; that Mr. Grote was utterly illiterate, had
never written, and could not write a history of Greece,
and had never been favourable to vote by ballot,—I
would say of this person, not that he had got what is
truth to himself, but that he had not reached truth at
all. Were I to allow myself to think that a certain
London banking-house of high repute is on the point of
bankruptcy, and that those who manage it are a band
of rogues and robbers, I should in the very act be guilty
not only of error but of sin; and I am sure that were
I to give expression to such a thought, I should be
justly exposed to punishment.

Mr. Grote represents his doctrine as forming the
basis of the principle of toleration, and the opposite
doctrine as fostering intolerance (p. 362). I reverse
this account, and declare that the person who avows
that he cannot distinguish between truth and error, is
not in circumstances to exercise the virtue of tolerance;
for he has not discovered an error which he is bound to
tolerate; and Mr. Grote's principle would lead him to
refuse toleration, if ever he did reach positive truth.

The principle of toleration, as I understand it, is, that I am bound to tolerate what I believe, what I may know, to be error; that the power of punishing error as error has not been put into my hands, has in fact been mercifully withheld from me by One who claims to be Himself the Judge. I am quite sure that there is a God who rules this world in justice and love, and yet I feel that I must bear even with the " fool who says in his heart, There is no God." This is my idea of toleration, which I reckon a much deeper and juster one than that held by those who say that truth varies with the individual, the age, and the circumstances.

But then Mr. Grote tells us " no infallible objective " mark, no common measure, no canon of evidence, re- " cognised by all, has yet been found " (p. 360). I admit freely that we cannot obtain what a certain school calls an absolute criterion of truth; for I admit that the word ' absolute' is about the most unintelligible in the language, whether as used by those who favour or oppose the doctrine it is employed to designate. I allow, further, that it is in vain to search for any one criterion which will settle for us what is truth in all matters. But we have tests quite sufficient to determine for us what is truth and what is error in many matters, both speculative and practical; these I shall endeavour to unfold in a future chapter (see XIX.) I have intuitive evidence of my own existence; and evidence from testimony of the existence of India, which I never saw; and evidence from induction and deduction of the existence of the law of gravitation,—and I declare of any one who denies any of these that he is in error, and this however strong his beliefs may be.   To believe without evidence, and not to believe when we have evidence, may both be sinful when our belief or unbelief involve duties which we owe to ourselves, to our fellow-men, and to God.

CHAPTER XI.

MAN'S POWER OF CONCEPTION AS A TEST OF TRUTH.

THE word 'conceive,' with its derivatives 'conceivable' and 'inconceivable,' is one of the most ambiguous in the philosophic nomenclature of this country. When I say I cannot conceive the distance of a star which requires hundreds of thousands of years to transmit its light to our earth, I use the term in the sense of 'image' or 'represent.' When I affirm that I have a conception of the animal kingdom, I mean that I have a general notion of beings possessing animation. When I declare that I cannot conceive that God should be unjust, I signify that I cannot so believe or decide. These three senses are at once seen not to be the same when the difference is pointed out. We cannot easily imagine the distance of a fixed star, but we decide on the evidence produced, or believe on the authority of astronomers, that it is at the distance it is said to be. We cannot image the class 'animal kingdom,' for it includes innumerable objects, yet we can intellectually think about it, that is, about objects possessing the common attribute of animal life. We cannot be made to decide or believe that Cleopatra's Needle should be in Paris and Egypt at the same time, yet with some difficulty we can simultaneously image it in both places.

It could easily be shown that the phrase is used in all these senses in philosophy, as well as in our current literature. " By conception," says Stewart (*Elem.* c. iii.), " I mean that power of the mind which enables us to " form a notion of an absent object of perception." Sir William Hamilton professes to use the word in the same sense as the German *Begriff*, that is, for the general notion formed by an indefinite number of objects being joined by the possession of a common attribute. With or without avowing it, philosophers have also employed it in the third sense. Hamilton often explains conceive by " construe in thought," which must denote an act of judgment ; he must employ it in this sense when he says it is inconceivable that space should have limits. Dr. Whewell's arguments in favour of necessary truth are valid only when he uses it in the signification of judging, as when he says, " we cannot conceive reasoning to be merely a series of sensations" (*Phil. Ind. Sciences*, i. 44).

The question arises, and must now be settled, in which of these senses, or in what other, is the word employed when man's power or impotency of conception is supposed to be a test of truth. It is clear that it cannot be employed in the first-mentioned sense. Man's capability of imaging an object is no proof of its existence : I can picture a hobgoblin without supposing it to be a reality. Man's incapacity to image or represent an object is no proof of its non-existence ; a blind man cannot have an idea of colour, but this does not prove even to him that colour has no existence. Nor can it be used in the second signification above intimated. I can form a notion of a class of mermaids without being convinced that mermaids were ever seen by any human being. In these senses of the words there is much conceivable by man which has no existence, much inconceivable by man which has an existence. Conceivability and inconceivability can be employed as a test of truth only in the third meaning of the term, as signifying " construe in thought" (whatever that may mean), judge or decide.

Both the defenders and opposers of intuitive truth have been in the way of going from the one of these meanings to the other. Hamilton uses the phrase both in the first and third of these significations without perceiving that they are not the same ; and it is very much because of this ambiguity that he is able to make it appear that there is a contradiction in human thought. He says, on the one hand, that we cannot conceive space or time as without bounds ; which must mean, when properly interpreted, that we must always give a boundary in the image we form of it. But then he tells us, on the other hand, that we are altogether unable to conceive space or time as bounded ; that is, when rightly understood, we cannot be made to judge or decide that it has bounds. He has constructed a set of opposed propositions as to space, time, and infinity, the seeming contradiction arising very much from the

double signification of the word 'conceive' (see Art. on
" Unconditioned" in *Discussions*).   But the philosopher
who has made the most frequent use of the impossibility
of conceiving the opposite as a test of truth is Dr.
Whewell.   He tells us that necessary truths are those
" in which we cannot, even by an effort of imagination,
" or in a supposition, conceive the reverse of that which
" is asserted."   " Necessary truths are those of which
" we cannot distinctly conceive the contrary" (*Phil.
Ind. Sc.*, i. 55, 59).   The phrase 'imagination' and the
phrase 'distinctly' might lead us to think that by
'conceive' we are to understand 'image,' yet we must
attach a different meaning to it when he tells us more
accurately of necessary truths that we " see" them—
which must mean 'judge' them—"to be true by thinking
about them, and see that they could not be otherwise"
(*Ib.*, p. 20).   But so loosely does he use this test, that
he declares that laws acknowledged to be discovered by
experiment, such as the laws of motion and of chemical
affinity, are such that it is inconceivable that they
should not be true.   " For how, in fact, can we conceive
" combinations otherwise than as definite in kind and
" quantity ?"   " We cannot conceive a world in which
" this should not be the case" (*Ib.*, i. 400).   When the
defenders of fundamental truth fall into such ambiguity
of phraseology, and apply their test so unsatisfactorily,
there is some excuse for those who criticise and oppose
them when they take advantage of their mistakes.

   I say 'some excuse,' for I cannot allow that this is
an entire justification of Mr. Mill when he uses the

word, as I shall show he does, in so many different senses ; and when, in criticising Hamilton and Whewell, he employs it in a way they would not have allowed. Mr. Mill is aware that, when Sir William Hamilton is wishing to bring out his full meaning, he uses such phrases as " think" and " construe in thought;" and Dr. Whewell, while he also uses the word " think," is careful to represent Conceptions as modifications of Fundamental Ideas, which he enumerates and classifies. Mr. Mill always employs the phrase in a vague manner, and often in more than one signification. He must use it in the sense of 'image' or 'picture' when he says, " We cannot conceive a line without breadth ; we can " form no mental picture of such a line" (*Logic*, B. II. c. v. § 1). This is all true, but it is also true that we —can form an abstract notion of such a line. He states that Dr. Whewell's idea of necessary truth is " a pro- " position, the negation of which is not only false, but " inconceivable." But then, in criticising this test, he uses the word in quite a different sense : " When we " have often seen and thought two things together, and " have never in one instance either seen or thought of " them separate, there is, by the primary law of associa- " tion, an increasing difficulty, which in the end becomes " insuperable, of conceiving the two things apart" (*Ib.*, § 6). It is clear that while Dr. Whewell uses the phrases as applicable to a proposition declared to be true, Mr. Mill employs it in the sense of mental pictures joined by association. This is one other instance of an amphiboly, which we have noticed before, and which will require to be noticed again in examining Mr. Mill's attempt to explain necessity of thought by association of ideas.

He tells us, "The history of science teems with incon- "ceivabilities which have been conquered, and supposed " necessary truths, which have first ceased to be thought " necessary, then to be thought true, and have finally " come to be deemed impossible" (p. 150). And then he gives us once more his famous case of persons not being able to conceive of antipodes, being " merely the effect of a strong association." But let us understand precisely in what sense our forefathers had a difficulty in conceiving the existence of antipodes. It is evident that they could have little difficulty in imagining to themselves a round globe with persons with their feet adhering to it all around. Their difficulty lay in decid- ing it to be true ; and the difficulty was increased by the very vividness of the picture of men, as they would have said, with their feet upward and their head down- ward. It is clear that Mr. Mill, when he applies it to such a case, must be using the word in the sense of 'judge' and ' believe.' But let us understand on what ground our ancestors felt a difficulty in yielding their judgment and belief. Not because of any supposed intuition or necessary truth,—I am not aware that they ever ap- pealed to such ; not even because of a strong association : but because the alleged fact seemed contrary to a law of nature established by observation. A gathered experi- ence seemed to show that there was an absolute up and down, and that heavy bodies tended downwards, and

thus, and not on any *a priori* grounds, did they argue
that there could not be antipodes, as persons so situated
would fall away into a lower space. As a narrow experience had created the difficulty, so it could remove
it by giving us a view of the earth as a mass of matter,
causing human beings to adhere to it over its whole
surface. And such a case does not in the least tend to
prove, that truths which are seen to be truths at once,
and without a gathered experience, could ever be set
aside by a further experience : that a conscious intelligent being could be made to regard himself as non-
existing; that he could believe himself as having been
in existence before he existed ; or that he could be led
to allow that two straight lines might enclose a space
in the constellation Orion.

It is in the highest degree expedient, at the stage to
which mental science has come, that the word 'conceive,' and its derivatives, should be abandoned altogether in such a connexion; as being fitted to confuse our
ideas and mislead our judgments. The greatest and
wisest philosophers have not appealed to the possibility
or impossibility of conception as tests of truth or falsehood, but have pointed to other and clearer and more
decisive *criteria*.[1]

---

[1] The printing of this work had proceeded thus far, when I observed
that Mr. M., in 6th edition of *Logic*, just published, has been obliged, in
defending himself against Mr. Spencer, to notice that 'conceive' might
signify 'to have an idea' or 'to have a belief' (i. 303). But he himself
continues to take advantage of the ambiguity, which is greater than he
yet sees. I have been labouring for years to make metaphysicians perceive the ambiguity.

CHAPTER XII.

SELF-EVIDENCE AND NECESSITY THE TESTS OF INTUITION.

Mr. Mill freely admits the existence and the veracity of intuitive perceptions. But he has not inquired into their nature, their mode of operation, their laws, their tests, or their limits. What he has failed to do must be undertaken by others; and in the process it will be seen that intuition has quite as important a place in the mind as sensation, association, or any of Mr. Mill's favourite principles, and that it must be embraced and have a distinct place allotted to it in a sufficient theory of our mental operations.

Our intuitions are all of the nature of perceptions, in which we look on objects known or apprehended: on separate objects, or on objects compared with one another. Sometimes the objects are present, and we look on them directly, by the senses and self-consciousness. In other cases they are not present, but still we have an apprehension of them, and our convictions, whether beliefs or judgments, proceed upon this apprehension. A very different account has often been given of them. According to Locke, the mind in intuition looks at

ideas, and not at things. According to the theory ela -
borated by Kant, and so far adopted by Hamilton, it is
possessed of *a priori* forms, which it imposes on objects.
Such views are altogether indefensible, and have in
fact hindered the ready reception of the true doctrine.
Making our intuitions mere ideas or forms in the mind,
they have very much separated them from realities.
The intuitions I stand up for are all intuitions of things.
In opposition to M. Comte and his school in all its
branches, I hold that man is so constituted as to know
somewhat of things, and the relations of things. What
we know of things, with their relations, on the bare inspection or contemplation of them, constitutes the body
of intuitive truth, and the capacity to discover it is called
intuition. Taken in this sense, the exercise of intuition
is not opposed to experience, but is in fact an experience:
only it is not a gathered experience; it is a singular experience at the basis of all collected experiences.

Our intuitive perceptions are all, in the first instance,
individual or singular. Thus, by the external senses,
we observe an extended and coloured surface before us,
or by the internal consciousness we experience ourselves
in a certain state of thought and feeling. Our very intuitive judgments or comparisons are singular. On
finding that a particular rod, A, is of the same length
as another rod, B, and that B is of the same length as a
third rod, C, we at once declare that A is equal to C.
But we can generalize these intuitive judgments, and
then they become maxims or axioms. We see that
what is true of the rods A, B, C, would also be of the

rods D, E, F, or of any other objects found equal to one another, and we feel ourselves entitled to declare that 'things which are equal to the same thing are equal to one another.' As the generalization is the result, not of an intuitive, but a discursive process, it is possible that error may creep into it, that the generalized expression of our original perceptions may be mutilated or exaggerated. But on the supposition that the generalization has been properly conducted, the maxim is as certain as the individual perception is allowed to be.

By standing up for this distinction between what we may call our spontaneous and our generalized intuitions, we can answer an objection urged against the existence of necessary truth by Mr. Mill. " The very fact that " the question is disputed, disproves the alleged impos- " sibility. Those against whom it is needful to defend " the belief which is affirmed to be necessary, are un- " mistakable examples that it is not necessary" (p. 150). But what is the dispute? It is commonly not as to the belief, but simply as to whether it is intuitive, which, as Mr. Mill knows and asserts, is not to be settled by intuition. Take only one example : the sums of equals are equals ; there is no dispute as to the truth of this. What Mr. Mill's school objects to is, that it should be represented as intuitive. But again, what the upholders of necessary truth maintain is, not that every man must hold speculatively by intuitive truth, that is, hold by it in the generalized form given it by philosophers ; but that all believe in, and spontaneously act upon, their individual primitive perceptions. It is quite possible for Mr. Mill

to maintain that the law of cause and effect is not
necessary or universal, and that there may be a phenomenon without a cause in the Dog-star; but meanwhile
it will be found that on any given occurrence presenting
itself, he will look for something as producing it.

If we look carefully into the nature of the intuitive
perceptions of the mind, they will be found to be of
three kinds. Some of them are of the nature of Primitive
Cognitions : the object is now present, and we look upon
it. It is thus we are conscious of self as existing in a
particular state. This being self-evident, we cannot be
made to regard ourselves as non-existent, and not in
that particular state. In other exercises our intuitions
are of the nature of Primitive Beliefs : the object is not
present, but we contemplate it, and discover that it is
of such a nature. It is thus that we believe of space,
that it does not cease when our eye is no longer able to
follow it : this appears from the very nature of space ;
and having such a conviction, we cannot be made to
believe that space, at the point at which it ceases to be
invisible, should come to a termination. Again, some of
our intuitions are of the nature of Primitive Judgments,
in which by bare inspection we discover relations between things apprehended. Thus we are told first of
one man that he died at the age of fifty, and then of
another man that he died at the age of fifty, and we at
once declare that the two men died at the same age ;
and this being evident from the contemplation of the
things, we cannot be made to decide otherwise.

The truth reached by intuition in these its three

forms is of course limited,—is confined, indeed, within very stringent boundaries. It is narrowed, first of all by the original inlets, which are the outward and inward senses ; and secondly, by the limited capacity of man to discover what is involved in this primitive stock. What intuition may do of itself is best seen in mathematical demonstration ; in which every step taken is seen to be true at once, on the bare contemplation of the figures or numbers ; and by which we reach a body of truth of immense scientific value. But the main service of intuition consists in its furnishing a point from which experience may start, and a foundation on which to build. Our original perceptions lie at the basis of all our acquired ones. I allow that our acquired ones, obtained by a gathered experience, carry us far beyond our primitive perceptions. But in fact intuitions, for example those of sense and consciousness, mingle with all our mental operations, and upon them we must fall back in the last resort, when required to specify the ground on which experience rests.

Keeping these explanations and distinctions in view, it should not be difficult to find tests of intuition. The primary mark I hold to be Self-Evidence. The evidence is in the objects, and is discerned by the mind on the bare contemplation of them. From the mere inspection of consciousness we perceive self in some action or under some affection. From the simple apprehension of $2+2$ we see that it makes 4. And wherever there is Self-Evidence there will also be Necessity. But let us observe carefully what this necessity consists in. It is not a fatalistic necessity imposed upon us from without, and for anything we know in an arbitary manner. It is necessity arising solely from the nature of things as the same is perceived by the mind.[1] This conviction of necessity may assume two forms, a positive and a negative. On the bare contemplation of $2+2$ I see that it must make 4 : this is the positive form. I am further constrained to decide that it cannot be otherwise, that $2+2$ cannot be 3, or 5, or any other number : this is the negative form. These two forms depend on each other, or rather they both depend on the Self-Evidence ; and we may in argument of any kind employ the one or other as may suit our purpose. And as is the nature of the original perception, so is the precise nature of the conviction of necessity. We have seen that our intuitions may be of the nature of cognitions, of beliefs, or of judgments ; and whatever the intuition be, we must adhere to it, and cannot be made to give our assent to the opposite. Thus, if our intuition be a cognition of an object as existing, we cannot be made to acknowledge it as non-existing : if I know self as thinking, I cannot be made to allow that it is not thinking. Again, if our intuition be a belief, such

---

[1] Mr. Herbert Spencer, following in this respect Sir William Hamilton, stands up for Necessity as a test of ultimate truth, but overlooks Self-Evidence, the evidence in the thing looked at. " No matter what he calls " these indestructible relations [of Consciousness, using consciousness in " a very vague and perverted sense], no matter what he supposes to be ." their meanings, he is completely fettered by them. Their indestructi-" bility is the proof to him that his consciousness is imprisoned within " them" (*Fortn. Rev.* No. v.) I have given a more pleasant account of them. The necessity is not a fetter or a prison, but a conviction arising from an immediate perception of the nature of the thing.

as that I saw a particular person yesterday, I cannot be
made to believe that I did not see him. The same is
true of our judgments : deciding that two straight lines
cannot enclose a space, I cannot be made to allow that
they can form a closed figure. Thus understood, the
necessity of conviction (and not the mere incapacity of
conceiving) becomes a criterion of fundamental truth,
clear and certain, and not difficult of application.

To these some have added Universality. But the
phrase has been used in two different significations.
As employed by some it means the universality of the
truth. In this sense the universality is involved in
the necessity, we cannot be made to believe that two
straight lines should enclose a space at any time or in
any world. Thus understood, the test of universality
is not different from that of necessity ; but as presenting the conviction under a very important aspect, it
may often be usefully employed in determining whether
a truth is intuitive. But Universality may also mean
being entertained by all men. This property of intuitive truth may be more appropriately designated by
Catholicity or Common Consent. This quality does
belong to all primary truth, and where it is found it
may be regarded as a presumption that the truth is
intuitive. But it is not a proof; for it may spring not
so much from any inborn principle as from the uniformity to be found in the experience of all men. All
men expect that the sun will rise to-morrow, not from
any intuitive principle, but from the gathered observations of the past carried forward to the future.

These two then, Self-Evidence, and Necessity with implied Universality, are the decisive tests of intuitive truth. All intuitive truths possess these characteristics; no others do. The question now to be discussed is, Can these marks be produced by Association of Ideas, or by Experience, the two principles from which Mr. Mill gets all our general convictions?

(1.) "As for the feeling of necessity, or what is termed a " necessity of thought, it is of all mental phenomena " positively the one which an inseparable association is " the most evidently competent to generate" (p. 299). In answer to this it can be shown, in the first place, that in many cases of immediate and necessary conviction we have not two ideas to be associated. This holds of our primitive cognitions and primitive beliefs. Take the con sciousness which the infant has of a sensation, or rather of self as sentient. Here we cannot point to two objects which have been often together: we have only one object, the sentient self as existing, and we cannot be made to know it as not existing or not sentient. Again, I remember that I was under a peculiar sensation of pain two days ago: I never had the same feeling before; the object is one, and there has been no repetition, and therefore no association can have been formed; and yet I have the most perfect assurance that I existed two days ago under that sensation, and I cannot be made to believe otherwise. These are cases of intuition allowed by Mr. Mill (see ε, ρ), but in which association cannot generate the conviction.

In other cases, I admit that there is a combination of

two ideas or two objects, that is, those in which we institute a comparison or pronounce a judgment. But even in such the judgment is pronounced not in consequence of the mere association, but on a comparison of the things brought together. What Mr. Mill means by the feeling of necessity, which can be generated by his examples, is evident from his examples. "Many "persons who have been frightened in childhood can "never be alone in the dark without irrepressible ter-"rors. Many a person is unable to revisit a particular "place, or think of a particular event, without recalling "acute feelings of grief or reminiscences of suffering" (p. 265). This is a very glaring example of mistaking the point to be proven. Mr. Mill is aware what those who hold necessary truth mean by it. "Necessary," says Mr. Mill, "according to Kant's definition, is, that of which the negation is impossible." But the necessity which he looks at and accounts for is of a very different character; it is not a necessity of conviction, of belief, or judgment, but is a mere association of two ideas or thoughts, so that the one never comes up without the other. He explains his meaning: "When an association "has acquired the character of inseparability—when the "bond between the two has been thus firmly riveted, "not only does the idea called up by the association "become, in our consciousness, inseparable from the "idea which suggested it, but the facts or phenomena "answering to those ideas, come at last to seem inse-"parable in existence: things which we are unable to "conceive apart, appear incapable of existing apart"

(p. 191). The word 'conceive' has here come in with all its ambiguity, and the two things denoted by it, having an idea, and judging or deciding, are here represented as being one. But the two are very different. The fright in childhood may long continue to raise up terror, but cannot of itself create conviction; as may be seen in the case of multitudes who experience the fear but have never believed in ghosts. When Pascal was crossing a bridge in a carriage, the two leaders took fright and plunged into the Seine; the shock broke the traces, and the carriage remained on the brink of the precipice; ever after he felt as if there was an abyss on his left hand, and had a chair placed there to tranquillize his mind. But this association, while it raised the painful idea, did not convince his judgment that there was actually a river ever running at his left hand. I never pass a particular spot without being reminded of a youthful companion whom I met there for the last time before his removal from this world; but this association of my friend and the spot has not convinced me that the two have any real connexion. The mother never thinks of a particular churchyard without remembering that her boy sleeps there; but she does not therefore think that her child will be there for ever; on the contrary, she may firmly believe that he will rise again.

(2.) Just as little can experience, I mean a gathered experience, create the self-evidence and its consequent necessity. A truth reached by an accumulation of instances cannot be self-evident, for the evidence is collected from the uniformity of many, perhaps of innumerable cases. Neither is it accompanied with any conviction of necessity. We do not affirm of a general law thus discovered that the opposite of it is impossible, and we allow that there may be exceptions. Some persons are so situated that they see crows daily, and they have never seen them with any other colour than black; they have sufficient evidence of the general law that crows are of this colour, and when the idea of a crow comes up before them, it will always be in a sable hue: but it is not self-evident that crows are black; and they do not decide that they must be of this colour, or that there cannot possibly be white crows in any other world which God has made.

We have seen in a former chapter that the mind is endowed with a capacity of observing relations. Some of these are discovered by a process of lengthened observation. It is thus we know that all matter attracts other matter, and that the elements of bodies have certain chemical affinities which can be expressed in numerical proportions. But there are other relations which can be discerned immediately. In saying so, I do not affirm that they are noticed independently of things compared; I mean that they are discovered on the contemplation, the bare contemplation, of the objects, and without a gathered experience or an induction of instances. Thus, on comparing my conscious self of the present moment with the remembered self of yesterday, I at once, and without any mediate proof, declare an identity of person. A triangle being a figure with three angles, I need no experiments to convince me that one of the angles being a part is less than the whole, and that the three angles make up the whole. I may never have tried whether I could enclose a space by two straight lines : I do not require to try it, for I see it at once ; and I would declare of any apparent or professed attempt to make them form a closed figure, that it must involve some deception, and that the two lines cannot be straight.

Mr. Mill derives what are usually reckoned intuitive truths by " simple enumeration without a known exception ;" a method which Bacon declares to be ' puerile' and useless, as the next instance may prove an exception. " The principles of number and geometry are duly and " satisfactorily proved by that method alone, nor are " they susceptible of any other proof" (*Logic*, B. III. c. xxi. § 2). This makes the evidence for mathematical axioms the same in kind as that which the Hindu has for water being always liquid ; as that which we have for crows being black all over the universe ; and for the alternation of day and night continuing for ever. We see now how he should be obliged in logical consistency to maintain that two and two may make five in other worlds. I meet this by showing that there is an essential difference between the two classes of cases. In the one we see nothing in the nature of things to necessitate the law ; we adhere to it simply on the ground of the number of instances ; and we can readily be made to believe that the law is limited in range, and that there are exceptions. But in the other class the relation is in the very nature of the things ; we discover it at once by looking at the things ; we believe it to hold wherever the things exist, and we cannot be made to decide otherwise.   In order to account for the conviction of necessity and universality which attaches to mathematical truth, Mr. Mill refers to the circumstance that geometrical curves admit of being distinctly painted in the imagination, so that we have " mental pictures of all possible combinations of lines and angles " (*Logic*, B. ii. c. v. § 5).   But what, I ask, makes he of algebraic demonstrations, where there can be no such painting of the imagination, while yet there is the same necessity ?   And I call attention to the circumstance that mental pictures do not constitute an accumulation of instances, or tend in the least to bring the case under the law of *simplex enumeratio*.   They do, however, serve a purpose.   They enable us to perceive more clearly the nature of the objects, and to conceive the " possible combinations of angles and figures," so that we see the certainty and necessity of the truth.   Supposing, he says, that two straight lines after diverging could again converge, " we can transport " ourselves thither ,in imagination, and can frame a " mental image of the appearance which one or both " the lines must present at that point, which we may " rely upon as being precisely similar to the reality."   The clearness of the image does help us, but it is simply in the way of giving us an apprehension of the " reality," and thus enabling us to pronounce a judgment on which we may " rely."

By means of these tests we can without much difficulty distinguish between truths which are intuitive, and truths which are reached by a gathered experience. We have seen that Mr. Mill proceeds on these *criteria* (see η, θ, ι). And if any one will take the trouble to look back upon the chapter in which I have collected his "Admissions," he will see that Self-Evidence, and Necessity with Universality, cover, sanction, and justify all the intuitive principles he has avowed. But as not following out these *criteria* consequentially, he rejects as intuitive, and labours to establish otherwise, truths which can stand these tests quite as clearly and decisively as those acknowledged by him. Hence the heterogeneous character of his theory, which looks as if it stood altogether on sensation, and was reared by association, but requires to be buttressed on all sides by intuition to keep it from falling. It is only by logically carrying out these tests that we can construct a consistent system of philosophy, in which we give to intuition what belongs to intuition, and to experience what belongs to experience. Let us now inquire whether our conviction as to causation can stand the tests of intuition.

CHAPTER XIII.

CAUSATION.

ON this subject a much sounder doctrine than that entertained by most metaphysicians has been laid down by Professor Bain, who, however, has neglected to unfold all that is in the mental phenomenon which he has noticed. "As regards muscular exertion, there is a "notable specialty, a radical difference in kind, signified "by such phrases as 'the sense of power,' 'the feeling "of energy put forth,' 'the experience of force or re "sistance.' This is an ultimate phase of the human "consciousness, and the most general and fundamental "of all our conscious states. By this experience "[observe, not a gathered experience] we body forth "to ourselves a notion of force or power." He believes that "the combined movements of locomotion are original or instinctive" (*Senses and Intell.*, pp. 98, 267). Here, then, we have a perception, original and intuitive, of things exercising power. We are immediately conscious of power exerted, and we find it producing an effect. Again, things become known to us as exercising power upon us, and we know an effect as proceeding from a cause. This perception of power exercised by us, and upon us, is the primary cognition of things on which all our judgments as to causation are founded. Our knowledge both of self and of external objects is of things effecting and being effected.

Mr. Mill tells us in his *Logic*, that he has no intention of entering into the merits of the question of causation " as a problem of transcendental metaphysics." And yet in his logical treatment of the subject he is ever introducing, I think unfortunately, metaphysical speculations. In the discussion he has confounded (in this respect like some of the Scottish metaphysicians) the principle of causation with that of the uniformity of nature. When we say that nature is uniform, we mean that nature constitutes a course or system ; that there is in it a determinate number of agents, or rather a fixed amount of energy, actual or potential, operating according to laws and in an arranged constitution. That there is an invariable uniformity in nature, is discovered by a long experience. It is certainly not an obvious truth forced upon us by an early and easy observation. Judging by first appearances, it looks as if nature often acted unsystematically, or was swayed by influences out of its sphere. The mother finds her child in health to-day, sick to-morrow, better the third day, and dead the next ; so far from showing a uniformity, it seems rather to indicate a change of agency, springing either from an unknown fatality or the will of a supernatural being. It is only as the result of long and patient research, conducted independently in the various departments of nature and of history, that we reach the reasonable conviction that there is a fixed system constituted amidst these seeming irregularities.

Now it is, in fact, of this uniformity of nature that Mr. Mill is treating in his chapter on the " Evidence of Universal Causation." He is right in saying of it, " There " must have been a time when the universal prevalence " of that law throughout nature could not have been " affirmed in the same confident and unqualified man- " ner as at present." He is further right, so far as the uniformity of nature is concerned, when he says that the reasons for our reliance on it " do not hold in cir - " cumstances unknown to us, and beyond the possible " range of our experience. In distant parts of the " stellar regions, where the phenomena may be entirely " unlike those with which we are acquainted, it would " be folly to affirm confidently that this general law " prevails, any more than those special ones which we " have found to hold universally on our own planet. " The uniformity in the succession of events, otherwise " called the law of causation, must be received not as a " law of the universe, but of that portion of it only " which is within the range of our means of sure ob- " servation, with a reasonable degree of extension to " adjacent cases." In this passage he identifies " the uniformity in the succession of events" with " the law of causation." But these are not the same. It is quite conceivable that there may be worlds in which there is a universal causation, and yet no self-contained system of natural causes. Some, or many, or in fact all of the phenomena might be produced by agents acting from above or beyond the phenomena themselves,—say by the Divine Being, or angels, or demons. In such a world spring might follow winter one year, and be prevented from following it the next by the action of a supra-mundane influence; and no one would be able from the past to anticipate the future. In this state of things there would be no uniformity of physical agencies, and yet there would be an invariable causation. Now the grand metaphysical question is not about the uniformity of nature, but about the relation of cause and effect. There is a momentary discovery of the difference of the two, and yet a studious identification of them in the following passage :—" There was a time " when many of the phenomena of nature must have " appeared altogether capricious and irregular, not " governed by any laws, nor steadily consequent upon " any causes. Such phenomena, indeed, were com " monly in that early stage of human knowledge as- " cribed to the direct intervention of the will of some " supernatural being, and therefore still to a cause."

It is admitted that the great body of mankind, whether they are or are not persuaded of the existence of a uniform system of nature, believe as to every effect, as to every new thing produced, or change upon an old thing, that it must have had a cause, whether natural or supernatural. The question is, Is this belief intuitive ?

This conviction can stand the tests of intuition. On

the bare contemplation of a new phenomenon, that is, of a new thing appearing, of a thing which did not exist before, we declare that it has had a producing cause. It certainly appears in very early life, before there can be a lengthened or wide observation or enumeration of instances. It is strong in very primitive states of society, long before mankind had observed an invariable uniformity in the occurrence of natural phenomena. It can be shown that it is necessary and universal. Mr. Mill indeed tells us, " I am convinced that " any one accustomed to abstraction and analysis, who " will fairly exert his faculties for the purpose, will, " when his imagination has once learned to entertain " the notion, find no difficulty in conceiving that in " some one for instance of the many firmaments into " which sidereal astronomy now divides the universe, " events may succeed one another at random, without " any fixed law ; nor can anything in our experience or " in our mental nature constitute a sufficient, or indeed " any, reason for believing that this is nowhere the case." The phrase, " fixed law," here employed, is ambiguous ; it may mean a mere natural or physical law, such as that of attraction. And I acknowledge at once that it is quite possible to apprehend and to believe that there may be worlds in which new phenomena, or changes on old phenomena, may be produced, without the operation of that law of gravitation which seems to act everywhere in our mundane system. But the real question is, would not the mind insist, and this according to " a fixed law" of our " mental nature." that the event must have a

cause in an agent physical or spiritual ? We may ob -
serve that the old misleading phrase, 'conceive,' is once
more casting up. I admit we can have the idea of, that
is, image to ourselves, a new phenomenon without any
necessary precedent. But I hold that we cannot be
made to judge, decide, or believe, that in any firmament
there could be a new event,—say a world springing into
being with no cause to produce it.

The mental phenomenon, the conviction and its attached necessity, Mr. Mill would explain by the association of ideas. But then, in order to save himself from
obvious and pressing difficulties, he is obliged to lay down
very stringent precautions as to when association can
generate a feeling of necessity. In order to produce the
inseparable association, the phenomenon must be " so
" closely linked in our experience, that we never perceive
" the one without at the same time, or the immediately
" succeeding moment, perceiving the other." Again, " No
" frequency of conjunction between two phenomena will
" create an inseparable association if counter associations
" are being created all the while" (p. 266). By help of
these two principles he tries to avoid the objection which
might be urged to his mode of accounting for the conviction of necessity. But he is seen to be involved in hope-
less perplexities when these laws are applied to causation.
For neither of them would allow the necessary conviction to be formed as to cause and effect from mere experience. For it is not the case that we never perceive
a cause without perceiving an effect, or that we never
observe an effect without also observing a cause. On

the contrary, the effects of causes operating, and the causes of effects falling under our notice, are very often concealed from us. Of how few of the occurrences happening in the circle of our experience, or in the times in which we live, are we able to estimate the consequences? In a large proportion of the physical effects which come under our notice, the cause is not discovered at the time, and is only found out in the end by a process of elaborate experiment, fitted to distract instead of aiding association; and in the case of a large number of the occurrences of our personal experience, or recorded in history, we never do rise to the discovery of the causes. Again, as to the other precautionary rule, we find that in the case of cause and effect there is a constant formation of "counter associations," by reason of the complexity of the conditions which meet in the cause, and of incidents which attach themselves to the effect, and of the combination of each of these with a host of concomitant circumstances to disturb the formation of an inseparable association. A friend dies: no doubt there has been a physical cause of the occurrence, but how many things prevent us from discovering or even inquiring about it; and finding little satisfaction in the contemplation, we dwell rather on the regard we had for the departed, on his excellent qualities, on the loss we have suffered; or if we think of what led to it, we prefer referring the whole to the appointment of God. That amidst all these complications, and in spite of appearances to the contrary, mankind should ever have clung to the belief that there is a cause, natural or supernatural, to every event, is a proof that the conviction is deeply seated in our nature.

When Mr. Mill confines his attention to the physical and logical nature of causation, he throws light upon the subject. "The statement of the cause is incomplete " unless in some shape or other we introduce all the " conditions." " In practice, that particular condition " is usually styled the cause, whose share in the matter " is superficially the most conspicuous, or whose re- " quisiteness to the production of the effect we happen " to be insisting upon at the moment." " The real cause " of the phenomenon is the assemblage of all the con- " ditions." There is new and important truth in this statement. But I am not sure that Mr. Mill has got a full view of the facts. In material nature there is always need of the action of two or more agents in order to an effect. If a ball moves in consequence of another striking it, there is need of the one ball as well as the other, and the cause, properly speaking, consists of the two in a relation to each other. But not only is there a duality or plurality in the cause, there is the same (Mr. Mill has not noticed it) in the effect. The effect consists not merely of the one ball, the ball struck and set in motion, but also of the other ball which struck it, and which has now lost part of its momentum. By carrying out this doctrine, we can determine what is meant by 'condition' and 'occasion' when the phrases are applied to the operation of causation. When we speak of an agent requiring a 'condition,' an 'occasion,' or 'circumstances,' in order to its action, we refer to the other agent or agents required, that it may produce a particular effect. Thus that fire may burn, it is necessary to have fuel, or a combustible material. In order that my will may move my arm, it is needful to have the concurrence of a healthy motor nerve. So much for the dual or plural agency in the cause. But there is a similar complexity in the effect, and we need a like phrase to designate the part of it which we do not require to consider at the time. Thus the steam which has raised a certain weight has expended meanwhile a certain amount of force; but persons striving merely to have the weight raised care nothing for the other, and may call it 'incidental;' which incidental part, however, may be the essential element in the view of the engineer who requires to generate the steam. In the proper enunciation of the cause and the effect—the invariable and unconditional cause and effect—there should be a statement of all the concurring antecedents, and all the involved consequents, including the conditions in the cause, and the incidents in the effect.

By carrying out this doctrine consistently, we are able to give (which Mr. Mill has not done) its proper place to the 'Agent' and 'Patient;' the distinction between which has been noticed in some form or other by most philosophers from the time of Aristotle. The agent and patient are certainly not to be identified with the cause and effect; but they are to be found in the cause, that is, in the assemblage of circumstances necessary in order to the production of the effect. These circumstances or agencies must concur, in short, must operate on each

other, in order to action and change. Thus, in order
to the production of water, there must be both oxygen
and hydrogen ; the two act on each other according to
their nature and laws ; and both are changed and appear
in the product. That which we consider as acting may
be called the Agent, that which we regard as acted on
may be considered as the Patient. It should be observed
and remembered, that the agent under one aspect is
always a patient under another, and the patient may
also be viewed as an agent; for that which acts is
always acted on, and that which is acted on always
acts ; and action is always equal to reaction. The
account now given enables us to settle a question
which has often been started, but never determined
satisfactorily. The question is, Is the effect always
posterior in time to the cause, or may it not be contemporaneous ? The answer is, that the complex effect
always follows the complex cause ; but that the con-
current agents which constitute the cause may be regarded as acting on each other simultaneously. The
oxygen and the hydrogen influence each other con-
temporaneously, and are followed by the production of
water as the effect.

The reader may compare the statement now offered
with that given by Mr. Mill in his chapter "Of the Law
of Universal Causation." Mr. Mill has not seen that
as the cause consists in an assemblage of conditions, so
the effect consists in an assemblage of consequences.
In the agents concurring in the cause there is a real
distinction between agent and patient, whereas he says

the distinction vanishes on examination, or rather is found to be merely verbal. He has discussed, but avowedly does not know how to settle the question as to whether the cause precedes the effect. He has also noticed the circumstance, that in some cases when the cause ceases the effect also seems to cease, whereas in others the effect appears to remain ; but he has not been able to give a full explanation of the phenomenon. The effect remains when the assemblage of circumstances which constitute the cause abides. It is thus a book remains on the table as long as the table is in a position to uphold it. It is thus oxygen and hydrogen abide in water till an element with a stronger affinity with one of them succeeds in drawing it off. In other cases the concurrence of agencies acting as the cause is ever liable to be broken up, and the effect ceases when the complex cause has disappeared. It is thus that the book is upheld in my hand, only so long as I stretch out my arm : thus that the room is illuminated by day only so long as the sun shines, and by night only so long as the lamp continues to burn. In all cases a change implies a new agent, or a new concurrence of agencies.

But we are now in the heart of our author's logical discussions. Mr. Mill's *Logic* has never been subjected to a careful review on the part either of his supporters or opponents. It deserves such an examination because of its excellencies, and it requires it because of its errors, which many students are accepting along with the truths. I undertake this review in the immediately succeeding chapters.

CHAPTER XIV.

THE LOGICAL NOTION.

FORMAL Logic is usually represented as dealing with the Notion, Judgment, and Reasoning. Mr. Mill has no separate exposition of the Notion. He treats instead, of Names : as if Names did not stand for Thoughts, the nature of which should have been previously investigated. This is surely a defect in an elaborate Logical Treatise. In his controversial work he has given us his theory of the Notion or Conception. It will be necessary to examine it.

The Notions, that is, apprehensions of things, which the mind can entertain, are of three sorts :—*First*, There is the Singular Concrete Notion, such as Homer, Virgil, Dante, Milton, this man, this dog, that daisy, that book. This notion is singular, as it embraces a single object. It is concrete, as it contemplates the object as possessing an aggregate of qualities. The consideration of the nature of this notion does not, properly speaking, come under Formal Logic, which has to do only with Discursive Thought ; that is, thought in which there is a process from something given or allowed to something founded upon it. It is furnished to us by intuítion, primarily by the senses and consciousness, and does not imply any logical operation. But then it comes into Logic when it is combined with the abstract and general notion in the proposition and argument. Thus, when we say, ' Locke was an independent thinker,' the subject is a singular concrete notion compared with a general notion in the predicate. Logic, therefore, cannot overlook this notion, but it may hand over the special discussion of its origin and validity to psychology or metaphysics. Mr. Mill gives us a correct enough account of it, though he does not specially investigate its nature : " A concrete name is a name which stands for a thing" (B. I. c. ii. 4).

Second, There is the Abstract Notion. It is the apprehension of a part of an object as a part, say of the head of a horse as the head of a horse. More technically it is the apprehension of an attribute. " An abstract name is a name which stands for an attribute of a thing" (*Ib.*) In this latter sense the part cannot exist separate from the whole : thus transparency cannot exist apart from a transparent object, such as glass or ice. But though an abstract quality cannot exist apart from an object, it is not to be regarded as a nonentity or a fiction of the mind. Rationality cannot exist apart from a rational being, but it has a real existence in a rational being, such as man.

On account of the defective view which he takes of the intellectual faculties of man, Mr. Mill has not been able to furnish an adequate account of the Abstract No-

tion.* Speaking of the notion of length without breadth,
" According to what appears to me the sounder opinion,
" the mind cannot form any such notion ; it cannot con-
" ceive length without breadth" (B. I. c. viii. 7).   And
in his recent work, " The existence of Abstract Ideas—
" the conception of the class qualities by themselves, and
" not as embodied in an individual—is effectually pre-
" cluded by the law of Inseparable Association" (p. 314).
The ambiguous word ' conceive' has once more cast up
without his telling us in what sense he employs it.   I
should say that in these passages he uses it in the sense
of ' image,' in which signification the statement is true.
I believe that length cannot exist except in an extended
object which has also breadth, and I am sure that I can
image length only in an extended object.   He adds, that
the mind " can only, in contemplating objects, *attend* to
" their length, exclusively of their other sensible quali-
" ties, and so determine what properties may be predi-
" cated of them in virtue of their length alone."   This
is not a sufficiently comprehensive account of the Abs -
tract Notion ; but it implies that there is more than a
mere image.   If we inquire carefully into its nature, we
shall find that as a *thought* it implies not only *attention*
but a comparative act.   We apprehend the attribute to
be an attribute of the concrete object, thus comparing
the part and whole.   This apprehension is the Abstract
Notion, and we can compare the attribute apprehended
with other attributes, or with concrete objects of various
kinds, and make affirmations or denials.   Thus, on perceiving a cone of sugar as a concrete object, we can in

abstract thought fix on the figure, and from the contemplation of it we might by a further abstraction fix on the conic sections, and by a process of reasoning evolve their properties. In all this we should be dealing, not with mere hypotheses, but abstracted realities : and the conclusions we reach will be found true of all cones, and of all sections of the cone, including the elliptic figures in which the planets move.[1]

Third, There is the General Notion, such as man, poet, animal. We are so constantly forming notions of this sort, that it should not be difficult to evolve the processes involved in it. The two first steps are,—(1.) that we observe a resemblance among objects ; (2.) that we fix on the points of resemblance. The first is accomplished by the mind's power of perceiving agreements, and the second by an operation of abstraction. No absolute rule can be laid down as to which of these processes is the prior. I believe that in most cases there is first a perception more or less vague of a likeness, and then the separate consideration of the points of likeness. But in other cases we seem rather to fix primarily on an attribute, and conjoin by it all the objects which we discover to possess it. Thus, in zoology the naturalist fixes on the possession of a backbone, and

---

1 Regarding Logic as the Science of the Laws of Discursive Thought, as above defined, the Abstract Notion is clearly embraced in it, as in it we draw an attribute out of the concrete object given, and we must endeavour to unfold the Laws of Thought involved in it. The following may serve provisionally till a better list be furnished :—I. The Abstract Quality implies a Concrete Object. II. When the Concrete Object is real the Abstract Quality taken from it is also real. III. When the Abstract is a Quality, it is not to be regarded as having an independent existence : its existence is in a Concrete Object.

makes it the bond of a class of animals. But there is more in generalization than either or than both of these steps. (3.) The consummating step is, that we constitute a class which embraces all the objects possessing the common attribute or attributes. Till this step is taken there is no generalization. When this step is taken the general notion is formed. Let it be observed that there is here an operation beyond the other two. In the first step we must have observed or contemplated more or fewer objects, and perceived them to resemble each other; still the number was limited. In the second step we fixed on a quality or qualities common to the objects noticed. But in the final step the number of objects is indefinite, and must include not merely those we have observed and compared, but all others possessing the mark or marks fixed on. On seeing only half a dozen red deer I may have been forcibly struck with their resemblance, and may have been able to fix on their points of likeness,—such as their shape and their noble antlers. But when I take the decisive step and form the class red deer, that class must include not only those I have seen, but all others with that form of body and horns; not only these six deer, but all other deer now living, and all deer that ever lived or shall live; not only so, but all imaginable deer, the deer sung of by all the poets, and the deer that may be created by the ever active imagination. A notion is not general unless it embraces all the objects possessing the mark or marks fixed on.

Now this consummating step has not been noticed.

or at least has not had its appropriate place allotted to it, by most psychologists and logicians.   Dr. Brown dwells very fondly on the feeling of resemblance, as he calls it (he should have said the observation of the relation of resemblance), but takes no notice of the all-important act by which the species is made to embrace all the objects having the resemblance.   This specially intellectual step was from time to time before the mind of Hamilton, as when he says, that "concepts have " only a potential, not an actual, universality; that is, " they are only universal, inasmuch as they may be " applied to any of a certain class of objects."   But with an occasional glimpse of the truth, he loses sight of it immediately after, and he talks of a mysterious " syn- " thesis in consciousness," wherein " the qualities, which " by comparison are judged similar, and by attention " are constituted into an exclusive object of thought,— " these are already, by this process, identified in con- " sciousness ; for they are only judged similar, inas- " much as they produce in us indiscernible effects" (*Logic*, Lect. viii.)   His whole exposition is confused and unsatisfactory, and it issues in his finding a con-tradiction in the general notion.   He loses his consis-tency and clearness in endeavouring to find some sort of reconciliation between nominalism and conceptualism. Mr. Mill has unfolded no elements in the general no-tion except the attribute and the name.   "We create " an artificial association between those attributes (to " which we wish to devote our exclusive attention) and " a certain combination of articulate sounds, which

" guarantees to us when we hear the sound, or see
" the written characters corresponding to it, there will
" be raised in the mind an idea of some object pos-
" sessing those attributes, in which idea those attri-
" butes alone will be suggested vividly to the minds,
" our consciousness of the remainder of the concrete
" idea being faint." " The association of that particular
" set of attributes with a given word is what keeps
" them together in the mind by a stronger tie than that
" with which they are associated with the remainder of
" the concrete image" (p. 322). There is a great oversight here. There is no reference to the discovery of
resemblances among objects as constituting the commencement of the whole process. He ascribes to the
name what is done by the possession of common qualities. " For a class is absolutely nothing but an in-
" definite number of individuals denoted by a general
" name. The name given to them in common is what
" makes them a class." But what makes the name
applicable to the indefinite number of objects? What
enables us, when we discover a new object, to say
whether it is or is not entitled to the name? The
answer to these questions will force us to look beyond
the name to the like attributes in the objects, as making
the objects pass under the same name, as enabling us to
understand what is denoted by the name, as being the
meaning of the name, and, in fact, constituting the bond
which joins the objects in a class. There is a passage
in which he has a glimpse of the consummating step,
and indeed of the whole process. " The only mode in

" which any general name has a definite meaning, is by
" being a name of an indefinite variety of things,
" namely, all things known or unknown, past, present,
" or future, which possess certain attributes" (*Logic*,
I. v. 3). This language does point to something else
than the name as bringing together "the indefinite number of individuals in the class :" it points to the possession of " certain attributes" in the " indefinite variety
of things ;" and it implies, though it does not just
state, that the class must include all the objects possessing these attributes. This account, consequentially
followed out, makes the common notion embrace three
elements : objects resembling each other ; points of resemblance ; and the inclusion of all objects having these
points. But Mr. Mill habitually loses sight of some of
these essential characteristics, and ever falls back upon
the attribute and the name. This omission in the
theory of the notion comes out in positive error in the
account of the judgment and reasoning.

According to the exposition now given, the Class-
Notion always includes both objects and attributes,
objects having a resemblance, and common attributes
possessed by them. So far as it embraces objects, it
is said to have Extension. So far as it contains attributes, it is said to have Comprehension or Intension.
This distinction was indicated in the *Port-Royal Logic*,
and was enunciated in several logical works published
in the end of the seventeenth and the beginning of the
eighteenth century.[1] It has been elaborated with great

[1] In particular, I have found it in a Compend of Logic, prepared and
printed (there is no evidence of its having been published) for use of the

care, at times with an excess of refinement, by Sir William Hamilton. That every general notion should have both these aspects, follows from the account I have given of its formation and constitution. In every General Notion there must be objects compared ; this constitutes the Extension. There must also be marks to bring the objects together under one head ; this is Comprehension. The former is got by observation and comparison, the latter by abstraction. We see that as the one rises the other falls, and that as the one falls the other rises. As we multiply the marks or attri butes, there must be fewer objects possessing them. As we multiply the objects, they must have fewer common marks. Hence the rule, that the greater the Extension, the less the Comprehension, and the greater the Comprehension, the less the Extension.

Upon this distinction the remark is, " that the Ex- " tension is not anything intrinsic to the concept ; it is " the sum of all the objects, in our concrete images of " which the concept is included : but the comprehension " is the very concept itself; for the concept means " nothing but our mental representation of the sum of " the attributes composing it" (p. 333). It is clear, that of the three constituents of common notions he gives the chief, or rather exclusive, place to the attributes. " All men, and the class man, are expressions which " point to nothing but attributes ; they cannot be inter-

Scottish Universities, by order of a Parliamentary Commission, 1795 : in an Introduction to Logic (2d edit., 1722) by Gershom Carmichael of Glasgow University ; and again in a Compend of Logic by Francis Hutcheson, which was used in Glasgow College till towards the close of last century.

" preted except in comprehension" (p. 363). In opposition to this, I maintain that the Extension of the notion is quite as important an aspect of it as the Comprehension ; that every common notion may be interpreted in Extension as well as Intension ; that in the class there must be objects to combine as well as attributes to combine them ; and that a mental representation must be inadequate which does not embrace the objects as well as the sum of the attributes possessed by them. The Universal Notion is of objects possessing common attributes, the notion including all the objects possessing the attributes. We see here, in Mr. Mill's logical doctrine, a taint at the fountain, which will be found running through the whole stream.

" General concepts, therefore, we have, properly " speaking, none." " I consider it nothing less than a " misfortune that the words Concept, General Notion, " or any other phrase to express the supposed mental " modification corresponding to a class name, should " ever have been invented. Above all, I hold that " nothing but confusion ever results from introducing " the term Concept into Logic ; and that instead of the " Concept of a class, we should always speak of the " signification of a class name" (pp. 321, 331). But surely it is desirable to have a word to express the " mental modification" when we contemplate a " class," and Conception or General Notion seems appropriate enough. I also think it desirable to have a phrase to denote, not the " signification of a class name," but the thing signified by the class name ; and the fittest I can

think of is Concept. Mr. Mill would replace Abstract and General Idea by " the connotation of the class name." I reckon the epithet ' connotation' a very good one for some purposes. It was used by the schoolmen ; it was a favourite one with Mr. James Mill ; and has had a clear meaning attached to it. " A connota-
" tive term is one which denotes a subject and implies
" an attribute." Thus, ' white' is connotative ; " it de-
" notes all things white, as snow, paper, the foam of the
" sea, etc. ; and implies, or, as it was termed by the
" schoolmen, connotes the attribute whiteness." But while ' connotative' is an expressive enough epithet, applied to certain predicates, it does not bring out what is contained in the class-notion. ' Horse,' for example, is a general notion, embracing an indefinite number of objects ; but all this is not expressed by applying the phrase ' connotative.' " It denotes a subject ;" but what is the subject ? This question is left unanswered. It can be answered only by saying that it consists of all the objects possessing the attributes ; and as to the phrase " signification of the class name," it leaves it unsettled what the thing signified is. I am inclined to think that the words Conception and Concept serve a good purpose ; they express the signification of the class name.[1]

The General Notion being formed in the way ex- plained, we fix it and preserve it, and think of it by

[1] The following are some of the Laws of Thought involved in the General Notion :—I. The Universal implies Singulars. II. When the Singulars are Real the Universal is also Real. III. The Reality in the Universal consists in the possession of common attributes by all the objects embraced in it. .

means of a Sign.   The Sign may be one or other of two
sorts.   Lauding the founder of his School, Mr. Mill
says, " It is a doctrine of one of the most fertile thinkers
" of modern times, Auguste Comte, that, besides the
" logic of signs, there is a logic of images, and a logic of
" feelings.   In many of the familiar processes of thought,
" and especially in uncultured minds, a visual image
" serves instead of a word" (p. 329).   Omitting the
consideration of the logic of feelings as not coming
specially before us, the doctrine attributed to Comte as
so " fertile" a thinker was long ago proclaimed by
Aristotle, and has floated ever since, in a more or less
correct form, in logic and speculative philosophy.   According to Aristotle, a notion is not the same as a
phantasm, but it is never found without a phantasm.[1]
The expression of Mr. Mill is much more loose.   He
talks of a " logic of images ;" whereas it is not a logic,
but a notion entertained by means of an image.   He
speaks of the image being a " visual sensation" and
" visual appearance ;" whereas it may be a phantasm
by any of the senses,—it may be of a smell, or a taste,
or a touch, or a sound.

I believe that the General Notion is kept before the
mind primarily by the phantasm.   In every such notion the objects are indefinite—are innumerable ; and
so the human mind (whatever angelic minds may do)
cannot image them all : but it images one as a sign of

---

[1] Distinguishing between Notions, νοήματα, and φαντάσματα, Aristotle
says (see *Anim.* III. 7), Νοήματα τινὶ διοίσει τοῦ μὴ φαντάσματα εἶναι, ἢ
οὐδὲ ταῦτα φαντάσματα, ἀλλ' οὐκ ἄνευ φαντασμάτων.

the others. The attribute, or aggregate of attributes, cannot be imaged apart from objects, but we labour to fashion an object which may give prominence to the one attribute, if there be only one, or combine them if there be many. This, I am persuaded, is the original and spontaneous agency by which we carry with us and compare our concepts. Mr. Mill has a glimpse of this, and nothing more, when he says that " in uncultured minds a visual image serves instead of words." The more correct expression would be, that in cultured minds the word often comes to serve the purpose of the image and to supersede it. I believe we naturally resort to the image ; but the image is always felt to be inadequate. Hence the common remark, that we cannot have an adequate idea, that is, in the sense of image, of a class. Suppose the notion to be ' quadruped :' when we think about the class, we may, and do commonly, image some sort of beast with four limbs ; but if the limbs be those of a horse, they cannot be those of a dog, and if they be those of a dog, they cannot be those of the horse ; and if they be different from either, they cannot be those either of the horse or the dog. All this does not prove that we cannot in thought form a general notion, or that we cannot legitimately employ it in judgment and reasoning; it merely shows that the image, as being single, is not equal to the indefinite number of objects, and, as being concrete, cannot be identical with the attribute, which is abstract. The fact is, the image, or, as I prefer calling it, with Aristotle, the phantasm, is a mere sign,—one for the many, that one being as far as possible a type of the many. The mind spontaneously forms such representations, and delights to do so; and when it can have them, the thinking is rendered much more vivid and pleasant, and is more readily accompanied with excitement and emotion.

But when the generalizations are very high, when the abstractions are very refined, and the common attributes are very numerous, or not very definitely fixed, it becomes all but impossible to construct a phantasm which will represent the class. We can form a pretty fair representative image of quadruped, but what phantasm could stand for such complex notions as civilisation, liberty, politics, art, and science? In striving to compass such notions, we naturally resort to artificial symbols, particularly language. If there be a word suitable to express the thought, it will employ it; if there be not, it will labour to invent one. But so far from images serving instead of words, the words serve our purpose as being images. It has been remarked by metaphysicians that most names were originally of individual objects. An individual object, or the image of it, was first taken to represent the class; and then the name of the individual, as a sound or a written character addressed to the eye, was used as a briefer and more convenient symbol. The advantage of such verbal signs, which are always, be it remarked, in a sense phantasms addressed to the eye or ear, is, that they do not distract us with the peculiarities of individual objects, and allow us in thinking to proceed only on the common qualities of objects. All this renders the notion less lively and emotional—unless indeed by those who resort to word-painting to raise up a phantasm—but at the same time better fitted for the conducting of rigid thought. The most perfect artificial signs for the limited end in view, are those employed in algebra, in which meaningless letters denote quantities known or unknown, and we can employ them according to the settled laws of reasoning in quantity without thinking of what they stand for, till we reach the result, when we translate the sign into what it signifies. When we lose sight for the time of what the sign stands for, this is what constitutes, properly speaking, Symbolical Thought. But it is always to be understood that the sign does stand for a notion, and has always a tacit reference to it; that we can predicate of the sign only what we could legitimately predicate of the notion; and that in passing it on from premisses to conclusion in a chain of reasoning, we must be sure that we proceed on principles which are applicable to the thing signified. And in order to determine whether we are or are not making a proper predication, we can always, and should often, require that the sign should be translated into the notion, and the notion compared with the thing.[1]

[1] The following are some of the Laws of Thought involved in the use of Signs as Instruments of Thought :— I. Every Logical Term stands for a Notion, which may be a Singular Concrete, an Abstract, or a Universal. II. According as it stands for one or other of these, so is it to be interpreted. III. We can predicate of the Sign only what might be predicated of the Notion. IV. In order to determine whether we are making a proper predication as to the Sign, we may demand at any time that the Notion be substituted for it. V. In order to determine whether we are making a proper predication as to the Notion, we must inquire what is the nature of the Things from which it has been formed.

A distinction of some importance may be drawn between two kinds of Concepts. In the one the class is determined by a single attribute, or by it together with the attributes implied in it. Such are the classes designated by adjectives, as generous, faithful, virtuous,—pointing to one quality of an object, along with those that may be involved in that quality. It is to these phrases that the epithet 'connotative' is specially applicable; they denote an attribute, and connote objects possessing it. In other cases the Comprehension of the class consists of an aggregate of attributes. Thus, we cannot fix on any one attribute of the class Man, and derive all the others from it. Rationality is one quality, but he has many others :

> " Men define a man
> The creature who stands frontward to the stars,
> The creature who looks inward to himself,
> The tool-wright, laughing creature. 'Tis enough ;
> We'll say instead the inconsequent creature man,
> For that's his specialty. What creature else
> Conceives the circle, and then walks the square ?"

The one kind of notions I would be inclined to call, when it is necessary to draw the distinction between them, the Generalized Abstract, because in it we seize on a single quality, and put all the objects possessing it into a class. The other I call the Generalized Concrete, because in it we bring together, by certain resemblances, individuals with their aggregate of qualities. It was to the latter that the schoolmen appropriated the phrase Species; I think they would scarcely have applied it to the Generalized Abstract such as 'rational' or 'irrational.' The Generalized Concrete evidently includes all natural classes, such as reptiles, fishes, birds, mammals, in the animal kingdom, and rosaceæ, cruciferæ, solanaceæ in the vegetable kingdom; the objects embraced in these have all a number of common qualities.

It is of importance to keep these distinctions in view in considering the nature of Definition. In defining the Generalized Abstract Notion, we have only to bring out the one common quality, and the work is completed. But in attempting to define the Generalized Concrete, we cannot fix on any one quality as being the essential one; and it often happens that the common attributes are so numerous, that it would be vain and presumptuous to attempt to specify all of them. Thus, no one can tell what are the properties embraced in horse, dog, metal, mineral. It fortunately, I believe providentially, happens that we have in nature classes called Kinds, the nature of which has been so well expounded by Mr. Mill. In these, one of the Marks is an invariable accompaniment, and therefore a sign of the others; and in specifying it we have truly fixed the significates of the notion, that is, comprised all the objects embraced in it and excluded others. Thus it is a good definition to say, "Man is a rational animal," for all his other special attributes are conjoined with rationality. If we call the attribute fixed on the Differentia, the others may be represented as Propria, if we wish to retain, after amending it, the distinction of Porphyry between Differentia and Proprium.

Mr. Mill has offered some valuable remarks on Definition, but from overlooking the distinction between the Extension and Comprehension of a Notion, he has not given us a thoroughly scientific account of the logical process. Sir William Hamilton is right in saying, after older logicians, that it is effected according to the Comprehension of a Notion; that is, it reflectively brings out the Marks by which those who spontaneously formed the concept combined the objects. From overlooking Extension Mr. Mill has omitted Division, a subject which ought to be discussed in all logical treatises. Logical Division proceeds according to the Extension of a Notion, and spreads out the co-ordinate species of a genus, according to marks added, so that the species exclude one another, and together make up the genus.

CHAPTER XV.

LOGICAL JUDGMENT.

THERE is no part of Logic which has greater need of being thoroughly cleared up than that which relates to Judgment. In particular, first, what precisely are the things compared, and in regard to which the affirmation or denial is made? In the common logical treatises we are said to compare two notions and declare their agreement or disagreement. Mr. Mill has made an important correction of this statement: " Propositions " (except when the mind itself is the subject treated of) " are not assertions respecting our ideas of things, but " assertions respecting the things themselves. In order " to believe that gold is yellow, I must indeed have the " idea of gold and the idea of yellow, and something " having reference to these ideas must take place in my " mind; but my belief has not reference to the ideas, " it has reference to the things" (*Logic*, I. v. 1). " Do " we never judge or assert anything but our mere " notions of things? Do we not make judgments and " assert propositions respecting actual things" (p. 346). There is truth here. But is the whole truth set forth?

The judgment is pronounced in regard to objects, but then, it must be of objects of which we have a notion. The judgment is not pronounced of our notions as mental phenomena, but neither can it be of things of which we have had no notion,—of such we can make no predication. He tells us again and again, " The judgment is concerning the fact, not the concept." But then he is obliged to allow, " that in order to believe that gold " is yellow, I must, indeed, have the idea of gold, and " the idea of yellow, and something having reference to these ideas must take place in my mind ;" and he adds, that in order to belief, " a previous mental conception of the facts is an indispensable condition." I ask, should not this indispensable condition have a place in the full statement of the nature of propositions ? There is a sentence in which he has got at least a momentary view of the correct doctrine : " The real object of belief " is not the concept, or any relation of the concept, but " the fact conceived" (p. 348). Yes, the *facts conceived* are what we compare. If we could get philosophers to reserve the word 'conception' for the mental operation, and apply the word 'concept' exclusively and consistently, not to the mental product as Hamilton does, but to the things conceived, then the proper account of Judgment, when we have a class-notion, would be, the act in which we compare two concepts. This account embraces the full mental operation, and throws us back first upon the notions that we may judge of them, and these throw us back on the things from which the notions have been formed.

This leads me to notice another misapprehension of our author's. Here, as all throughout his Logic, he makes us look to names rather than to thoughts. But surely Locke has shown, in that third book of his *Essay*, which Mr. Mill so commends, that names should ever carry us back to ideas, which ideas, as Bacon had previously shown, should ever carry us back to things. Logic has to do primarily with Thought as employed about Things, and with Names only secondarily and incidentally, as being the expression of Thoughts. It is thus only that we can employ the laws of thought, which are fixed, to enable us to examine and correct language, which is variable. But Mr. Mill reverses this order, and makes Logic deal primarily with the proposition or expression, and not with the judgment or comparison (p. 357).

But the important and unsettled question is, What is the precise relation between the two Concepts or Terms in Judgment? When it is said to be an agreement or disagreement, the language is far too vague for philosophic purposes. Sir William Hamilton vacillates in the account given by him. His common representation is that the relation is one of whole and parts. " We " may articulately define a judgment or proposition to be " the product of that act by which we pronounce, that, " of two notions thought as subject and as predicate, " the one does or does not constitute a part of the other, " either in the quantity of extension or in the quantity " of comprehension " (*Logic*, I. p. 229). In other places the relation seems rather to be spoken of as one of equa-

lity, and he would interpret " all men are mortal" as
" all men = some mortals." Again, he seems to make
the relation one of identity ; for he says that the law of
identity " is the principle of all logical affirmation and
definition" (*Ib.* p. 80), and he speaks of the two notions
being " conceived as one" (*Ib.* p. 227).

It is not very easy, amidst Mr. Mill's criticisms of
others, to find his own theory. He tells us, " Existence,
" Co-existence, Sequence, Causation, Resemblance, one
" or other of these, is asserted or denied in every pro-
" position without exception." But then he explains
away the affirmations and denials as to Existence and
Causation ; for Existence, that is, noumenon, is unknown
and unknowable, and Causation is unconditional sequence. There remain only three relations, and the
judgment is a recognition of a relation " of a succession,
a co-existence, or a similitude between facts" (p. 353).
But he has a way of still further reducing the number
of relations. For propositions which assert a resemblance, such as ' this colour is like that colour,' " might
" with some plausibility be brought within the descrip-
" tion of an affirmation of sequence, by considering it
" as an assertion that the simultaneous contemplation of
" the two colours is *followed* by a specific feeling, termed
" the feeling of resemblance." And as to the allegation
that the propositions of which the predicate is a general
name, affirm or deny resemblance, he says, that what is
declared is the possession of " certain common peculiarities," " and those peculiarities it is which the terms
" connote, and which the propositions consequently

" assert, not the resemblance" (*Logic*, I. v. 6). By this subtle but not satisfactory process, in which, as usual, he reaches simplicity by overlooking the peculiarities of the phenomenon, he makes propositions to declare " that a certain attribute is *either* part of a given set of " attributes, or invariably co-exists with them" (p. 361). His final reduction is thus expressed: " Propositions in " which the concept of the predicate is part of the con- " cept of the subject, or, to express ourselves more phi- " losophically, in which the attributes connoted by the " predicate are part of those connoted by the subject, " are a kind of Identical Propositions : they convey no " information, but at most remind us of what, if we un- " derstood the word which is the subject of the propo- " sition, we knew as soon as the word is pronounced. " Propositions of this kind are either definitions, or parts " of definitions.   These judgments are analytical : they " analyse the connotation of the subject-name, and " predicate separably the different attributes which the " name asserts collectively.   All other affirmative judg- " ments are synthetical, and affirm that some attribute, " or set of attributes, is, not a part of those connoted by " the subject-name, but an invariable accompaniment " of them" (p. 359).   This analysis accords thoroughly with Mr. Mill's psychological theory, and helps to prop it.   It makes all judgments relate to attributes, and simply to proclaim either an identity, or co-existence among them,—which attributes are in the end sensations, or possibilities of sensation.   But it is not in accordance with the revelations of consciousness, which show us

T

that the mind pronounces judgments not as to abstract attributes, but as to things with attributes ; and not only of identity and co-existence, but of whole and parts, of resemblance, of space, of quantity, and active property (see *supra*, pp. 202, 203).

Much clearness, as it appears to me, may be introduced into this subject by distinguishing three classes of judgments, corresponding to three classes of notions :

(1.) There are judgments in which the objects compared are Singular Concretes ; as when by the eye I see two marbles and judge them to be of the same size, or by the ear hear two sounds and declare one of them to be louder than the other. In the order of time these are the first judgments pronounced by the mind. It is by a succession of them, that is, by observing resemblances among a number of individual objects that we form the General Notion. It is to these, as I understand his doctrine, that Dr. Mansel applies the term Psychological Judgments (*Proleg. Log.*, p. 63). I have already expressed my opinion, that the relations which the mind can perceive among objects are very numerous and diversified—much more so than Mr. Mill supposes. What is the nature and what the best classification of these comparisons ; these are very important questions in psychology, but do not specially fall under the science which treats of discursive thought.

(2.) There are judgments in which we compare Abstracts, by which I do not mean mental states or modifications, but *things abstracted*. For example, ' Honesty is the best policy,' where both ' honesty' and ' the best

policy' are Abstracts, being neither Singular Concretes
on the one hand, nor Common Concepts on the other,
that is, they do not denote separately existing things,
such as ' this man,' nor an indefinite number of objects,
like ' man.' Under this fall all definitions such as
' Logic is the science of the laws of thought.' Here
both the subject, ' Logic,' and the predicate, ' the science
of the laws of thought,' are not independently existing
things on the one hand, nor do they embrace indefinite
objects on the other. In this same class I place judgments regarding space, time, and quantity, such as ' the
zenith is the point of the visible hemisphere directly
over the head of the observer;' ' mid-day is 12 o'clock
in the day;' and ' $2 + 2 = 4$.' Here both the terms are
abstract. We never met with such separate things
as $2 + 2$ or 4; nor can we describe either $2 + 2$ or 4
as a class embracing objects; in fact we cannot say
of such abstract notions that they have Extension.

In all such judgments the relation is one of identity
or of equality. The judgments are convertible or substitutive ; that is, we can change the position of the
terms, or substitute the one for the other, without any
change ; in fact we can make either term the subject
or the predicate, as may suit our purpose. Thus we
reverse the order given above, and say, ' the science of
the laws of thought is logic;' ' the point of the visible hemisphere directly over the head of the observer is
the zenith;' ' 12 o'clock in the day is mid-day;' and
' $4 = 2 + 2$.' Great clearness is introduced into this part
of Logic by separating these judgments, in which we

compare Abstracts, from those in which we compare Singulars or Concepts.

(3.) A more important, but a more complicated, class of judgments remains for consideration. It consists of those in which there is an attributive, and in fact, or by implication, a Concept or a class-notion. This language requires to be explained. When we say, 'this cow ruminates,' we have abstracted an attribute and ascribed it to the animal. In this proposition the subject is singular. But in judgments of this kind the subject may be a class-notion ; thus we say, 'cows ruminate,' meaning that the whole class do so. A judgment of this description is called attributive. One of the terms is, properly speaking, the subject, and the other the predicate. And the terms cannot be converted simply ; in other words, the predicate cannot be made the subject without limitation. Because all cows possess the attribute of rumination, we cannot say all ruminating things are cows.

All Attributive judgments are judgments in Comprehension, but they may also be made judgments in Extension. For we may reckon 'ruminant' as a class embracing not only the cow but other animals, such as the sheep and the deer. It will be admitted that this is always possible. On the other hand, I do not affirm that this is always done. In by far the greater number of propositions the primary and uppermost sense is in comprehension. Thus, when we say 'larks sing,' we probably mean not that larks are among the class of singing birds, but that they have the capacity of singing.

But we may always interpret in Extension the proposi
tion which is primarily in Comprehension. This follows
from the account given in last chapter, of the mutual
relation and dependence of the two. When we have a
mark, we may always form a class, embracing the objects
possessing the mark. The mind in its discursive operations tends to go on from Comprehension to Extension. When the predicate of a proposition is a verb, as
in the example just given, the thought is in Comprehension. But then we have also adjectives and common nouns as predicates. When we say the 'man
hoards money,' the thought is in Comprehension ; but
we also say that ' he is penurious,' and the thought is
rising to Extension ; and when we say ' he is a miser,'
the thought is in Extension as well as Comprehension,
for we have established a class, ' miser,' to which we
refer the individual. Mr. Mill seems to get a momentary view of this ; for while he holds that all judgments
(except where both the terms are proper names) are
really judgments in Comprehension, he allows that " it
" is customary, and the natural tendency of the mind,
" to express most of them in terms of Extension." The
" tendency" to do this must surely proceed from some
law of thought as applied to things ; and the possibility
of doing it surely implies an intimate relation between
the Comprehension and the Extension. In not a few
propositions the uppermost thought is in Extension.
Thus, when the young student of Natural History is
told that ' the crocodile is a reptile,' his idea is of a
class, of which he may afterwards learn the marks. As

in the other cases, the mind tends to generalize the attribute, and make the proposition one in Extension, so in this case it should go on to translate the idea in Extension into one in Comprehension. That propositions can always be interpreted in both ways, is a clear evidence of the indissoluble connexion of the operations.

It appears then that in all judgments belonging to this head the relation is always one of Comprehension, and may also and always be one of Extension likewise. This cannot be said of the second class, or those in which we compare mere Abstracts. We cannot call such attributive; thus there would be no propriety in saying that 4 is an attribute of $2 + 2$. Nor can such judgments be intelligently explained in Extension. At this point we see that Sir William Hamilton has fallen into error, from looking merely, in his Logic, to the Conception or General Notion, and overlooking the Abstract Notion. He makes all logical propositions capable of being interpreted both in Extension and Comprehension. But when we affirm that $4 \times 4 = 16$, we have no General Notion, and the phrases Extension and Comprehension are not applicable. In all cases, however, in which the predicate is a formed class-notion or Concept, the proposition should be interpreted both ways. Not only so, but when the predicate is merely attributive, it is still possible to interpret the proposition in both; and we shall see in next chapter that in reasoning its uppermost meaning is always in Extension rather than Comprehension.

At this point we see the error of Mr. Mill, as at the other we saw that of Sir William Hamilton. Mr. Mill maintains that " the supposed meaning in Extension is " not a meaning at all, until interpreted by the meaning " in Comprehension ; that all concepts and general " names which enter into propositions require to be " construed in Comprehension, and that their Compre- " hension is the whole of their meaning." Again, " The " Extension of a concept is not, like the Comprehension, " intrinsic and essential to the concept ; it is an exter- " nal and wholly accidental relation of the concept, and " no contemplation or analysis of the concept itself will " tell us anything about it" (pp. 362, 364). There is an accumulation of mistakes in this statement, all arising from the inadequate view taken by him of the elements involved in the General Notion. We have seen that in the General Notion there are objects as well as attri- butes ; objects to combine as well as attributes to com- bine them. In all propositions falling under this head the Extension has quite as distinct a meaning (it con- notes objects) as the Comprehension (which denotes attributes) ; and both are " intrinsic and essential to the concept." Extension is involved in every concept, and should always be noticed when we are using the con- cept, and brought out into distinct view when we ana- lyse it. Even in cases in which the primary sense of the predicate is attributive, we may also turn it into a class-notion and explain it in extension ; and we shall see that we always do so think it when we use the pro- position as a premiss in an argument.

Looking upon all judgments of this class as having both Extension and Comprehension, we can obtain from any given proposition a set of what have been called by Kant Syllogisms of the Understanding, and by Hamilton Immediate Inferences, or what I call Implied or Transposed Judgments. Thus, the judgment being given, ' All men are responsible,' we can by Extension derive such judgments as the following :—that man is a species in the genus responsible ; that some responsible beings are men ; that any one man is responsible ; that it is not true that no men are responsible ; or that some men are not responsible ; that men of genius are responsible with their genius ; and that God who calls men to account is calling to account responsible beings. Again, by Comprehension we can say, that responsibility should always accompany our notion of man ; that responsibility exists, being found in man who really exists ; that no man is irresponsible ; that irresponsible beings cannot be men ; and since responsibility is to God, man being responsible is responsible to God. These implied judgments bring us to the very verge of mediate reasoning. By subalternation we declare that all men being responsible, some men are responsible : there is but a step between this and mediate reasoning, in which we argue that all men being responsible, the New Zealanders who are men, that is, some men, are responsible. These Transposed Judgments appeared in the old Logic under the heads of Opposition and Conversion ; and in the New Analytic they have been drawn out fully in Archbishop Thomson's

Laws of Thought (p. iii., where, however, they are not drawn by Extension and Comprehension). It is a defect in Mr. Mill's work, professedly *A System of Logic, Ratiocinative and Inductive,* that it does not discuss such topics.

CHAPTER XVI.

REASONING.

IN order that they may reason, and reason validly, it is not necessary that persons be logicians. Man reasons spontaneously. The logician reflects upon the natural operation, and seeks to unfold its nature and its laws; and he strives also to lay down rules fitted to guide and guard us as we reason. The grand question to be determined in scientific logic is, what is the regulating principle of spontaneous ratiocination? On this subject there is a general agreement, and yet considerable diversity of opinion, among logicians. Almost all admit that the principle (when the conclusion is affirmative) may be expressed, 'Things which agree with one and the same agree with one another.' But this form is too vague, for it does not specify the nature of the agreement. And so logicians have endeavoured to make the statement more definite. According to the Dictum of Aristotle, the things must agree in being both under some higher class or genus. The form has sometimes been put, 'Things are the same which are the same with a third.' Mr. Mill expresses it, 'Things which co-exist with the same co-exist with one another.' The distinctions which have been drawn in the two last chapters in regard to the Notion and Judgment will be found, if followed out, to throw light on some of these points.

First, There are simple cases of reasoning in which the terms are Singular or Abstract :—

> Thomas à Kempis was the author of the 'Imitation of Christ ;'
> Gerson was not Thomas à Kempis ;
> .·. Gerson was not the author of the 'Imitation of Christ.'

Or the unfigured syllogism of Hamilton :—

> Sulphate of iron is copperas ;
> Sulphate of iron is not sulphate of copper ;
> .·. Sulphate of copper is not copperas.

In the same class may be placed all reasoning in which the propositions are definitions or substitutive : as, ' Logic is the science of the laws of thought ; Ethics is the science of the laws of our moral nature ; therefore Logic is not Ethics.' Under this head I put all quantitative reasoning ; as, ' $A = B$; $B = C$; therefore $A = C$.' In such examples none of the notions is properly a class-notion or attributive. As none of them has quantity or extension, so we cannot speak of a minor or major term, or of a minor or major premiss. The division into figures has no place ; for, as any one will at once see on trial, the middle term may be made, as we please, the subject or the predicate of either premiss. The regulating principle in all such cases is either, ' Things are the same which are the same with a third,' or ' things which are equal to the

same are equal to one another.' Much confusion is
avoided by allotting reasoning of this description to a
separate head. As there is no class-notion the Dictum
cannot be the regulating principle.

Second, There is more complex reasoning in which
there is an attributive predicate or a class-notion. In
this the old Aristotelian Dictum remains, after all discussion, the fundamental regulating principle : ' Whatever is predicated of a class may be predicated of all
the members of the class.' No other proposed Dictum
has lived beyond the age of its inventor. I am convinced that the same fate awaits that propounded by
our author (*Logic,* II. I-IV.).

The " really fundamental axiom of ratiocination," as
announced by him is, " Things which co-exist with the
same thing, co-exist with one another ;" and "a thing
" which co-exists with another thing, with which other
" a third thing does not co-exist, is not co-existent
" with that third thing." But the phrase ' co-exist,' if
limited to co-existence in respect of time or space, does
not include most important cases of reasoning ; and if
widened beyond this it becomes meaningless. When
we argue that the man having committed murder deserves punishment, the premisses and the conclusion
have reference, not to space or time, but to far different
relations. When we infer from A being equal to B, and
B to C, that A is equal to C, we are not making affirmations about co-existence. In explanation, he tells
us (p. 202, *footnote,* 6th ed.), " the co-existence meant
is that of being jointly attributes of the same subject."

This statement is still vague, and is not adequate, for it does not specify what is " the same subject," and it does not bring out that the attribution involves Extension : but it contains partial truth, and it has a meaning, which we can examine.

This new Dictum gives him the following universal formula :—

> Attribute A is a mark of Attribute B ;
> A given object has the mark A ;
> ∴ The given object has the attribute B.

But what does this first premiss mean when we translate it from abstractions into concrete realities ? As there cannot be an Attribute existing separately or apart from objects, it must mean, 'Whatever objects have the attribute A have the attribute B.' And what is this but the major premiss of the old syllogistic formula ? The second premiss requires an explanation. " A given object has the mark A :" this object may be one object or a class of objects. In order to give the formula a meaning, we must interpret it, 'Whatever individual or class has the attribute A has the attribute B ; a given object or class C has the attribute A ; therefore it has the attribute B.' The new Dictum and new Syllogistic formula are just bad versions of the old ones. I call them bad versions, for the phrase " co-exist" does not bring out the precise relation of the terms on which the thought proceeds ; and the phrase, " Attribute A," requires to be interpreted in order to have a relevant signification.

But he has given us another form, which he represents

as " an universal type of the reasoning process. We
" find it resolvable in all cases into the following ele-
" ments : Certain individuals have a given attribute ; an
" individual or individuals resemble the former in certain
" other attributes ; therefore they resemble them also in
" the given attribute" (*1b.* II. III. 7). It may be observed
that the phrase ' co-exist' has disappeared, and another
and equally vague one has taken its place ; it is a
" resemblance" in certain attributes, and in other attributes. It is allowed that this is not " conclusive from
the mere form of the expression." By itself it would
sanction fallacious reasoning quite as readily as valid.
' All men have immortal souls ; the brutes resemble
them in certain attributes (as instincts and bodily
organs) ; they must also have immortal souls.' We shall
see immediately that Mr. Mill allows that the syllogism
is an admirable test of the validity of reasoning, which,
it is conceded, this alleged " universal type" is not. It
wants the essential testing element, the general rule
that guarantees the conclusion, and which in the
syllogistic formula is embodied in the major premiss,—the necessity of which is pressed on us by the
Dictum.

But may there not be reasoning in Comprehension as
well as in Extension ? In answering this question it
should be admitted fully, that reasoning in Extension
may always be translated into reasoning in Comprehension. The reason of this is very obvious : it follows
from the account given of the nature of the Concept.
Extension always implies Comprehension ; that is, the

objects in the class are joined in the class by the possession of common marks :

> He who has intelligence and free agency is responsible ;
> Man has intelligence and free agency ;
> ∴ Man is responsible.

This reasoning in Extension may be put in Comprehension :

> Responsibility is an attribute of all who have intelligence and
> free agency ;
> Intelligence and free agency is an attribute of man ;
> ∴ Responsibility is an attribute of man.

Mr. Mill maintains that all reasoning is in Comprehension, and not in Extension. "All propositions into
" which general names enter, and consequently all rea-
" sonings, are in Comprehension only. Propositions
" and reasonings may be written in Extension, but they
" are always understood in Comprehension" (p. 363). I
have granted that, so far as propositions are concerned,
spontaneous thought is chiefly in Comprehension. In
simple affirmation and denial, we commonly mean to
do nothing more than declare or deny that an object
or class of objects has or has not a certain attribute,
but without turning the predicate into a class-notion,
or inquiring whether there may or may not be other
objects, which have or have not the same attribute.
When we say that 'the horse is warm-blooded,' we
may be looking exclusively to the attribute, without
caring, at the time, whether there are other warm-
blooded animals. But it seems to me to be different
in regard to reasoning, the uppermost thought in
which is always in Extension. It seems to me to be
so when, not knowing whether the horse is or is not

warm-blooded, we call in a middle concept, and argue
'that the horse being a mammal, and all mammals
being warm-blooded, the horse must be so.' Here we
place the horse in the class mammal, and mammals
among warm-blooded animals, and thus reach the
conclusion. Again, to take an example of negative
reasoning (falling naturally into the second figure) :
When we argue that 'the rat, not bringing forth its
young by eggs, is not a reptile,' we find in thought
that the class rats, not being in the class of animals
which bring forth their young by eggs, cannot be in
the class reptiles, which always bring forth their
young by eggs. Here, as in all other cases, we understand the attributive terms—such as bringing forth
their young by eggs—as class-notions in order to draw
a conclusion. This is seen very clearly when we have
to determine whether our conclusion should be universal or particular ; that is, of the whole class, or a
part. We argue (in the third figure) that 'as the connexion of soul and body, though incomprehensible, is
yet to be believed, that therefore—not all things, but—
some things to be believed are incomprehensible ;' and
how do we reach this conclusion ? Because in thought
we have made a class of 'things to be believed,' and
found that in this class are things incomprehensible.[1]

Such considerations convince me that our spontaneous reasoning is in Extension. I allow that Sir W.

[1] Mr. Kidd, in his very able work, *A Delineation of the Primary Principles of Reasoning*, shows, p. 121, " The conception of a class is present
in every instance of reasoning."

Hamilton has furnished a valuable contribution to Logic by exhibiting the forms of reasoning in Comprehension. But I look on these as secondary and derived, and not entitled to the same primary rank as those in Extension. Most logicians—teachers and taught—have shrunk from his 108 Modes as being an oppressive burden on the mind, both on its memory and its intellectual apprehension. I am inclined to think that all the purposes of Logic will be accomplished by retaining the old forms of reasoning in Extension, and showing how, when any end is to be served, they can be turned into the forms of Comprehension. As to Mr. Mill, he has got a partial and imperfect view of reasoning in Comprehension, but has not taken the trouble of showing us how his theory is adequate to explain the processes of spontaneous reasoning.

He utters an emphatic denial regarding the syllogistic form and its rules, that they are not " the form and the " rules according to which our reasonings are neces- " sarily, or even usually, made." But all wise logicians have allowed that in spontaneous reasoning persons have not before them the Dictum of Aristotle, and still less the modes and figures of the syllogism. The former of these is the regulative principle of reasoning, and the latter are expressions constructed to test the validity of ratiocination. What I maintain is that the mind in all reasoning grasps the three notions, that is, things apprehended, and the relation between them. We see a new kind of leaf that never fell under our view before, and we notice that it is netted in its veins, and we

infer that the plant on which it grew must be dicotyledonous : we do so on the principle, gathered probably
from botanical books, that all netted-veined plants are
dicotyledons; and we see the relation of ' this plant, having netted leaves, and being dicotyledonous.' But we do
not enounce the Dictum, nor do we spread out major,
minor, and conclusion. We leave all this to logicians, who
construct a reflex science out of a spontaneous process.

He makes two most important admissions in favour
of the syllogistic analysis. One is that all reasoning
can be reduced to the formula of the syllogism ; and the
other, that this formula is admirably fitted to expose
invalid reasoning. The value of the syllogistic form,
and of the rules of using it correctly, is said to consist
" in their furnishing us with a mode in which those
" reasonings may always be represented, and which is
" admirably calculated, if they are inconclusive, to bring
" their inconclusiveness to light." But I ask, how does
it happen that all our reasoning can be reduced to this
form ? How is it that it comes to test so admirably the
conclusiveness and inconclusiveness of all reasoning ?
It is surely strange that there is a rule to which all
reasoning is conformable, and which acts as a criterion
of all reasoning, and yet is not the natural law of
reasoning. I believe that all arguments can be made to
take this form, because it is the right one. I believe it
is a crucial test of the soundness or unsoundness of all
arguments, because it is the law of thought, springing
from the mental constitution with which our Maker has
endowed us.

I suppose Mr. Mill would account for the conform-
ableness of all reasoning to the syllogistic form, and for
its aptness to act as a test, by saying that, though all
reasoning is naturally in Comprehension, it can be
represented in Extension. But if this be so, it would
show, I think, that propositions and reasoning must,
contrary to what Mr. Mill alleges, have a meaning in
Extension as well as in Comprehension. And if reasoning be naturally in Comprehension, we should expect
that formulæ drawn out on that principle must be
better fitted than those derived from Extension to exhibit the validity or invalidity of arguments. Mr. Mill
has, unfortunately, not favoured us with a development
of the forms of reasoning according to Comprehension.
We are therefore not in a position to say whether these
would or would not be superior, as a means of testing
inference, to those furnished in the old Logic. I am
convinced that such forms, constructed even by so clear
a thinker as Mr Mill, would have a more artificial, a
more twisted and translated look, and would be far less
fitted to expose fallacies in reasoning. I rather think
that we should have to translate them back into Extension before we could fully recognise their meaning.
Looking upon reasoning as proceeding naturally by
classification, rather than attribution, I maintain that
the great body of logicians, from Aristotle downwards,
have acted properly in drawing out their formulæ
according to Extension, and that it is when they are
thus drawn out that they are most easily understood
and readily applied. Mr. Mill has made a most im-

portant admission (p. 429) :—" The propositions in Ex -
" tension, being, in this sense, exactly equivalent to the
" judgments in Comprehension, served quite as well to
" ground forms of ratiocination upon : and as the validity
" of the forms was more easily and conveniently shown
" through the concrete conception of comparing classes
" of objects, than through the abstract one of recognis-
" ing co-existence of attributes, logicians were perfectly
" justified in taking the course which, in any case, the
" established forms of language would doubtless have
" forced upon them." The two circumstances, that the
validity of the forms is more easily and conveniently
shown by comparing " classes," and that the established
forms of language, which are expressions of the natural
processes of the mind, would have forced an expression
according to classes on logicians, is surely a presumption, if not a proof, that the forms in Extension are the
development of spontaneous thought.

" I believe that, in point of fact, when drawing in-
" ferences from our personal experience, and not from
" maxims handed down to us by books or tradition, we
" much oftener conclude from particulars to particulars
" directly, than through the intermediate agency of any
" general proposition." Now, nearly all philosophers
have allowed that the mind begins its observations with
particulars, or, to use a better phrase, singulars. Having observed a number of individuals, it can reach a
general conclusion ; but it is only by a process which
the logician should fully unfold. Having observed or
heard that crows everywhere are black, we conclude

that the crow which we hear, without seeing, is black. But we can argue thus only on the condition that the induction is such as to justify the general proposition that all crows are black. The syllogism is so admirable a means of bringing to light the inconclusiveness of fallacious reasoning, just because it requires the general proposition to be expressed in one of the premisses.

" All inference is from particulars to particulars ; " general propositions are merely registers of such infer- " ences already made, and short formulæ for making " more." He thinks that the error of the syllogistic theory arises from not distinguishing between " the in- " ferring part and the registering part, and ascribing to " the latter the functions of the former." Now I admit that the general proposition may be the record or regis- ter of a previous induction. And if there has been reasoning in the process of induction by which this has been reached, there must have been a prior general pro- position got by an earlier induction, or given by in tuition. But in any given argument we do not look to the previous accumulation of particulars, but to the register embodied in a general proposition. The gene - ral proposition is certainly no part of the *inference,* but it is an essential part of the assumption *from which* we infer the conclusion, and should therefore have a dis- tinct place allotted to it in the premisses. Mr. Mill has a partial view of the truth when he says (*Ib.* c. iv.), " In " drawing this inference we conform to a formula which " we have adopted for our guidance in such operations, " and which is a record of the criteria by which we

" thought we had ascertained that we might distinguish
" when the inference could and when it could not be
" drawn." In any given argument, as an argument, all
that we have to do is to look to this register, or record,
or general proposition. If doubts arise as to its accuracy,
we must go back on the processes by which we reached
it ; and if there be reasoning in the processes, we must
test them in the same way. But our record being
settled, the general proposition in which it is announced
is implied in the argument, and should therefore have
a place in the formula of reasoning. We have already
noticed that " universal type of the reasoning process,"
according to which we find that ' certain individuals have
a given attribute, and that an individual or individuals
resemble the former in certain attributes, and therefore
resemble them in the given attribute.' We remarked
upon the vagueness of this type as leaving us in doubt
as to what are the " certain attributes" which entitle us
to infer the presence of the " given attribute." It is the
general proposition embodied in the major premiss,
which spreads out the rules which, when we take the
minor premiss along with it, entitles us to draw the
conclusion.

But it is asked, if all reasoning implies a major proposition, where do we get our first major, that with
which we start ? Aristotle did not overlook this question, and he answered it. He tells us again and again
that the beginning of demonstration cannot be demonstration, and that all demonstration carries us back to
Intuitive Reason ($\nu o\hat{v}\varsigma$, see *Anal. Post.*, I. 3, 22, 23).

In certain acts of reasoning, primitive perceptions, such as 'the effect has a cause,' give us the one proposition, and ordinary observation the other, and the two necessitate the conclusion. But in far the greater number of arguments the general proposition is the result of a gathered observation. The criteria of these gathered or inductive general laws will come under our notice in next chapter.

"The child, who, having burnt his fingers, avoids to "thrust them again into the fire, has reasoned or in- "ferred, though he has never thought of the general "maxim, Fire burns. He knows from memory that he "has been burnt, and on this evidence believes, when "he sees a candle, that if he puts his finger into the "flame of it, he will be burnt again. He believes this "in every case which happens to arise; but without "looking, in each instance, beyond the present case. "He is not generalizing; he is inferring a particular "from particulars. In the same way, also, brutes "reason." "Not only the burnt child, but the burnt "dog dreads the fire." I am inclined to think that in these cases, that of the child and the dog, the process is very much one of the association of ideas and feelings. The fire and the sensation have been together, and upon the fire presenting itself there is a tendency to a feeling which causes shrinking. There is really no conclusion from observed, from remembered, from gathered particulars. Should the fire only once have burnt the child it will turn away from it, possibly without remembering the previous case, certainly with-

out an induction of particulars, or an inference from
them.

I have called attention to the circumstance that
while Judgment and Association are not the same,
they do yet conspire in their action (pp. 181, 182, 206,
207). I have now to apply this remark to reasoning
and suggestion. Inference is not to be confounded with
mere association. In all reasoning there is comparison,
there is the perception of a relation between things
about which we reason. Thus we argue, 'A deer, being
horned, is ruminant.' Here the mind grasps the three
concepts and their relation : 'deer,' 'being horned,'
'are among ruminant animals.' Unless there be a
positive perception of the connexion of the things
there is no reasoning. Herein is argument at once distinguished from association, which does not imply any
connexion between the things which have been together in the mind, any comparison, or any observed
relation. But while the two mental operations are not
the same, association greatly helps reasoning. In all
inference there is a discovered relation, and the related
things may often have been together, and thus the one
tends to suggest the others. Some think that it is a
native law of the mind that correlated things, such as
like things, and cause and effect, call up each other.
However we may account for it, whether from things
being often together or an original tendency, correlated
things come up simultaneously, altogether independent
of our observing the relation. Indeed it is often the
circumstance that they have come up together which

invites or constrains us to notice the connexion. Now all this helps us to conduct the operation of reasoning. Thus fire suggests the burning sensation, and we collect cases till we reach the general truth that fire burns, and then the process may become one of inference. It is in this way we are to account for the readiness, the rapidity, and for what is often called the unconsciousness of the reasoning process. The laws of association call up correlated objects, and the mind perceives the correlation and draws the inference. Thus 'deer' suggests 'horned;' and having heard that horned animals are ruminant, 'horned' suggests 'ruminant;' and perceiving the class relation of the terms, we draw the conclusion that horned animals are ruminant.

I believe that very much of what some regard as reasoning in the brute creatures arises from mere association, without the relation of the things being discovered. In like manner the laws of suggestion operate in children to excite fears and expectations, before there are those observed relations which must enter into reasoning. All our lives we act on impulses produced by mere association, without any accompanying argument. A loud noise will raise up fear, without our having inferred that it proceeds from a cause implying danger. The person who has been seriously hurt by a horse or dog can never look on a horse or dog without a feeling of tremor. In such mental action I admit that there is no class-notion, no general proposition, no regulating principle of Extension. But just as little is there an

induction of particulars, or attribution, or reasoning in
Comprehension ; there is no such process as 'Attribute
A being a mark of Attribute B, and C having the mark
A.' But then it is one aim of intellectual teaching, and
one very special end of Logic, to raise us above the animal state and the infant state ; to keep us from being
driven along passively by more casual associations ; and
train the mind to look narrowly into the relations of
things that pass before it, and of which it must have
some conception, that it may thereby reach sound conclusions which can be justified. In all such processes of real reasoning, it will be found that there is a
general proposition involved, and this should have a
place in the formula which systematizes the spontaneous operation.

But Mr. Mill tells us that " in every syllogism con-
" sidered as an argument to prove the conclusion, there
" is a *petitio principii.*" But did any one ever maintain
that the syllogism is " an argument to prove the conclusion ?" It has usually been represented as the form
to which the argument can be reduced. The *petitio
principii* is a fallacious mode of reasoning; but the
syllogism cannot with any possible propriety be represented as a mode of reasoning, valid or fallacious, for it
is not reasoning, but the formula of reasoning. I suppose Mr. Mill meant to affirm that all reasoning in
syllogistic form involves a *petitio.* If so, then he is
caught in inextricable toils, for he admits that all
reasoning can be reduced to syllogistic form, which
seems to imply that it involves a begging of the ques-

tion. The *petitio principii* is a fallacy in which one of
the premisses is either the same as the conclusion, or
depends upon it. But in reasoning, according to the
syllogistic analysis, the conclusion follows, not from one
of the premisses, but from the two, or rather from the relations between the things compared and the premisses.
It is when the relations predicated in the two propositions are brought before the mind that we see the force
of the inference. We wish to determine—what we are
not expressly told in the gospels—whether the Baptist
was a priest : give us only one premiss, as, that 'the Baptist was the son of a priest,' or, that 'the sons of priests
were priests,' and we can infer nothing ; but place the
two together, and the conclusion is necessitated. The
one of these premisses is a particular fact, the other is
a general proposition, and both are necessary to the
validity of the conclusion. Both premisses are, in the
reasoning, assumptions—they must be given or granted :
but neither of them is an assumption of the conclusion ;
the two are assumptions which warrant the conclusion.
As to whether the assumptions are or are not warranted,
this is to be determined by a previous investigation, to
be tested by the criteria of induction, intuition, or
reasoning. And it should be for ever pressed on Mr.
Mill, that the objections he brings against the Dictum
of Aristotle are quite as applicable to his own. "Things
" which co-exist with one and the same thing co-exist
" with one another;" this is quite as much a truism as
the old Dictum, while it is much more vague ; and
reasoning proceeding upon it must be quite as liable to

the charge of being a begging of the question, as reasoning according to the syllogistic formula.

It should not be omitted that Mr. Mill does not enter upon any special consideration of the nature of Conditional Reasoning, whether Hypothetical or Disjunctive. This is a great defect in a work which professes to give us a full Logic of Inference. There are very important questions started as to the regulating principle of Conditional Arguments, and these should be discussed in every logical treatise worthy of these advanced times. He tells us, in his " Examination of Hamilton," that a Hypothetical Judgment is " a judgment concerning judgments ;" but he does not attempt to enounce the principle which connects the 'judgment' with the 'judgments' with which it is concerned. He further lets us know that he looks on a Disjunctive Judgment as compounded of two or more Hypotheticals, but he does not inform us what is the relation of these Hypotheticals to one another (pp. 454, 455). I confess I should like to see his attributive theory of reasoning tried by its application to Conditional, and specially to Disjunctive reasoning. When we argue that 'the season when a particular event took place not having been spring, summer, or autumn, must have been winter,' we seem to proceed on the principle of Division, which is made according to the Extension and not the Comprehension of a concept. But I allude to these topics here, not in order to discuss them, but to show that as Mr. Mill has avoided the discussion, he cannot be said to furnish a full system of Logic.

CHAPTER XVII.

SECONDARY LOGIC ; OR THOUGHT AS DIRECTED TO PARTICULAR CLASSES OF OBJECTS.

I AM inclined to justify Mr. Mill in introducing into the science other topics besides those treated of in what we may call Primary Logic. The effort made by certain purists to exclude such matters as Demonstration, Induction, and Evidence generally, must fail, and ought to fail. It is of vast moment to have these subjects discussed in a scientific manner, and Logic is the field for the discussion ; and our definitions of the science are too narrow if they exclude them, and should be so widened as to give them an acknowledged place. In treating of such topics, or at least two of them, Induction and Evidence, our author occupies a far more distinguished place than he does in Formal Logic. Still, even in this department, his work, while possessed of great merits, may be charged with grave errors, springing, I believe, from his mistaken views of fundamental truth.

I have commented already (Chap. xii.) on his account of Necessary Truth generally. His defective appreciation of intuition has led him to an erroneous exposition of the nature and office of Mathematical Definitions and Axioms (*Logic*, II. v.-vii.) Definitions are represented as hypotheses, and the necessity of the truths derived from them consists in the relation between the supposition and the conclusions drawn from it. " Axioms are " experimental truths; generalizations from observation. " The proposition, Two straight lines cannot enclose a " space—or in other words, Two straight lines which " have once met, do not meet again, but continue to " diverge—is an induction from the evidence of our " senses."

I reckon these views as radically erroneous. Definitions are Abstracts, that is, things abstracted from known concrete realities. ' A line is length without breadth,' that is, we consider the length without regarding the breadth. ' A superficies has breadth and length without depth,' that is, in all reasoning we agree to look to the length and breadth without taking the depth into account. But Mr. Mill tells us " there exist no real things exactly conformable to the definition;" there exist no lines without breadth, no surfaces without depth. I admit that there can be no such lines or surfaces with a separate or independent existence. But still they have a reality; they have a reality in extended objects—which have, besides, length and breadth. Man's mind is so constituted that he can think about them, and draw deductions from them. But he tells us, " A line, as defined by geometers, is wholly inconceivable," where the word that covers so much confusion appears once more, and in his latest edition. We certainly cannot image such a line, but we can image an extended object, and think about its length. I believe that all further mathematical truths are derived from Definitions. But when I say so, I do not mean that they are obtained from ideas in the mind, but from things abstracted from concrete realities, and having a reality in existing concrete objects. As there is a reality in the things defined, so there is also a reality in all the conclusions logically drawn from them. The deductions derived two thousand years ago from the definition of the ellipse, are found to be realized in the planetary bodies, so far as they move in elliptic orbits. I cannot see how this should follow, unless the thing defined had been a reality.

Mr. Mill thinks that demonstrative truths follow from Postulates and not Definitions. We postulate that there may be a line with length without breadth, and get deductions from our assumptions. True, in all deduction the premisses are assumptions, but in mathematical definitions the assumptions are abstracted realities. Here, as in so many other departments, his acuteness has given him a partial view of the truth, and he says that "our reasonings are grounded upon matters of fact in our definitions." When I say that mathematical demonstration is founded upon definitions, I mean upon the matters of fact or things defined, which no doubt are postulated, but postulated as realities, giving us corresponding realities in all legitimate deductions from them. To support his confused theory, he is obliged to give a twofold view of defini-

tions.   The definition of a triangle, he says, obviously
comprises not one but two propositions perfectly distin-
guishable.   The one is, 'There may exist a figure
bounded by three straight lines;' and the other, 'this
figure may be termed a triangle.'   But there is no
advantage secured, in the way of clearing our thoughts
or otherwise, by drawing such a distinction ; for demonstration relates throughout not to the word, but the
thing, a figure bounded by three straight lines.   He
argues that definitions, as such, are the premisses only
in the reasonings which relate to words, and that if we
take any other view, "we might argue correctly from
true premisses, and arrive at a false conclusion."   Thus
let the definition be, 'A dragon is a serpent breathing
flame,' out of this we may carve the following syllogism :
'A dragon is a thing which breathes flame ; but a
dragon is a serpent : therefore, some serpents breathe
flame,'—" in which both premisses are true, and yet
the conclusion false."   But surely the premisses are
here true or false according to what we understand as
to the objects compared.   If we are speaking throughout of imaginary things, the conclusion is true in the
same sense as the premisses are.   If we are speaking
of actually existing things, both the premisses and the
conclusion are false.

After what I have said in regard to necessary truth
(Chap. xii.), it is not necessary to dwell on his theory of
Mathematical Axioms.   They are represented as mere
generalizations of an outward experience.   I believe,
indeed, that in the axiom in its generalized form there

must be generalization. But they are not generalizations of an outward or sensible experience. On the bare contemplation of a whole object, say a table, we declare it to be larger than a part of it, say its leg. I do so at once on the mere sight or thought of the object as known to me, and not from any induction of particulars falling under my experience in time past. Perceiving that I would do the same in every like case, I may generalize the judgment and put it in the form of an axiom, that 'the whole is greater than its part.' But this general truth is not the generalization of a lengthened experience ; it is not reached by our having observed a thousand times or ten thousand times that a whole thing is greater than a part of the same thing : we see it at once on the bare inspection of any one thing; our conviction could not be made stronger by multiplying examples ; and we cannot allow that there should be an exception. I may have observed of ten thousand plants with netted leaves that they have all sprung from two seed-lobes, and I feel justified in laying down the general rule, that 'netted-leaved plants are dicotyledonous;' but the law is reached by a gathered experience. I do not assert that it can have no exceptions ; and when I learn that there is a tribe of plants (including *Arum*, etc.) which have netted leaves, and yet spring from one seed-lobe, I may wonder at the fact, but I do not say that it is impossible. But the mind having discovered, from its knowledge of the nature of things, that the whole is greater than a part, I cannot be made to allow that there is anywhere an exception.

X

To apply these remarks to mathematical truth : In proceeding with its demonstrations, the mind pronounces its judgments immediately on the objects defined being presented to it, and it does not need the axiom in its generalized form; indeed it feels the force of the reasoning quite as clearly before as after the maxim is announced. In learning geometry, the beginner seems to discover the truth of the axiom from the judgment pronounced in a given case, rather than to recognise the validity of the argument in the particular example by the maxim. Still the axiom is the expression of the regulating principle of reasoning, and it serves important purposes to enunciate it at the commencement of the demonstration. It is one of the greatest defects of Mr. Mill's work on Logic, that in consequence of mistaking the nature and functions of definitions and axioms he has not been able to give a correct account of the Method employed in Demonstration. That Method I call the Joint Dogmatic and Deductive. I call it Dogmatic, for it begins with assumptions, with truths not proven, with truths perceived by intuition; and I call it Deductive, for it draws other truths from its assumptions. The criteria of its assumptions are the tests of intuitive truth, that is, Self-Evidence and Necessity ; the criteria of its deductions are the forms of reasoning.

Mr. Mill's Book on Induction is far the most valuable part of his Logic ; it contains the best exposition which we have of the Method of Induction in our own or in any other language. His Canons of Causes are a great improvement upon the Prerogative Instances of Bacon,

and are an advance upon the rules proposed by Sir J.
Herschel. But, while he has admirably expounded the
functions of Prerogative Instances or Canons in physical
science, he does not seem to see what is the precise
·logical purpose, that is, the purpose in thought, served
by them. Induction consists of two parts: the gathering
of individual facts, which, however numerous, must
always be limited; and the derivation from them of a
law announced in a general proposition. In the first of
these, there is no special exercise of reasoning; the
whole is the work of observation and trained sagacity.
But in the derivation of the law from the scattered and
incomplete facts there is inference. Now, what is it
that justifies the inference? If there be any truth in
the Aristotelian or syllogistic analysis, there must be a
general principle involved, which, when the reasoning
is put in syllogistic form, becomes the major premiss.
Now, such rules as these, involved in the Prerogative
Instances of Bacon, and the Canons of Mr. Mill, are the
general propositions which supply the major premiss;
and the particular set of facts give us the minor premiss;
and the two necessitate the conclusion. I drank brandy
on Monday, Wednesday, and Saturday, and had a headache the succeeding mornings; I drank no brandy on
Sunday, Tuesday, Thursday, and Friday, and had no
headache on the following days. When I conclude
that my drinking brandy was the cause of the headache,
I have, as my major premiss, such a general proposition
as the Canon of Difference: 'If, in comparing cases in
which the effect takes place with other cases in which

it does not take place, we find the latter to have every antecedent in common with the former except one, that one circumstance is the cause, or a part of the cause;' and as my minor premiss, the facts as constituting such a case; and the conclusion follows syllogistically. The excellence of Mr. Mill's Canons is, that they are the simplest and most complete yet enunciated of the general principles which guide us in rising from the collection of individual facts to the causes. Had Mr. Mill clearly perceived that there is reasoning in all induction, he would have been prevented from reversing the natural order by representing the reasoning process as an induction.

But the discovery of causes is not the sole end of science. In some departments the object is to resolve the compounds of nature into their elements. This is one of the main ends sought in chemistry, and also in psychology. There should, therefore, be Canons of Composition[1] as well as Canons of Causes.

[1] In the absence of an attempt by any Logician to supply them, we may give the following :—(1.) We have decomposed a compound when we have decomposed it in separation from all other substances. (2.) Having found the elements of a compound in one case, we have found them in all. A caution requires to be added, that the elements reached are to be regarded as such merely provisionally. The first rule theoretically guards against a mistake, which is difficult to avoid in practice. The second shows that one decisive experiment may settle the whole question of the decomposition of a substance. Hence it is that in Chemistry we may not require a large induction, such as is necessary in Natural History and many departments of Natural Philosophy. As Chemistry did not exist in the days of Bacon, he does not seem to have contemplated the possibility of so rapid a method of reaching a law ; and his rules as to the necessity of a wide induction, and the gradual rising from particulars to minor, middle, and major axioms do not apply to this science, at least in its present advanced stage,—though I rather think they did at its earlier stages, before the nature of chemical

In another important group of sciences, those called the Classificatory by Dr. Whewell, the end sought is not the discovery of Causes or of Composition, but of Classes; that is, Natural Classes.[1] I mention these things to show that, while Mr. Mill has given us the best exposition we yet have of the Logic of Induction, he has by no means completed the investigation. Much remains to be done by other men and by other ages.

There has been an important discussion between Dr. Whewell and Mr. Mill as to whether we may now expect more from the Method of Induction or of Deduction. Mr. Mill maintains that in most departments of science our hope of discovery lies more in Deduction than in the Induction of Bacon. On the other hand, Dr. Whewell holds that, whatever may be the case with the social sciences, in the physical sciences discoveries may be expected to be made in time to come, as they have been

affinity had been ascertained. The caution guards us against concluding, when we have reached certain components, we must have got the ultimate elements. Every chemist allows that these sixty elements are to be esteemed such, merely till there has been a successful decomposition of them.

[1] The following Canons of Classes may serve till better are furnished:—
(1.) We have found the resemblance among the objects in many and varied cases. (2.) We must be in circumstances to say that if there be exceptions we should most probably have fallen in with them. These two rules will prevent us from drawing rash generalizations from a few cases, or cases confined to a limited region. But in order to determine whether the class is or is not a Natural Class, we require a more important rule. (3.) The class may be regarded as a natural one when it is one of Kinds; that is, when the possession of one mark is a sign of a number of others. Thus we may reckon Mammal as a Natural Class; for though founded on the single circumstance of the animals belonging to it suckling their young, it is found that this characteristic is a sign of others,—as, that they are warm-blooded, and that their heart has four compartments. Such Orders as Ranunculaceæ, Cruciferæ, Rosaceæ, are obviously Natural Classes, for the plants included in each have a number of resembling points.

in time past, by a patient induction. Much confusion
has crept into this controversy from the circumstance
that these two eminent men have not come to an agreement as to what is involved in the processes about which
they dispute. According to Mr. Mill, the Deductive
Method consists of three operations : the first, one of
direct induction ; the second, of ratiocination ; and the
third, of verification (*Logic*, III. xi.) Now, of these three
steps, the first, the direct induction of particulars, and
also the third, the verification by facts, are essentially
inductive ; they consist in collecting facts, with the view
of determining the law of the facts. What Mr. Mill
calls Deductive, I am inclined to designate the Joint
Inductive and Deductive Method. In those departments
of science which are yet in their infancy, we must trust
mainly to a careful collection of facts, and allow the
facts to suggest the law, at which we may not yet be
able even to guess. But in advanced sciences in which
laws have been established, and are ready to form the
general or major proposition, advances may be expected
mainly from the combination of Deduction with Induction. Dr. Whewell and Mr. Mill have both done much
to unfold the steps of this Joint Method. But much yet
remains to be done, by showing what is the separate
province of each, and how they may be combined so as
best to yield the wished-for results in the different
departments of science.

CHAPTER XVIII.

LOGICAL DISCUSSIONS : THE PROVINCE OF LOGIC.

In this country Formal Logic is dealt with in four different ways at this present time.

I. By some it is reckoned antiquated and exploded, and never referred to without a sneer. Though these persons are not likely to attend to me, or favour me with an answer, yet I beg to ask them whether it would not be very desirable to have a Logic to unfold the laws of thought, and direct thought in its various walks—in which it is so apt to err? If they can be induced to reply candidly in the affirmative, I would then invite them to look into what earnest and able thinkers have done ; and I would show them how the Aristotelian Logic has cast up again and again, in spite of all efforts to suppress it ; and that no other Logic has stood longer than a single age : in particular, no one now sets any value on the attempts that were made to construct a logical science by the school of Locke and the school of Condillac.

II. There are those who accept the Aristotelian Logic without criticism or modification. Most of these are

inclined to accept it in the form in which it is put by
Whately, who, by his new and fresh illustrations and
examples, threw such life into the bones which had
become dry. The mastering of Whately's *Elements* is
certainly a most profitable gymnastic to all young men,
and is fitted to exercise a salutary influence upon their
intellectual habits, which is likely to continue with
them all their lives. But those who have a taste for
the study ought not to content themselves with such an
elementary exposition; they should go on to make themselves acquainted with the discussions in our day in
regard to logical forms ; and neither young nor advanced
students must be allowed to forget that we have now a
Logic of Induction quite as important as the Logic of
Deduction.

III. There is a British modification of the Logic of
Kant which has able supporters, the leader having been
Sir W. Hamilton, who has had able and learned fellow-
workers in Dr. Mansel and Archbishop Thomson. The
Logic of this school has many excellencies. It has
allotted a distinct and intelligible province to the science,
which is described as that of the Laws of Thought. It
has so defined the department as to make it embrace
the Concept and the Judgment, as well as Reasoning.
Sir W. Hamilton has revived the distinction between
the Extension and Comprehension of the Concept, and
has evolved and applied it in a more scientific
manner than was ever done before. Not satisfied with
the Dictum of Aristotle as the one and universal regulating principle of reasoning, the school is seeking to

enunciate a wider Canon, and important minor rules derived from it. It has successfully shown that reasoning may be put in the form of Comprehension as well as Extension. It has subjected all the forms of reasoning, Categorical and Conditional, to a sifting examination, which has introduced greater scientific accuracy into the technicalities of Primary Logic. With unsurpassed acuteness and erudition, Dr. Mansel has introduced us to important Aristotelian and scholastic distinctions. Archbishop Thomson has given us an admirable chapter on Language as the instrument of thought, has clearly expounded the distinction between Substitutive and Attributive Judgments (though he has not seen what is the precise nature of the forms), and drawn out a comprehensive scheme of Immediate Inferences.

But on the other hand the Logic of the school is tainted throughout with the false metaphysics of Kant, and should not be accepted without important explanations and modifications. It proceeds all along on the principle that there are subjective forms in the mind itself, which impose on objects as we think about them, much that is not in the objects themselves. From this general error there arise several particular ones.

(1.) The school represent Logic as an *a priori* science. Now this doctrine cannot be allowed without an important explanation which changes the whole theory. It is all true that the mind in logical thought proceeds according to native principles. But the principles, as general rules, are not before consciousness. It is upon the bare inspection and comprehension of the case before it that the mind proceeds in the exercises of thought. It being understood that a crocodile is a reptile, and that all reptiles bring forth their young by eggs, we at once conclude that the crocodile must do so ; but without having consciously before us the Dictum, that whatever is predicated of a class may be predicated of all that is contained in the class. It needs objects to call the native capacities of the mind into exercise. Not only so, but the exercises are always individual. It is by a process of generalization that we derive the general law from the individual cases ; and as there may be oversights and inaccuracies in the generalization, so there may be discussions and disputes about the expression of the general law. The laws of thought may be in the mind *a priori*, but we cannot discover and unfold them *a priori*. In order to find the general principles of logical thought, and to construct a science of Logic, there must be a careful and extensive observation of thought as directed to objects, and various classes of objects.

(2.) Kant represents Logic as " making abstraction of " all content of the cognition of the understanding and " of the difference of objects, and having to do only " with the form of thought." Sir W. Hamilton makes a like statement : " Logic is conversant with the form of thought to the exclusion of the matter" (*Logic*, I. 15). Now this account contains both a truth and an error. It is quite true that Logic does not look to the objects of thought, but to thought : but it is equally true that thought must be employed about objects. If Logic, then, considers thought, it must consider thought as employed about objects,—only it considers the thought and not the objects. Taking this view, we see that we are warranted (though, perhaps, Kant was not, according to his principles) in adopting the division of the science, which we shall explain further on in this chapter, into Universal and Particular Logic.

(3.) From the same mistaken view of thought, the whole school represent the Notion or Conception as being formed by the mind, according to *a priori* laws, not altogether independent of objects, but imposing on objects what is not in them. Hamilton speaks of "an " act of thought as the recognition of a thing as coming " under a concept;" and again, "Thought is a know- " ledge of a thing through a concept or general notion, " or of one notion through another" (*Ib.* p. 43). This language proceeds on the idea that there is a concept prior to the thing, above the thing, and ready to be imposed upon it, so as to shape and colour it. But surely the correct statement is not that thought is through a concept, but that a concept is a thought formed on the contemplation of things. The General Notion is fashioned by the mind on the apprehension of objects, by putting together the objects, real or potential, having common properties.

(4.) The whole Kantian school omits the Abstract Notion in the construction of logical science. Sir W. Hamilton, indeed, gives a brief but correct account of it in his *Metaphysics* (Lect. xxxv.), showing that it implies comparison, and that "there is nothing necessarily connected with generalization in abstraction." But in his *Logic*, the laws which he lays down apply only to the Concept or General Notion. This omission not only leads to a defective account of Simple Apprehension in the first part of Formal Logic, but makes him overlook a class of judgments and a species of reasoning in which the terms are abstract.

(5.) In consequence of neglecting to give the Abstract Notion a separate place, Sir W. Hamilton and Archbishop Thomson have been led to represent every Notion as having Extension and Comprehension. Now, these are properties exclusively of the General Notion. The Abstract Notion, say tranquillity, cannot be said to have Extension, for it denotes not objects, but an attribute.

(6.) In a previous chapter I have shown that Sir W. Hamilton has not unfolded fully nor accurately the nature and the relations of the things compared in Logical Judgment. He represents the comparison as between two conceptions or concepts as mental products, whereas it is between concepts as things conceived. He vacillates in the account which he gives of the relation discovered between the concepts, speaking of it at times as being identity, at other times as that of whole and parts, and in some places as equality.

(7.) One of Sir W. Hamilton's supposed improvements in Formal Logic consists in his insisting that the predicate should always be quantified; that is, declared to be either universal or particular. Thus the proposition, 'All men are mortal,' he would write, 'All men are some mortals.' He defends this on the general principle, that whatever is in thought should be unfolded in the statement which professes to express thought. I admit the principle, but I do not admit that it requires the predicate to be quantified. For I have endeavoured to show that in by far the greater number of propositions the uppermost thought is in Comprehension, and we do not think at all of the Extension. When we say 'the dog barks,' we mean that the dog is engaged in the act of barking, and we may not think of a class of barking animals; we certainly do not trouble ourselves with inquiring whether there are or are not other animals that bark. Even in propositions in which the Extension is in the thought, we do not always settle whether the subject is or is not co-extensive with the predicate. Thus, when we say 'Man is rational,' we may not have determined whether there are or are not other rational beings besides man. It is sufficient to lead us to form the judgment that man has the attribute rationality, or that he is in the class rational, whether this class include other beings or not. I hold that in the vast majority of propositions the predicate is not quantified in thought. I urge, further, in opposition to the doctrine, that in those propositions in which the terms are abstract, the predicate, properly speaking, has no quantity or extension, for it is not a class-notion. When we say that $3 \times 3 = 9$, neither subject nor predicate has an indefinite number of objects embraced in it. I admit that in reasoning, when the predicate is known to be distributed, we can convert the subject into the predicate, and the predicate into the subject, without any change, and draw a conclusion which we should not otherwise be entitled to do. Thus when we have it demonstrated, both that 'all equilateral triangles are equiangular,' and that 'all equiangular triangles are equilateral,' we can, upon a given triangle being found equilateral, declare it to be equiangular. Such cases are worthy of special notice, and might have a separate place allotted them in logical treatises, but, being so limited, should not be allowed to change the whole analytic of reasoning.

(8.) The new Canon of Reasoning adopted by the school is very vague. It is thus stated in the *Outlines of the Laws of Thought:* "The agreement or disagree-" ment of one conception with another, is ascertained " by a third conception, inasmuch as this, wholly or " by the same part, agrees with both, or with only one " of the conceptions to be compared" (§ 93). Now, the phrase 'agree' is not explicit; it does not specify what the concepts agree or do not agree in. This defect may be remedied by distinguishing between those cases in which the terms are singular or abstract, and those in which one at least is general. In the former the regulating principle is 'things which are the same with, or equal to, one and the same thing, are the same with, or equal to one another.' In the latter, in which we have a general conception, the main regulating principle is, I believe, the Dictum, which the founder of Logic propounded. While this is the main law of thought, I am convinced that there may be others involved, such as that of whole and parts, and of division in all disjunctive reasoning. A thorough analytic of logical forms should unfold all these laws, and give each its separate place.

(9.) Sir W. Hamilton places reasoning in Comprehension on the same level as reasoning in Extension, or rather he gives it a prior and higher position. I have stated my reasons for thinking that reasoning is primarily in Extension. It may, indeed, always be translated into the forms of Comprehension, and it is desirable that students should know how to do this, and do it when any purpose is to be served by it. But it is not necessary to burden the mind with the numerous modes which appear when we insist on always quantifying the predicate, and join on the same footing reasoning in Comprehension and reasoning in Extension.

IV. There is a large class who accept implicitly the Logic of Mr. Mill. [1] These consist chiefly of persons who are disgusted with the scholastic Logic as being so abstract and technical, and are not prepared to give their adherence to the Kantian reformation, as they feel that its forms keep us too far removed from things. Now, I rejoice to proclaim that there are remarks, as true and important as they are fresh, scattered throughout Mr. Mill's treatise. In Book First he has many useful observations on Naming, which make us regret the more that they are indissolubly mixed up

---

[1] I should here have referred to the very able attempts of Prof. De Morgan and the late Prof. Boole to give us a mathematical theory of reasoning. But it would take us altogether out of our present line of thought to discuss it thoroughly, and I think it better not to enter upon it.

with sensational metaphysics.   His Book on Induction
is by far the most valuable part of his work, though it
is much injured by doubtful speculations as to the
nature of our belief in causation.[1]   There are practical
lessons of much utility conveyed in his Book on
Fallacies, only it is to be regretted that in pointing out
with so much keenness and relish the errors of the old
philosophy, he leaves unnoticed the still more glaring
fallacies of the nescience and association schools.   His
closing Book is very defective as a full Logic of the
mental and social sciences, more particularly in not
estimating what is involved in man's essential freedom ;
but is of value as the commencement of a discussion
which must grow in interest and importance.   I propose to sum up the defects of the work as gathered from
the survey taken in the last four chapters.

(1.) He denies that Logic is entitled to be regarded
as a separate science.   "So far as it is a science at all,
" it is a part or branch of Psychology ; differing from
" it on the one hand as a part differs from the whole,
" and on the other, as an Art differs from a Science "
(p. 388).   Now, there is no doubt that Logic is closely
connected with Psychology, is in fact largely dependent
on it for some of its elementary truths.   The same may
be said of Metaphysics, or the science of the laws of

[1] I regret to see that in the later editions Mr. Mill is crowding his work
with still more of metaphysical discussion.   Students would feel it to be a
great advantage to have his book on Induction in a separate form, and
with the discussions on Intuitions left out.   This would leave them at
liberty to get their Formal Logic elsewhere, and to resort to his complete
work when they want to know his theory of the mind and his other
opinions.

intuition ; of Æsthetics, or, as I prefer calling it, Kalo-
logy, the science of the laws of the Feelings ; and
Ethics, the science of the laws of our motive and
moral nature. It is no doubt one part of the office
of Psychology to gather from an observation of the
operations of the mind the laws of discursive thought,
as it is also to find out the laws of our immediate
perceptions, of our emotional and moral nature. But
having ascertained that there are such laws, and shown
how they act in the mind, it does not seek in a special
way to formalize them, to inquire into their relation to
external things, or to apply them to scientific or practical
ends. Psychology leaves all this very appropriately
to the other mental sciences, which are no doubt her
daughters, but have their separate households, where
they are married to their different objects, each with
its own alliances. In particular, Logic strives to give
a strictly scientific form and expression to the mode of
the mind's procedure in apprehending, judging, and
reasoning, and in gathering laws and causes ; and from
these it draws rules for the guidance of thought in its
various walks of investigation. Logic has the proper
characteristics of a science ; it is systematized truth,
systematized natural truth.

(2.) He does not give its proper place to the element
of thought. No doubt he has done great service to the
study, by calling our attention to the objects of thought,
which the scholastic and Kantian logicians had very
much declined to look at. But Logic has not to do
with things as things. This it leaves to other, and what

Y

have been called material, or real, or what in such a connexion might be called objective, sciences. Logic has to do not with objects, but with thought as employed about objects. If this distinction is not kept constantly in view, the logician is ever tempted to mix up physical or psychological questions with those that properly belong to Logic.

(3.) He makes Logic treat of Names, Propositions, and Arguments, and not, as our more philosophical logicians make it, with Simple Apprehension, Judgment, and Reasoning. Every one allows that Apprehensions may be expressed in Names, Judgments in Propositions, and Reasoning in Arguments, and that Logic should look to these incidentally, as the expression of thought. But the science should deal primarily and throughout with the laws of thought, always as applied to things, leaving the laws of language to a special department of science now being formed. It is to be remembered, that as a term may consist of one word, or twenty words, we cannot by merely looking at words so much as know what the term is; and that we cannot make an intelligent predication in a proposition without knowing the meaning of the terms : all which shows that Logic should expound thought rather than names. Nor is it to be forgotten that the laws of thought constitute the fixed element, while the names or phrases differ not only in their sound, but in what they express and embrace in different languages. And then the forms of language are often defective, and not unfrequently erroneous, and need to be amended by the

invariable and, I believe, unerring laws of thought :
which we should endeavour so to analyse and formalize
as to aid the advancing Science of Language,—which
will again, as it makes progress, greatly help the Science
of Thought.

(4.) In looking at language instead of thought, he has
given a very imperfect account of the topics usually expounded in the first part of Formal Logic, that which
deals with Simple Apprehension. Instead of examining
the various classes of apprehensions, and carefully distinguishing them, he confines his own attention and
that of his readers to the name and its connotation,
without regard to the notion which the name expresses,
or bringing out accurately what things, or aspects of
things, the notion embraces in its different forms.

Owing to his defective psychology, he has no adequate idea of the capacity of the mind to discover
relations among things, and he has failed to give us a
full or accurate exposition of the relation of the two
apprehensions in logical Judgment. He makes us look
not at the act of comparison, which is surely the
primary and main element, but at the attribute connoted, overlooking, in the General Notion, the class of
objects combined by the attribute, and the mental concept combining them.

(5.) The error goes up into his analysis of reasoning,
and makes him give a very partial exhibition of the
process, in which he sees only the attribute, and overlooks the general conception and general proposition,
which are involved in the validity of the inference.

(6.) Mr. Mill has given us the most valuable contribution since the days of Bacon to one important department of Logic, that which treats of Induction. But still there are very grave mistakes in his exposition of the topics that fall under Particular or Secondary Logic. These spring from his erroneous theory of Demonstration, more particularly of the nature, functions, and value of mathematical definitions and axioms ; from his mixing false metaphysics with his logical exposition of causation ; from his not seeing that the discovery of the Decomposition of compounds and of Natural Classes are among the ends aimed at in science, and requiring Special Canons : and finally, from an imperfect view of the nature of the phenomena of the mind, which it is the office of Psychology to co-ordinate, and for the aid of which Logic should furnish a method.

It now only remains to gather from this discussion what is the Province of the science of Logic. It has to do with thought : but what is meant by thought in such an application ? It must evidently be so explained as not to include the motive exercises of the mind, and to exclude intuition, in which we perceive objects or truths at once, and which has always been allotted to Metaphysics. By thought, in the technical sense in which the word is used in Logic, is meant Discursive Thought, in which we proceed from something given or allowed to something else derived from it. It implies a process, which must have laws. In order to construct the science of Logic, we must endeavour to gather the laws of thought, by a careful observation of the operations of thought.

Kant has a twofold division of the science, as Logic of the universal or of the particular use of the understanding. " The first contains the absolutely necessary " laws of thought, without which no use whatever of the " understanding is possible, and gives laws therefore to " the understanding, without regard to the difference of " objects on which it may be employed. The Logic of " the particular use of the understanding contains the " laws of correct thinking upon a particular class of objects" (*Kritik of Pure Reason,* Meiklejohn's trans., p. 46). This language is not unexceptionable, more particularly as pointing to laws independent of the observation of objects; and it is doubtful whether Kant, in consistency with his account of the science, which " makes abstraction of all content of the cognition, that is, of all relation of cognition to its object" (*Ib.* p. 49), could adopt such a division. But if we take the proper view of thought, as always engaged with objects, then we can accept and justify the arrangement. We have, first, a Universal, or, as I prefer calling it, a Primary Logic (identical with what is commonly designated Formal Logic), conversant with the laws of thought, not independent of objects, but *whatever be the objects.* We have, secondly, a Particular, or, as I would call it, Secondary Logic, considering the operations of thought as directed to particular classes of objects, say to intui tive perceptions, as in Demonstration; and the collection of scattered facts, external or internal, as in Induction.

Under the first head Logic treats of Simple Apprehension, Judgment, and Reasoning, which, no doubt, all look to objects, but are the same for all objects. It has to consider, first, our apprehensions. Some of these are of objects singular and concrete, what we may call Percepts, as being immediately perceived by the mind. Some of them, again, are of Abstracts, or parts considered as parts of a whole, more particularly of attributes of objects. Others are of Concepts, or of things having common attributes, and joined in a class which embraces all the objects possessing the attributes. All Concepts have both Extension and Comprehension. Logic does not deal immediately with the formation of Percepts, which are intuitive; but it evolves the laws involved in the construction of Abstracts and Concepts. In Judgment we compare two of these Percepts, Abstracts, or Concepts. This process also has laws, such as, when the things compared are Abstracts the relation is one of identity or of equivalence; and, when there is a general notion the relation is both of Comprehension and Extension. There are also laws involved in Reasoning, in which we compare two of our apprehensions by means of a third. These are derived very much from the nature of the apprehensions compared. Thus, in cases in which we compare Abstracts, the regulating principle is that of identity or equality, " things which are the same with a third, or equal to a third, are the same with, or equal to one another." But when there is a class-notion involved—and there is so wherever there is attribution,—then we must proceed according to the class-notion, and the regulating principle is, ' whatever is predicated of a class may be predicated of all that is contained in that class.' While these are the main ruling principles involved in all cases of reasoning, there may also be other principles implied in all cases, or in special cases. Thus the principle of whole and parts is involved when we include an individual in a class, or a species in a genus. The Comprehension of the Notion is to be taken along with us, when we translate reasoning in Extension, so as to make Comprehension the uppermost thought. A principle of Division, that the co-ordinate sub-classes must make up the class, is involved in all Disjunctive Reasoning : thus when we argue that this man, being either a knave or a fool, and not being a fool, must be a knave, it is implied that knave and fool make up the class to which this man must belong.

Taking this view of Logic, we do not separate it so entirely from realities as the scholastic logicians did, and as the Kantian logicians still do. It has not, indeed, to do with things directly. Many of Mr. Mill's discussions would lead us to think that it has, and we are thus involved in questions which can be settled only by the sciences—material or mental,—which deal with objects. Logic has to do not with objects, but with thought as directed to objects. This account makes it quite competent for Logic to consider not only Apprehension, Judgment, and Reasoning, which are the same for all objects, but also Thought as directed to particular classes of objects. The great body of thinkers in

modern times have felt that Logic ought to embrace
other topics besides those treated of in Formal Logic,
in particular that it ought not to exclude the Method of
investigation propounded by Bacon. The exposition I
have given makes it include not only Induction but
other modes of discovering truth.

It may consider thought as proceeding in the way of
Demonstration. Here all that is assumed in start-
ing, and all that is assumed throughout, must be seen to
be true intuitively. The Method of Investigation is
what I call the Joint Dogmatic and Deductive. It is
Dogmatic, in that it assumes ; but then it should assume
only what is seen to be true on the bare contemplation
of the nature of objects. It is Deductive, in that it
derives other truths from these assumptions by a process of reasoning. But this Method is applicable only
within a very limited range, only so far as we have an
immediate intuition of the nature of things. In most
walks of investigation Demonstration is not available.
What we have before us are individual and scattered
facts, falling under the senses or the consciousness. It
is out of these that we must gather the law. So far as
we observe and co-ordinate the facts with the view of
rising to their law, whether this be a class, or a cause,
or the constitution of compound objects, the Method
pursued is the Inductive. In this process we gather the
facts and tabulate them, and, without 'anticipating'
nature, we allow the facts to suggest the law, which is
accepted only when it embraces and explains all the
facts. But as science advances, by this method we

reach laws, which may be regarded as at least provisionally established, and we inquire—in certain departments
with the powerful aid of Mathematics—what consequences would follow from these laws ? Another, and a
very powerful Method, now becomes applicable. I call
it the Joint Inductive and Deductive, in which we inquire what results must follow from certain supposed
laws, and then compare these with facts got by observation or experiment. In all our advanced sciences this
must now be the principal mode of investigation.

I am inclined to think that Whately is right when
he represents Logic as both a Science and an Art. It
is a science, inasmuch as it is a systematized body of
natural truth. It is reared by the observation and co-
ordination of the spontaneous operations of discursive
thought. But it may also become an art, or a body of
precepts drawn out to enable us to accomplish a particular end, that is, to think correctly, and expose confused thought or invalid reasoning. It should aim at
nothing less than the discovery of the laws of thought
operating in the mind as it contemplates objects. When
we have accurately apprehended and expressed them,
we may then apply them to test and correct actual
thought. For this purpose we may derive from them
rules, and put these in various formulæ, which admit
of a ready and useful application to our everyday thinking, and to scientific investigation. In particular, Logic
is of great use in clearing our notions ; it shows what
notions are singular and what universal ; what concrete
and what abstract ; and guards us against using a general

term as if it were a singular concrete. It cannot tell us what judgments are true and what false (this must be done by the departments of knowledge which deal with objects), but it tells us what is the precise relation between the Percepts, Abstracts, and Concepts compared, and thus places our notions in such a light that we are better able to say whether a given proposition is true or false. Again, the syllogistic analysis lets us see that in reasoning we have to look to the relation of three notions, Percepts, Abstracts, or Concepts ; and that when one of the notions is a Concept, we always need by implication a general proposition ; and the formulæ derived from this analysis unfold the various possible forms of reasoning, and enable us to test our own inferences and those of others. In the Secondary (but not less important) Logic, there can be tests laid down, such as those of self-evidence, necessity, and catholicity, sufficient to decide readily and certainly what truths are intuitive, and so entitled to become assumptions in Demonstration ; while the processes of deduction from intuitive truth may all be tested by the syllogism. The Canons of Causes enunciated by Mr. Mill settle for us, when we are entitled to argue that we have discovered the cause of a given phenomenon ; and I hope that in due time we shall have Canons of Decomposition and Canons of Classes, to determine when we have reached the elementary constitution of bodies (provisionally), and when we have discovered natural classes. We have already some Canons of Historical Investigation to aid us in finding whether the evidence

is sufficient to establish the alleged facts, and these
Canons should be adopted into Logic, and made as suc-
cinct and comprehensive as possible.   Logic has thus a
wide and most important field as an art ; it furnishes
guiding rules and tests in every path of inquiry.   It is
thus fulfilling some of the old pretensions made in its
behalf.   I do not like the phrase, ' Art of Thinking,' for
men think spontaneously, without any science or art ;
but Logic supplies rules to guard against confused and
erroneous thinking.   It is in a special sense the ' Science
of Method ;' that is, of the Method to be pursued in
discovering scientific and historical truth.   It is the
' Science of Sciences,' not because superior to other
departments of knowledge, but because it supplies rules
to guide and guard in every other science.

CHAPTER XIX.

WHAT IS TRUTH ? CRITERIA OF TRUTH.

IT is very evident that Mr. Mill has a pleasure in seeing himself and his opinions reflected in the convictions and writings of young men. On the other side, the youth who give themselves up to his guidance seem as if they could look only straight before them in the path in which he leads them, and as if they were incapable of taking a comprehensive view of things lying on either side. As, however, they will be obliged to do so sooner or later, it might be as well if they now stopped for a little, in order to look round them and inquire whither he is leading, and where he is to leave them ? What have we left us according to this new philosophy ? We have sensations ; we have a series of feelings aware of itself, and permanent, or rather prolonged ; and we have an association of sensations, and perceived resemblances, and possibilities of sensations. The sensations and associations of sensation generate ideas and beliefs, which do not, however, either in themselves or their mode of formation, guarantee any reality. We have an idea of an external material world ; but Mr. Mill does not affirm that there is such a world, for there are laws of the series of feelings which would produce the idea, whether the thing existed or not ; and our belief in it may be overcome,—just as our natural belief in the sun rising is made to give way before the scientific conviction that it is the earth that moves. He thinks he is able by a process of inference to reach the existence of other beings besides ourselves. But the logic of the process is very doubtful. I believe that neither Mr. Mill nor any other has been able to show how from sensations, individual or associated, we could ever legitimately infer the existence of anything beyond. What he claims to have found is, after all, only other 'series of feelings.'

But have we not, it is said, a body of scientific truth, for which Mr. Mill has done as much as any living man, by showing how it may be best arranged. I acknowledge that in the view of those who believe in the reality of things, and who further believe in a God who made and arranged, and still upholds them, this systematized truth is a glorious body,—like the sun itself, with a central solidity which keeps it firm, while it holds other bodies circling round it, and with a gloriously illuminated atmosphere, scattering light and heat all around. But what is all this when interpreted in philosophic accuracy? It is simply possibilities of sensations, coming in groups, and in regular succession, and with resemblances which can be noticed. And is this the sum of what has been gained by the highest science of the nineteenth century ? As we contemplate it, do we

not feel as if the solid heart of truth and the radiating
light were both gone, and as if we had left only a series
of systematic vibrations in an unknown ether? Does
this satisfy the convictions and the longings of man?
Does not the intelligence declare that it has something
deeper than this? Does not the heart crave for something higher than this? And when the youths, who
are led on so pleasantly by the clear enunciations of Mr.
Mill, stop at any time to inquire what he has given
them, must they not feel that they are, after all, in
darkness, with only a camera obscura displaying figures
before them, always according to sternly scientific laws?
If they are satisfied with this, are they not in the act
abnegating the deeper capacities, and refusing to follow
the higher aspirations of their souls, which, for want
of proper exercise, will become dry, and shrunk, and
withered? And if they are not satisfied—as our higher
minds will certainly not be,—how piteous must be the
wail of disappointment and anguish coming from the
depths of their bosoms, as they crave for truth on the
one hand, and feel that they can never catch it on the
other? I do fear for the consequences, when our pro-
mising youths awake, and in despair of attaining truth,
are tempted to plunge into deeper and yet deeper darkness. Fortunately such a state of things—the deeper
instincts of human nature being so strong—cannot continue for any length of time; and however lamentable
may be the experience and history of individuals, the
hour of thickest darkness will be found to excite the
cry for the returning light. .

" By nature," says Aristotle, " man is competently
" organized for truth; and truth in general is not beyond
" his reach." Truth is usually defined as the agreement
of our ideas, or apprehensions, with things. Profound
thinkers have assumed, or laboured to prove, that, on the
one hand, man has ideas ; that, on the other hand, there
are things; and that man can reach ideas which correspond with things. Let us inquire what view must
be taken of truth by those who follow out Mr. Mill's
system to its consequences ?

Mr. Mill acknowledges that we have ideas. But he
takes great pains to show that these originate in sensations, and grow out of sensations, according to the laws
of the association of sensations. I am not sure whether
he acknowledges the existence of material things out of,
and independent of, sensations. He often uses language
which seems to imply that he does ; but his system all
tends the other way. This is certain, that even if body
exists we can never know anything of it, except as " the
possibility of sensations." All that we know of objects
is the sensations which they give us, and the order of
the occurrence of those sensations. " There is not the
" slightest reason for believing that what we call the
" sensible qualities of the object are a type of anything
" inherent in itself, or bear any affinity to its own nature.
" A cause does not, as such, resemble its effects; an east
" wind is not like the feeling of cold, nor is heat like the
" steam of boiling water : why then should matter
" resemble our sensations ?" (*Logic*, I. III. 7). Then as
to the internal world : all that we know of it is a series

of feelings, with a prolongation in time, which again is identical with a series of muscular sensations (*supra*, p. 133).   I suppose he would further say—though I do not remember any passage in which he does say it,—that we do not know what is the nature of these sensations.   As things are thus unknown, and must be unknown with our present faculties, and in the condition in which we are placed, so man seems to be precluded from reaching any truth beyond the consciousness of present sensations, and the possibility of other sensations.

But some have defined truth as the accordance, not of our own ideas with things, but of our ideas with one another.   This is a view which I do not think worth the pains of defending.   It is quite compatible with the existence of a universal system of delusion and deception, provided always that this system were consistent with itself.   Give a mathematician such a false assumption as that matter attracts other matter inversely according to the distance (and not the square of the distance), and he might construct from it an imaginary world, every part of which would be in agreement with every other, but no part in accordance with the reality of things. It is imaginable that the truth which man discovers is all of this description : a consistency between an unfounded hypothesis, and the results following from it according to the laws of our ideas.   Some ideal philosophers would be content with such a view of truth. But then they think that this consistency is given by the laws of reason, and that man can actually reach truth, not it may be in congruity with phenomenal things,

but, with the principles of reason —some of them would
say absolute and eternal reason.   But truth thus understood is, according to our author's system, quite as much
beyond the reach of man as truth in the other sense.
For any accordance that there may be between our
ideas might be produced, not by independent reason, or
consequential reasoning, but by the association of ideas,
by the laws of contiguity or resemblance.   When two
phenomena have been very often experienced in conjunction, and have not, in any single instance, occurred
separately, either in experience or in thought : " When
" the bond between the two ideas has thus been firmly
" riveted, not only does the idea, called up by association,
" become, in our consciousness, inseparable from the idea
" which suggested it, but the facts or phenomena answer-
" ing to these ideas come at last to seem inseparable in
" existence : things which we are unable to conceive
" apart appear incapable of existing apart" (p. 191).
Thus 2 and 2 having been associated in our experience
with 4, we give them a relation in the nature of things :
but if 2 and 2 had been followed by the appearance of
5, we should have had a like assurance of $2 + 2$ and 5
being equal.   Truth in Mr. Mill's philosophy is not
even a logical or rational consistency between ideas : it
can be nothing more than an accordance of our ideas
with sensations, and laws of the association of sensation :
which sensations come we know not whence, and are
associated by resemblances, existing we know not how,
or, more frequently by contiguity, implying no relation
of reason, no connexion in the nature of things, and

z

very possibly altogether fortuitous, or absolutely fatalistic.

We see now the issues in which the doctrine of the relativity of knowledge, as held by Mr. Mill, lands us. The geometrical demonstrations of Euclid and Apollonius and Newton may hold good only within our experience, and "a reasonable distance beyond." The mathematics taught in Cambridge may differ in their fundamental principles from those taught in the corresponding university of the planet Jupiter; where two and two may make five, where two straight lines may enclose a space, and where the three angles of a triangle may be more than two right angles. Mr. Mill is exceedingly indignant at Dr. Mansel for maintaining that the Divine morality is not to be measured by human morality, declaring that "it is simply the most morally pernicious doctrine now current" (p. 90). But I can discover no ground on which the rebuker can stand, in pronouncing such a judgment on Dr. Mansel's application of the doctrine of the relativity of knowledge. Any one with half the acuteness of Dr. Mansel could show that if two and two may make five, it is also supposable that lying may be a virtue, and veracity a vice, in other worlds; and that God (if there be a God) may commend deceit in the constellation of the Plough, even as He encourages truthfulness in our world; and this doctrine, I rather think, is quite as "morally pernicious" as any now current, and certainly much more so than that entertained by Dr. Mansel, who holds resolutely (whether consistently or not) by an absolute morality, which does not change with times or circum stances.[1]

Some represent Mr. Mill as falling back upon the position of Berkeley. And I suppose we may reckon Mr. Mill as favouring all the negative statements of Berkeley; but he has discarded all those grand views and elevating sentiments which render his system so attractive to certain minds. No consistent thinker can stay at the place taken up by the Irish metaphysician : he had to give way before the Scotch one,—who used the arguments against the independent existence of matter, to undermine our belief in the independent existence of mind.[2] Our author's system, both in its

[1] " We can point to a doctrine which cannot be less morally pernicious than Mr. Mansel's, than which none indeed can be more morally pernicious." " If in some other world two and two may make five ; in some other world what we regard as virtue may be vice, and our wrong may come forth there as right" (*London Quarterly Review*, Jan. 1866). A very able contributor to that periodical has anticipated Mr. Mill in many of his objections to Hamilton's philosophy, but rejects Mr. Mill's philosophy as a substitute.

[2] Some are looking with extreme anxiety to the course which the pupils of Hamilton may adopt at this crisis in the history of philosophic thought. It is clear, from their published writings, that Dr. Cairns and Dr. Calderwood will be prepared to defend natural realism, and the veracity of our native convictions. But what line is to be taken by those who occupy chairs of philosophy, and have students under them ? I am convinced that they cannot now stand where their illustrious master endeavoured to stand,—half way between Reid and Kant—between realities and forms. Are they to fall back on an intuitive perception of things and necessary truth ? Or, abandoning the position taken by Hamilton, and defended by him in many a brave fight, are they to betake themselves to the lines occupied by Kant or by Berkeley, and which have been found so utterly untenable? If they take the latter course, it will be seen by every shrewd observer that they cannot stand one hour before the keen play of Mr. Mill's musketry, or Mr. Spencer's heavier artillery. Those of their pupils who may try to stand on the sliding-scale, will only thereby be made to fall more rapidly to the base—where the school of Mill will welcome them.

premisses and conclusion, has many striking analogies
to that of Hume. Does the one begin with sensations,
these are very much the same as the impressions of the
other. The later metaphysician is only following the
elder, in labouring to show we get our ideas out of
sensations and impressions, by means of association.
They concur in not knowing very well what to make of
time and space; but neither allows them any separate
reality. Both hold that there is no such thing as sub
stance; that all we can know of mind is, that it is a
bundle of states or a series of feelings, to which we give
some sort of unity or permanence, not justifiable by
reason or any higher principle; and that body is an
unknown something, from which we suppose we get our
sensations. Both deny that we have any intuitive
conviction as to cause and effect; and both make the
relation between these to consist in invariable or unconditional conjunction, within the limits of experience.
Both admit some sort of original power: Hume stands
up for innate instincts; and Mr. Mill for an ultimate
belief in memory; and it should be added that neither
knows very well what to make of these inborn principles. Both derive our motives originally from sensations
of pleasure and pain; and both, it is well known, were
clear and eloquent expounders of the utilitarian theory
of morals. Nor is it unworthy of being mentioned, that
both point not unobscurely to changes, which they think
ought to be made, in the marriage relation. It should
be admitted, that with these prominent points of correspondence there are also points of difference. Hume's

account of the relations which the mind of man can discover, is much more comprehensive than that of Mill.
On the other hand, it is pleasant to find that the writer
of this century assumes a higher moral tone than the
writer of the last ; both, however, concurring in overlooking or despising the special Christian graces. But
the main difference lies in this, that Hume discovers
flagrant contradictions in human intelligences ; whereas
the other maintains that the most certain principles
reached by us, being all the product of circumstances,
might have to give way before new circumstances or in
other conditions. Hume had to say, that " the *intense*
" view of these manifold contradictions and imperfections
" in human reason has so wrought upon me and heated
" my brain, that I am ready to reject all belief and
" reasoning, and can look upon no opinion even as more
" probable or likely than another." The modern author
is saved from all such contradictions ; for if one set of
experiences showed him that *two* and *two* make four, and
another that *two* and *two* make five, he would proclaim
both true in the different conditions. The consequence
is, that the one is an avowed sceptic or professed pyrrho-
nist—at least in many parts of his writings—delighting
to play off one dogmatist against another ; whereas the
other is a supporter of the doctrines of nescience and
relativity, holding that we can never reach truths which
may not be modified or set aside in other times and circumstances. I am not sure which of the issues is the
more blank : I rejoice that I do not feel myself required
to make a choice between them.

I hold that human intelligence begins with truth, and if it proceeds properly it ends with truth; which may at times be mysterious, but never contradictory; which may be indefinitely enlarged, but cannot be upturned or reversed. In the course of these discussions we have gathered the means of trying the supposed verities proffered for our acceptance. There is to us no one absolute criterion of all truth; but there are tests of the various kinds of truth, both of those with which we start, and of those which we reach in our progress. Of Intuition itself we have tests in self-evidence, necessity, and universality. Of Reasoning we have stringent tests in the forms of the syllogism. By these two combined we can try Demonstration, which consists in a union of intuition and deduction. We have tests, too, of truths reached in physical, in psychological, and in historical investigation, by the Collection of Facts. These are to be found in the Canons of Induction and in the Canons of Verification; which we may confidently expect to be more and more perfected in their formalization and expression as the separate departments of knowledge make progress.

It is admitted that these criteria demand that we leave unanswered many questions which the questioning mind of man can put. Whatever alleged truth cannot stand such tests should be regarded as unsettled, and allowed to lie for the present in the land of darkness. As we use the criteria we shall be led to see that there are very stringent limits set to man's power of acquiring knowledge. But we shall see at the same time how wide is the field of inquiry, and even of certainty, thrown open to us.   Geology can carry us back in the history of our earth to periods removed from us by millions of years.   Astronomy, aided by mathematics, lets us know of the existence of bodies millions of miles away ; and, aided by chemistry, gives us an insight into the composition of the atmosphere of a body so far removed from us as the sun.   Nor is it to be forgotten that, by the observation of the evidences of design in nature, combined with the principle of cause and effect, and our moral convictions, we can rise to a most reasonable belief in the existence of an Almighty and All-Perfect God. Man should ever claim this wide field as an inheritance, and allow no one, on any pretence, to deprive him of it. And having such an inheritance he should be glad and grateful,—the more so as, attending always to the tests appointed to guide and guard, he can indefinitely widen and extend his possessions.

CHAPTER XX.

UTILITARIANISM.

In specifying the influences under which Mr. Mill's opinions were formed, I might have referred to Jeremy Bentham and his utilitarian theory, as having not a little swayed the opinions of the young thinker, either directly, or indirectly through his father, who was a friend of Bentham's. But in this treatise I meant to look more to Mr. Mill's general philosophic system than his specially ethical views; and however eminent as a jurist, Bentham had no name as a metaphysician. Our author's philosophy is essentially a combination of that of Mr. James Mill and of M. Comte,—however, the utilitarianism of the older Mill and of Bentham thoroughly fits into the system. It would require a volume instead of a chapter to discuss historically, psychologically, and ethically the utilitarian theory. We can touch here only on a few points intimately connected with the preceding discussions.

I. Can Mr. Mill's psychological theory account for the peculiar idea and conviction which we have in regard to moral good and evil? He admits that the mature man in the advanced stages of society has a conscience and moral ideas : let us inquire how he generates them. And first, let us try to ascertain what he makes the original motive powers or springs of action in the mind of man. " The utilitarian doctrine is, that " happiness is desirable, and the only thing desirable, as " an end" (p. 51). It is clear that he makes, as every other philosopher does, the desire of personal pleasure a primary motive to action. But I am not sure whether he makes the desire of promoting the happiness of other beings also an originating appetence in man. There are passages which look as if he did, or at least wished to be regarded as doing so. In rearing his theory he is ever appealing to " the social feelings of mankind ; " and he maintains with Bentham, that man is urged to the ' greatest happiness' principle both " by interest and sympathy" (pp. 45, 47). " The idea of the pain of " another is naturally painful ; the idea of the plea- " sure of another is naturally pleasure" (*Dis.*, p. 137). I am sure that the great British moralists who lived at the beginning of last century, have succeeded in demonstrating that man is not in his nature and constitution an utterly selfish being, but is capable of being swayed by a desire to promote the welfare of others ; and the arguments of Shaftesbury, Hutche son, and Butler have been repeated and strengthened by the Scottish school of philosophers generally, including Reid, Stewart, and Brown, and by M. Cousin, and the Eclectic school of France. But these writers have shown that the same facts and arguments which lead us to admit an original principle of sympathy, require us also to call in a cognitive and a motive moral power.

He allows as a psychological fact that virtue may become " a good in itself, without looking to any end beyond it," and that the mind is not in a right state unless it love virtue "as a thing desirable in itself" (p. 53). In indignantly repelling the objections of Dr. Sedgwick, he maintains, " It is a fact in human nature " that we have moral judgments and moral feelings. We " judge certain actions and dispositions to be right; " others wrong : this we call approving and disapproving " them. We have also feelings of pleasure in the con- " templation of the former class of actions and disposi- " tions—feelings of dislike and aversion to the latter ; " which feelings, as everybody must be conscious, do not " exactly resemble any other of our feelings of pain or " pleasure. Such are the phenomena ; concerning their " reality there is no dispute." He then seeks to account for the phenomena by his famous principle of the chemistry of the association of ideas. " The only colour " for representing our moral judgments as the result of " a peculiar part of our nature, is that our feelings of " moral approbation and disapprobation are really " peculiar feelings. But is it not notorious that peculiar " feelings, unlike any others we have experience of, are " created by association every day ?" (*Dis.* pp. 139, 140.) He instances the desire of power, the feelings of ambi- tion, of envy, of jealousy, and of the miser towards his gold. Now, as to some of these appetencies, I believe them to be natural. We see them working strongly in certain individuals, showing that they are elements of their inborn character. We see them descending hereditarily from father or mother, to son or daughter or grandchild; and we find them stronger in certain families and races than in others. As the love of power is a native appetence by which men may be swayed, surely the conscience and the felt obligation to do that which is right may be the same.

But our present question is one not so much of mere appetency or desires as of moral perceptions, judgments, and sentiments. I grant that persons may be led by mere prudence to attend to the duties of an outward morality, and by a kindly disposition to relieve distress, altogether irrespective of a moral sense. But there is a very special obligation felt in regard to those actions which we call moral, and which does not bear on other parts of our conduct; we are convinced that we ought to attend to them, and that if we neglect to do so our conduct is blameworthy. Whence the very peculiar and profound ideas denoted by the phrases ' obligation,' ' ought,' ' blameworthy.' Take the perception of conscience, that deceit is a sin. Take the conviction, that we are not at liberty to tell a lie when we might be tempted to do so. Take the judgment, that the person who has committed the act is guilty, condemnable, punishable. Take the feeling of remorse, which rises when we contemplate ourselves as having told a falsehood. We have here a series of mental phenomena quite as real and quite as worthy of being looked at, as our very sensations, or beliefs of the reality of the past in memory, or our expectation of

the future. I am convinced that as these last are admitted to be ultimate (see ρ, σ, τ), so are the others also. "This instinct," says Isaac Taylor, "flushes in
" the cheek of every sensitive child, and it prevails
" over the laborious sophistications of the philosopher.
" This belief is cherished as an inestimable jewel by the
" best and purest of human beings ; and it is bowed to
" in dismay by the foulest and the worst ; its rudiments
" are a monition of eternal truth, whispered in the ear of
" infancy ; its articulate announcements are a dread fore--
" doom ringing in the ears of the guilty adult. You say
" you can bring forward a hundred educated men, who,
" at this time, will profess themselves to be no believers
" in a moral system ; but I will rebut their testimony
" by the spontaneous and accordant voices of as many
" millions of men as you may please to call for on the
" other side."

I have already examined the general theory which generates a new idea by means of an association of sensations, and have shown how little truth there is in it (pp. 180-186). Give us mere sensations, say of sounds, or colours, or forms, or of pleasure and pain, and they will never be anything else in the reproduction of them than the ideas of sounds, colours, forms, pleasures, or pains,—unless, indeed, there be some new power introduced, and this new element in itself, or in conjunction with the sensations, be fitted to produce a new idea, and that very idea. In none of its applications is the theory seen to fail so utterly, as in the attempt thus to produce our moral perceptions. Provided we once had the ideas, the laws of association might show how they could be brought up again; how in the reproduction certain parts might sink into shadow and neglect, while others came forth into prominence and light; and how the whole feeling, by the confluence of different ideas, might be wrought into a glow of intensity; but the difficulty of generating the ideas, such ideas, ideas so full of meaning, is not thereby surmounted. The idea I have of pain is one thing, and the idea I have of deceit, that it is morally evil, condemnable, deserving of pain, is an entirely different thing—our consciousness being witness. On the supposition that there is a chemical power in association to create such ideas as those of duty and merit, sin and demerit, this chemical power would be a native moral power; not the product of sensations, but a power above them, and adapted to transmute them from the baser into the golden substance.

It will be needful at this place to correct a misapprehension into which Mr. Mill has fallen. He represents the intuitive school of morals as holding that "the principles of morals are evident *a priori*" (p. 3). Now I admit that influential members of the school have used language fitted to warrant this statement. But there are others, and these the wisest defenders of intuition, who have given a different account. Our intuitions are perceptions of individual objects or individual truths; and in order to reach an axiom or "principle of morals," there is need of a discursive process of generalization. Our author makes the intuitive

agree with the inductive school, in holding that "the
" morality of an individual action is not a question of
" direct perception, but of the application of law to an
" individual case." The proper account is that the law
is generalized out of our direct perceptions. On the bare
contemplation of an ungrateful spirit, the conscience at
once declares it to be evil, apart from the conscious
apprehension or application of any general principle.
The enunciation of the law is a reflective and not a
spontaneous process, and is undertaken when we wish
to construct a code of morals or a science of ethics.
This representation saves the intuitive theory of morals
from many of the specious objections urged against a
different version. Our moral intuitions are not *a priori*
forms, which the mind imposes on objects, but immediate perceptions of qualities in certain objects, that is,
in the voluntary dispositions and actions of intelligent
beings. Taking this view of them, I believe they can
stand the tests which settle what truth is intuitive.
They are self-evident : on the simple apprehension of
disinterested love we declare it to be good and commendable. They may be described, if we properly
explain the statement, as necessary : give us a correct
representation of a deed of intentional deceit for a selfish
end, and we condemn, and cannot be made to commend
it. They have, in a sense, even catholic consent
in their favour : all men will condemn deceit if it is
properly laid before them, but the deceit may be so
painted as that we do not see its true nature, and
then we give our approval,—not of the deceit, but of its

accompaniments. Mankind can be so deceived as to give diverse judgments on moral actions, only by the blinding influence of sin, disguising and distorting the real nature of things.

II. Does utilitarianism embrace sufficient sanctions to induce us to approve virtue and condemn vice? Our author labours to show that the motives usually supposed to lead to virtue are left untouched by this theory. But this is not the question, the main question; and if any defender of *a priori* morals had been guilty of such an *ignoratio elenchi*, we can conceive that the acute logician would have exposed it with extraordinary zest. The question is not about sanctions which other systems may employ, but it is, Does utilitarianism contain within itself a body of motives, or motive powers, fitted to lead to virtuous conduct? If it does not, if it is obliged to make us look elsewhere for motives, then it is without one of the essential constituents of an adequate theory of morals. Utilitarianism bids us seek to promote the greatest happiness of the greatest number. 'But why should I strive to attain this end?' asks the inquiring youth. Practically, and in reference to his future conduct, theoretically, and as interested in the science of ethics, he insists on a reply. 'Why should I give up my immediate ease and comfort and expected enjoyments, and restrain my strong native impulses and indulged habits in order to look after others, who may be quite able to look after themselves?' 'Or why, at the best, may I not content myself with attending to the feelings and immediate wishes of the few persons in my family or circle, with whose welfare my own is bound up, or of the single person to whom I am attached?' As he presses these questions he will not be satisfied to be told that other ethical systems have sanctions, and that utilitarianism leaves them where it found them.

But let us look at those sanctions with which it is said the theory does not meddle. We may find, as to some of the guarantees or sureties to which we are referred, that their credit is undermined, and that they are rendered bankrupt, by the principles of the new philosophy. Mr. Mill tells us, that if persons believe that there is a God, they may still have the motives derived from their religion to induce them to practise morality. This starts the question, what religion has our author's system left us? It is clear that utilitarianism deprives us of one of the arguments which has been felt by profound thinkers to carry the greatest weight, that derived from the moral law in the heart arguing a moral lawgiver. Nor is it to be forgotten, that our greatest moralists have not been in the way of appealing first to the Divine power or will, as a motive to lead us to do good, but have rather sought, by the principles of an independent morality, to show that we ought to obey God. We may omit entering further into this inquiry at present, as the whole subject of the relation of Mr. Mill's philosophy to natural theology will come to be discussed in next chapter. But we must look here at some other sanctions which it is supposed utilitarianism has left untouched.

" The internal sanction of duty, whatever our standard
" of duty may be, is one and the same, a feeling in our
" own mind ; a pain more or less intense attendant on
" violation of duty, which in properly cultivated moral
" natures rises, in the more serious cases, into shrinking
" from it as an impossibility ;" and " the ultimate sanc-
" tion, therefore, of all morality (external motives apart)
" being a subjective feeling in our own minds," he thinks
that utilitarianism has as powerful a sanction as any
other theory can have (pp. 40, 41). But it is not fair to
represent those who hold the opposite theory as making
the ultimate appeal, standard, and sanction, to be in
" feeling," in mere " subjective feeling," a " feeling of
pain" attendant on the violation of duty. It cannot be
said to consist in " feeling," except we use the phrase in
so wide and loose a sense as to include all mental operations, and the native principles of action from which
they spring. It should not be represented as a mere
" subjective feeling," for it points to and implies an
objective reality, a real good and evil in the voluntary
acts of intelligent beings, independent of our sense of it,
being in fact the object to which the sense looks. Still
less should it be regarded as a mere " feeling of pain ;"
it has been shown again and again by moralists, that the
feeling of pain rises in consequence of a prior perception of the evil of sin. According to our most esteemed
moralists, the mind, in looking at moral good and evil,
is exercising a higher attribute than mere feeling or
emotion. By some it is represented as a Sense looking
to and discerning a moral quality—as the eye discerns

colour and surface. More frequently it is described as Reason, or as analogous to Reason, and the Moral Reason, which perceives at once the good and the evil, and distinguishes between them, declaring the doing of the one and the avoiding of the other to be obligatory on all intelligent beings, and the one to be of good desert and rewardable, and the other of evil desert and punishable ; and the feeling of pleasure or pain is the consequent and not the essence of the conviction.

But then the feeling, which is the essence of conscience, is "all encrusted over with collateral associa- " tions, derived from sympathy, from love, and still " more from fear ; from all the forms of religious feeling : " from the recollections of childhood and of all our past " life ; from self-esteem, desire of the esteem of others, " and occasionally even self-abasement." "Its binding " force consists in the existence of a mass of feeling, " which must be broken through in order to do what " violates our standard of right, and which, if we do " nevertheless violate that standard, will probably have " to be encountered afterwards in the form of remorse" (p. 41). He reckons this complicated feeling as furnishing quite as strong a sanction, and one quite as likely not to be violated, as that which might be awakened by a distinct moral faculty. Now, I concede at once, that other and secondary motives may and should gather and cling round our primary conviction of duty, to aid and strengthen it. But meanwhile, as the centre, and in the last resort, as the support of them, there should be recognised obligations of morality. The intelligent youth, when he comes to rise beyond his educational beliefs, and to think for himself, will not be satisfied with the mere existence of the mass of feeling; he will ask, Is it justifiable, is it binding? If satisfied on this point, then he will feel himself called on to encourage all these associations, and to live under their influence. But if not satisfied, if taught they have no obligation in reason or the nature of things, then why should he not uncoil them, as he does some other hereditary prepossessions; or even if he should be inclined to retain them, will they not be apt to give way before the strong and seductive temptations which are ever assailing him? Let it be observed of many of these associations which have been gathered, and sentiments which have been gendered, that they have been generated in individuals, or grown up in a state of society, entertaining and cherishing the belief that there is an independent rule of duty. Such, for example, are our "religious feelings;" such, too, our "remorse;" such our "self-abasement,"—they arise mainly from the promptings of a conscience, which carries with it its own authority and its own sanctions. Remove the support which bears them—as the stake bears up the vine—and they will speedily fall, or rather will never rise to any height. Let the school beware lest, in striving to destroy the inborn sense and native perceptions of good and evil, they be not doing as much as within them lies to cut down the tree that has borne the fruit; or, to use a still more familiar image, to kill the hen that has laid the golden eggs. And as to the "recollections of childhood and of our past lives," and the feelings of "sympathy" and "self-esteem," and "the desire of the esteem of others," these can foster virtuous sentiment and lead to virtuous conduct only where there is a high moral and religious standard in the family, and in the community, and may tend the opposite way in other states of society; as, for instance, that which existed in ancient Rome in the decline of the empire, or among the educated classes in France in the age before the Revolution, or which may be found in certain circles in Paris at this present time. The vessel, which is sailing along gracefully with its present structure, may be speedily dissolved and its crew wrecked, when a magnet (to refer to a well-known fable) has been applied, which draws out the bolts that kept the parts together.

I deny that the two kinds of sanction are on the same footing and of equal strength. The one sort is derived from a mere agglomeration of feelings, which are generated by associations created independently of our choice, and mainly by outward contiguities. Some of these, such as those mentioned by Mr. Mill, may be laudable, and may tend to promote virtuous conduct. But others, though arising from like associations, produced by the same circumstances, may be of an opposite character. Such are the fears which spring from a degraded superstition with its horrid ceremonials; such are the animal lusts that may grow up along with a purer love; such are the jealousy, malice, and envy gendered by the rivalries of trade and fashion; such are the expectations excited when large pleasure and profit to ourselves or others may be had by one bold deed of selfishness; and such is the despair awakened when there has been a failure in the favourite ends of a man's life. These feelings, growing from the same root of associations and circumstances, will tend to moral evil as the others do to good; and surely it is of moment to have a moral obligation above either, and calling on us while we allow the one to disallow the other. How vastly inferior must be the sanction supplied by this conglomeration of associations to that which the higher moral theory furnishes, when it declares that certain affections, such as gratitude, and love, and justice, are themselves good, and that certain other affections, such as ingratitude, and malice, and deceit, are evil in their very nature; that the mind is organized to discern the distinction between good and evil, just as it discovers the difference between truth and error: that the moral power by which it does this is not only in the mind, but claims to be supreme there; that it implies and points to a God who is the guardian of the law, and will call every man to account for the deeds done in the body, whether they have been good or evil.

III. Does utilitarianism furnish a sufficient test of virtuous acts and of virtuous motives? It tells us that a good deed is one tending to promote the greatest happiness of the greatest number. But in the complicated affairs of this world, the most far-sighted cannot know for certain what may be the total consequences of any one act: and the great body of mankind feel as if they were looking out on a tangled forest, and need a guide to direct them.   Utilitarian moralists, like Bentham, may draw out schemes of tendencies for us; but the specific rules have no obliging authority, and, even when understood and appreciated, are difficult of application, and are ever bringing us into cross avenues into which we may be led by self-deceit.   With no other standard than ultimate tendency, the timid will ever be afraid to act as never clearly seeing their way, while the bold will ever be tempted at critical junctures, and in order to gain ends which are dear to them, and which they have identified with the good of their country,—as when Julius Cæsar crossed the Rubicon, and Louis Napoleon ventured on his *coup d'état,*—to commit crimes in the name of virtue.   I am aware that on any theoretical system men will commit sin ; but on this system they will commit crimes of the highest order, and justify themselves as they do so, on the ground of the great advantages to be secured by themselves and others.

Mr. Mill's defence of the theory proceeds on the principle, that there may be a distinction drawn between the virtuousness of the act and the virtuousness of the agent.   " He who saves a fellow-creature from " drowning does what is morally right, whether his mo- " tive be duty, or the hope of being paid for his trouble ; " he who betrays the friend that trusts him, is guilty of a " crime, even if his object be to serve another friend to " whom he is under greater obligations " (p. 26).   The test of a virtuous act is beneficial tendency, but what is the test of the virtuous motive ?   Is it, too, beneficial tendency? Is the agriculturist who improves the soil, so as to make it feed more men and cattle than it did before, or the master manufacturer who sets up a large public work which gives food to thousands, necessarily virtuous, and this in proportion to the good done, and though in the depths of his heart he may be influenced by no other consideration than the love of gain? We do run a considerable risk in these times of the prevalence of a cosmopolitanism, originating in a deeper selfishness, and prosecuted in a spirit of self-righteousness, and going on to overwhelm and supersede the gentler and the humbler private and domestic virtues, which our fathers so valued before utilitarianism was heard of. But Mr. Mill is too wise a man to make beneficial tendency a test of excellence in the agent. " The motive has nothing to do with the morality of the action, though much with the worth of the agent." He tells us that it is a misapprehension of the utilitarian mode of thought to conceive it as implying so wide a generality as the world or morality at large, and he says of M. Comte, that " he committed the error which is " often, but falsely, charged against the whole class of " utilitarian moralists : he required that the test of con " duct should also be the exclusive motive to it" (*Comte and Posit.*, p. 138). It is not very clear what constitutes a virtuous agent, according to our author. The following statement is sufficiently vague, and yet it is the clearest I can find on a point which should not be left in uncertainty for a moment : " The great majority of " good actions are intended not for the benefit of the

" world, but for that of individuals, of which the good of
" the world is made up : and the thoughts of the most
" virtuous man need not on these occasions travel be-
" yond the particular persons concerned, except so far
" as is necessary to assure himself that in benefiting
" them he is not violating the rights, that is, the legiti-
" mate and authorized expectations, of any one else"
(p. 27). There is some truth here, but it is surely far from
being the full truth.   The impelling motive of an action
entitled to be called virtuous is love, leading us to perform that which is right; that is, according to moral law,
the law of God.   The love is a well-spring ready to
burst forth, and the law is the channel provided in
which the stream may flow.   Without the love there is
no virtue ; and without the love regulated by law there is
no virtue—in the agent.   It is to the credit of M. Comte
that, separating himself from cold utilitarianism, he
reckoned love as of the essence of excellence : but it is
an evidence of the narrowness and bigotry which so
distinguished him, that he does not see that he has derived this principle from Christianity, which he represents as deriving all its motives from the selfish fear of
hell and hope of heaven.

And what makes an action sinful according to this
philosophy ?   It is still more difficult to find what is the
answer to that question.   Sin is quite as much a fact of
consciousness and of our moral nature as even virtue.
' Thou shalt not kill ;' ' Thou shalt not commit adultery ;'
' Thou shalt not steal ;' ' Thou shalt not bear false witness,'—these laws are clear, and the violation of them is

sin according to Scripture, and according to conscience. But what is sin according to utilitarianism? It is acknowledged not to be the mere omission to look to the general good. What then does it consist in? Mr. Mill speaks of "reproach" being one of the checks on evil; but when is reproach justifiable? Not knowing what to make of sin, the system provides no place for repentance. The boundary line between moral good and evil is drawn so uncertainly, that persons will ever be tempted to cross it without allowing that they have done so,—the more so that they are not told what they should do when they have crossed it.

IV. Does utilitarianism embrace all the virtues? In answering this question, it should at once be allowed that the system contains an important body of truth; it errs only so far as it professes to embrace and unfold the whole of morals. It is a duty devolving on all to promote the happiness of their fellows. So far as the system recommends this, it can have nothing erroneous, —it should be added that it has nothing original. But even at this point where it is supposed to be strongest, it is found to fail when we narrowly examine it. For whence can utilitarianism draw its motive and obligation to constrain us to look after the general happiness? He says, " No reason can be given why the general hap " piness is desirable, except that each person, so far as he " believes it to be attainable, desires his own happiness " (p. 52). But it would need more acuteness than even Mr. Mill is possessed of to show that this principle requires us to promote the best interests of others. It is proper to refer to this here; but I need not dwell upon it, as I have urged it under another head.

Utilitarianism has a special merit in all questions of jurisprudence. The reason can be given. The end of legislation is not the maintenance of the law of God, but the promotion of the interests of the nation. But even in this department a higher morality has a place, though only a negative one. The governing power is not entitled to enact what is in itself sinful, on the pretence of adding to the pleasures of the community. The people of this country are right in their religious and moral instincts when they declare that on no pretence whatever should the Government take upon itself the licensing of places of prostitution, even on the pretence of regulating them, and restraining the evils that flow from them. Nor is the magistrate at liberty to punish an act unless it be sinful; for example, he would not be justified in punishing a person, who, without meaning it, had brought infectious disease into a city, whereby ten thousand inhabitants had perished; whereas he would be required to inflict a penalty for the theft of a very small sum from a rich man who never felt the loss. Why the difference? Plainly because the former act is not a sin, that is, implied no evil disposition, whereas the other does. But while the civil government should punish only when sin has been committed, and has thus to look to the moral law, it does not punish sin as sin, but as inflicting injustice on others, and injurious to the best interests of society. The utilitarian theory, as developed by Bentham, has.

consequentially and historically, been the means of alleviating the harshness of our penal code, and giving a more benignant aspect to legislation generally.

Mr. Mill has given a contribution to public ethics in his treatise on *Liberty*. The work is stimulating in its spirit, but at the same time far from being satisfactory in its results. It might have been expected in a renewed discussion on such a subject, after all that has been written during the last two centuries, that we should have had some principles laid down to guide us as to the moral limits to be set to the expression of sentiment, and the attempt to create a public feeling against what we believe to be evil. A gentleman, let me suppose, settles in my neighbourhood, of polite manners, of cultivated mind, and apparently of general beneficence. But he has a wife and a mistress, and maintains that he is justified in having both, and might allowably have more. What is to be my demeanour towards him? Am I to ask him to my house, and introduce him to my sons and my daughters? Am I never to speak against him and his conduct, never to warn my family against being influenced by his example? Am I to hasten to elect him to places of honour and trust in the parish or in the town? Or, if I decline thus to countenance him, am I to be declared intolerant? Rising beyond such personal to public questions, am I not to protest against a public evil, and seek to create a public sentiment against it? If I am not at liberty to do this, Mr. Mill is laying down a doctrine of liberty which is interfering with my liberty. Such questions as these start points, on which many anxious to cultivate a spirit, not only of toleration, but what is far higher, of charity, are anxious to have light, which is not vouchsafed in this treatise.

The spirit which it is fitted to engender is that of 'individualism :' and when it has had time to produce its proper fruits, it will be found to have raised up a body of young men who reckon it a virtue to be peculiar in their opinions, and rather commendable to be eccentric. The spirit of hero-worship produced indirectly by German pantheism, and directly by the writings of Carlyle, has happily lost its sway over our young men, and is now to be found, in some of the remains of it, only among literary gentlemen of respectable middle age.   But we are sure to be flooded in the coming generation with something still more intolerable, in ambitious youths each affecting to strike out a path of his own, in opinion and sentiment, speculative, practical, and religious.   This spirit, as it runs to excess, will be quite as deleterious, and will be more foolish and offen sive, than the old habit of subjection to authority or reverence for the great.   The genuine temper is not a prostration before antiquity or before genius on the one hand ; but just as little is it a love of novelty or a love of change on the other : it is a love of indepen dence, which, believing that truth in all important mat ters is attainable, sets out earnestly in search of it ; not rejecting the old because it is old, or accepting the new because it is new, but willing to take light from what ever quarter it may come.

While giving to utility an important place, I deny that it is the only thing to be looked at as a good, as a test, or as a standard. Take the duties we owe to God, the love and reverence we should cherish towards Him, and the worship we should pay Him in private and in public. Surely man's moral nature justifies him in holding that there are such duties : but on what foundation can utilitarianism rest them ? Is it on beneficial tendency to the individual or to society ? So far as the individual is concerned, the salutary influence is produced on his spirit only when he pays the service, because it is right. If he is constrained to render it from any other motive, it will rather chafe and irritate, and end in unbelief and rebellion. And as to worship paid to God merely for the good of the community, it is the very consummation of public hypocrisy—which in the end would deceive no one. The defenders of the utilitarian theory, in the form given to it by Bentham, have never attempted to build upon it a code of religious duties. I believe that any attempt of this description would only show that the foundation was not broad or deep enough to bear such a superstructure. The same may be said of not a few of the duties we owe to our fellow-men. Take gratitude for undeserved favours. I would not choose to found it on the mere desire to promote our own happiness or that of the person from whom the benefit has come: in order to be a virtue, it must spring from a sense of the duty we owe to the benefactor.

There are symptoms of a renewed attempt being made

in our age to construct a morality without a godliness.
I speak of it as a renewed attempt, for it has been tried
before.   In the second century, when paganism was
losing its hold of educated minds, and young Christianity
was advancing with such rapid strides, an attempt was
made by the Neo-Platonic School of Alexandria to
construct a theology, and, by the Stoic School of Rome
a morality, higher than that of the Bible.   Every student of history knows how these schemes were soon
seen to terminate in a humiliating failure.   The Neo-
Platonic ecstasy evaporated into empty air, and the
Stoic self-sufficiency hardened into offensive pride ; and
neither offered any effectual resistance to the triumph-
ant march of a religion suited in every way to the
wants of man's nature.   Analogous projects have been
devised and are being recommended in our day.   For
some time past the God of the Bible has been represented as not sufficiently pure——as being too anthropo-
morphic ; and mystic thinkers have sought to picture
to us a God of a more spiritual and ethereal character.
This style of thinking in Germany has issued from, or
culminated in, a shadowy pantheism, which, followed
to its logical and practical consequences— as it will be
in this country—must identify God with the evil as
well as with the good, or in fact make evil only a form
of good.   And now it looks as if we are to have persons
presenting to us a morality higher and broader than that
of the New Testament.

After speaking in very exalted terms of the doctrines
and precepts of Christ, Mr. Mill asserts " that many

" essential elements of the highest morality are among
" the things which are not provided for, nor intended to
" be provided for, in the recorded deliverances of the
" Founder of Christianity, and which have been entirely
" thrown aside in the system of ethics erected on the basis
" of those deliverances by the Christian church. And
" this being so, I think it a great error to persist in at-
" tempting to find in the Christian doctrine that com
" plete rule for our guidance, which its author intended to
" sanction and enforce, but only partially to provide." "I
" believe that other ethics than any which can be evolved
" from exclusively Christian sources, must exist side by
" side with Christian ethics to produce the moral regene-
" ration of mankind" (*Liberty*, pp. 91-92). Now, it may
be admitted that the precepts of the Word of God do not
contain specific directions as to what mankind should
do in the infinitely varied positions in which they may
be placed. The Christian system first shows the sinner
how he may be delivered from the burden of past sin,
which so weighs him down in his efforts after regenera-
tion. It then furnishes motives to induce him to perform the duties which devolve upon him. It enjoins, as
the regulating principle of our conduct, love to God and
love to man. It lays down many and varied precepts
as to how we should feel and what we should do, in
very many and varied situations, and supplies numerous
warnings against evil, and examples of good. Speaking
as unto wise men, it leaves the rest to ourselves, to the
motives which it has called forth, and the royal law
of love, which is its grand moving and ruling principle.

Mr. Mill is not very specific as to what he supposes
the code of Christian morality to be deficient in.
He complains of our "discarding those secular standards
" (as for want of a better name they may be called)
" which heretofore co-existed with and supplemented
" the Christian ethics." But I believe this has been pro
vided for in such passages as these, scattered everywhere : " Whatsoever things are true, whatsoever things
" are honest, whatsoever things are just, whatsoever
" things are pure, whatsoever things are lovely, whatso
" ever things are of good report; if there be any virtue,
" and if there be any praise, think on these things."
Narrow Christians may have overlooked some of these
graces and virtues; but in order to correct them, we do
not require to go beyond the Scriptures themselves.
He fixes on one department of duty which he supposes
to be neglected in the Word of God, and that is the
duty we owe to the State : " In the purely Christian
ethics, that grand department of duty is scarcely noticed
or acknowledged." I am amazed, I confess, at this
charge. The history of ancient Israel, recorded in the Old
Testament, exhibits the most fervent patriotism in every
page. How nobly does it burst forth in the exclamation
of the Psalmist, " If I forget thee, O Jerusalem," etc.
Paul has caught the same spirit : " Brethren, my heart's
desire and prayer for Israel is, that they might be saved."
We find it burning and flaming in the bosom of our
Lord himself: "O Jerusalem, Jerusalem, how often would
" I have gathered thy children together, even as a
" hen gathereth her chickens under her wings, but ye

" would not." The Word of God requires obedience from the subject : " Render therefore to all their dues : tribute to whom tribute is due, custom to whom custom, fear to whom fear, honour to whom honour." But he adds, " It is essentially a doctrine of passive obedience : " it inculcates submission to all authorities thought " established, who indeed are not to be actively obeyed " when they command what religion forbids, but who " are not to be resented, far less rebelled against, for " any amount of wrong to ourselves." I admit that the Bible does not give minute rules as to when subjects may claim the right to refuse obedience,—nor do I know of any moral code that does. But it prescribes the function of governors : "A minister of God to thee for good," " sent for the punishment of evil-doers, and for the praise of them that do well." I do believe that Christians are not at liberty to rebel merely because of wrong done to themselves personally. But when the governor commands what is evil in itself, when the government ceases to fulfil its proper office, Christians have thought themselves entitled, always with excessive reluctance, to resist, and have drawn their warrant from the Word of God. So at least thought the Huguenots of France, and the Puritans of England, and the Covenanters of Scotland, and the Bishops at the Revolution Settlement : and their descendants, who have inherited the blessings secured through them, have been proud of the example they set.

Mr. Mill and his school have, unfortunately, not drawn out this code of morality, which is to be purer and nobler

2 B

than the Christian. But we may gather what it would be from occasional statements. With perhaps some few additions, it would probably be such as we find in the *Meditations* of Marcus Aurelius Antoninus, the Roman emperor who so rigorously opposed the progress of Christianity. Mr. Mill says of his writings, that " they are the highest ethical product of the ancient mind," and that they " differ scarcely perceptibly, if they differ at all, from the most characteristic teachings of Christ " (*Ib.* p. 49). Surely Mr. Mill forgets that Jesus began his public teaching by " preaching the " gospel of the kingdom of God, and saying, The time is " fulfilled, and the kingdom of God is at hand: repent " ye, and believe the gospel " (Mark i. 14, 15) ; that the first beatitude and the second beatitude in the Sermon on the Mount are, " Blessed are the poor in spirit ; " " Blessed are they that mourn ; " and the prayer commanded is that of the publican, " God be merciful to me a sinner." I have met with no such injunctions, no such spirit, in the *Meditations* of Antoninus. This work of the heathen emperor was much read by the moral school of divines last century ; and the precepts enjoined were those they recommended. We know the result. The self-righteous system, whether recommended by the stoic moralists in ancient times, or by the rationalists of last century, was favourably regarded by a few persons belonging to the middle class, mostly in comfortable worldly circumstances, and not in a position to be much in fear of poverty, or the deeper trials of life. In them it produced or favoured a spirit of self-sufficiency and pride, which tended to make their characters hard and unlovely, and exposed them often to grievous falls, from which it could not lift them. And as to the great body of the people of all classes, but especially the poor, the tried, and the unfortunate, they turned away from it with loathing, as not adapted to their wants and circumstances, pretending, as it did, to keep up by their own strength those who felt that they needed higher support, and providing no means of raising the lapsed or comforting the mourner. I do not allow that it would be an elevation of morality to set aside the peculiar Christian graces of penitence, meekness, and humility, and to substitute for them a sense of honour, a sense of our own merits, and a spirit of selfsufficient independence.

CHAPTER XXI.

NATURAL THEOLOGY.

THE School of M. Comte, both in its French and British departments, is essentially a *Sect*, separated from other philosophies, and with very narrow sympathies. It has been made so partly by the circumstance that its adherents were at first few, and had to meet not only with opposition but with contempt from the leading metaphysicians of the age ; but it is so essentially, because it has cut itself off from the streams which flow down from the past, and, like a pool, it has no connexion with anything beyond itself. Though no longer a small body, and though by their intellectual power and perseverance they have compelled their opponents to respect them, the disciples have still the exclusiveness of a sect : they read one another, they quote one another, and they criticise one another, they are incapable of appreciating any other philosophy. The two articles of their creed, and the two points that unite them, are the theory of nescience, and that of the steps by which knowledge has made progress. I have been examining the first all throughout this work. Before I close I must notice the other.

The famous law of sociology, as developed by M. Comte, is about as rash a generalization as was ever made by a Presocratic physiologist, a mediæval schoolman, or a modern German speculator. It realizes the description given by Bacon of empiricists, who are represented as rising at once from a limited observation of facts to the highest and widest generalizations. The theory contains a small amount of truth, which it has misunderstood and perverted. In the early ages of the world, and in simple states of society at all times, mankind are inclined to see God or the gods as acting without any secondary instrumentality, in operations which are found subsequently to take place according to natural law. The reason of this is very simple, and very obvious, and has often been noticed : it is that mankind are prompted by the native principle of causation to seek for a cause to every event, while they have not so large an experience as to enable them to discover the uniformity in the cosmos. This state of society constitutes what M. Comte calls the Theological Era ; which, however, does not imply that men are more disposed to see God in His works, and to worship, love, and obey Him, than in other ages ; but simply that they believe Him to act or interpose by a free operation, independent of all physical causation.

As observation widens and intelligence advances, men learn to abstract and generalize upon the phenomena of nature. They are apt to do so in the first instance—as being the easiest method—by mere mental force or inward cogitation. Not having learned to perform experiments, they cannot distinguish between the various subtle powers and elements which operate in nature, nor to make what Bacon calls the necessary " rejections and exclusions." Generalizing the obvious facts, they represent the sun and stars as moving daily round the earth, and, as they find they cannot thus explain the whole phenomena, they give a special motion to the moon and planets, and call in eccentrics and epicycles. Or, abstracting what seems common in the obvious operations of earthly agents, they represent the components of the universe as being the fiery, the aërial, the aqueous, and the solid powers ; and speak of certain bodies being in their very nature light and others heavy. This is what is called the Metaphysical Era. Not that mankind are then inclined to cultivate metaphysics in any proper sense of the term, or more than any other department of inquiry ; but simply that they hasten to grasp the operations of nature within and without them by mental acts, and have not learned—what it required a Bacon to tell us—that investigation must proceed gradually, and by means of enlarged observation and careful experiment. So far from being in any peculiar sense a metaphysical age, it sought to penetrate into all the departments of nature, and inquired into the origin and structure of the universe, and the movements of the celestial bodies. It did enter upon metaphysical subjects, but it was as it rushed into physiological and astrological speculations.; and it discussed them all in the same spirit. The Presocratic schools, for example, did inquire into the nature of knowing, and being, and the human soul; but it was as they inquired into the primary principle or elements of the universe. They satisfied themselves with a few common observations, and then proceeded to apply thought to them. In pure metaphysical questions they distinguished in a rude way between Sensation and Reason, and when this division was found insufficient, they called in a vague intermediate principle called Opinion or Faith. Such ages have no special title to be called the Metaphysical Era: they treat physics and metaphysics in the same undistinguishing and uncertain manner. Nor are they to be regarded as necessarily non-theological ages. No doubt there were curious questions started, which could not be settled, as to the relation between these rapidly generalized and abstract powers, and the gods who ruled in heaven. There were thus stirred theological questions which tended to undermine the old superstitions, and to prepare the way for a better era. It was at this time—'the fulness of time' —that Christianity was introduced as a seed into a soil ploughed to receive it.

In the natural advancement of intelligence, especially after the great awakening of thought in the sixteenth century, it was felt that the old methods were waxing old, and must soon vanish away. These methods are happily described by Bacon as the 'Rational' so presumptuous, the 'Empirical' so narrow, and the 'Superstitious' which made religion accomplish what could be done only by science. At this time there appeared such men as

Galileo practising careful experiment, and Bacon himself to expound the general principles of the true mode of procedure—of which method the Positive Philosophy is merely a monstrous outgrowth. This Era should be called the Inductive. It may be quite as metaphysical as the previous ones, only it will conduct the investigations in a new spirit and mode, that is, according to the Method of Induction. This new spirit (though the method was not yet properly understood) sprang up in the seventeenth century, and was fostered by such men as Descartes, who taught us to look into the mind to discover its operations, and by Locke, who appealed to experience. Since that time an inductive mental science, distracted from time to time by an ambitious *a priori*, or by a narrow empirical philosophy, has run parallel to physical science. Nor is this era necessarily an untheological one. Never were questions of divinity discussed so keenly as in the ages when the inductive spirit sprang up, and was applied to the study of the human mind. And I believe that there is as much, and as intense, religious feeling in our country at this present time as there ever was in any country since man appeared on the earth ; and sooner or later there will be a tremendous reaction against the present attempt to deaden the religious instincts among our young men by a cold unbelief. No doubt educated men cannot now see the constant interpositions of God which were noticed in early ages ; but it is because they take an enlarged and enlightened view of the course of nature, which they regard as ordered by God in infinite wisdom, and as the

expression of His will, and not requiring to be inter-
fered with. It is all true that men with a proud and
self-dependent spirit may now find it easier to dis-
believe in a personal God, and to hand over the universe
to unconscious natural law. But the truth is, persons
who do not like to retain a pure and holy God in their
hearts, had at all times an outlet. That outlet was furnished in ancient times by superstition, which degraded
the Divine character, and in modern times by infidelity,
which denies His existence or His constant operation.

It is a pleasant circumstance to reflect upon, that
nearly all the great philosophers of ancient and modern
times have been anxious to show that their systems
favour religion. There is every reason to believe that
the Ionian physiologists recognised the Divine existence
and the Divine agency : certainly Anaxagoras, who
seems to have been the greatest of them, allotted the all
important place in his system to the Divine Intelligence.
The founder of the Eleatic School, Xenophanes, while he
ridiculed the popular mythology, represented God as the
essential existence. We know little of the Pythagorean
system, but it is clear that it had a Zeus as the centre
of the order which it delighted to unfold. The two
great truths which Socrates held by firmly, amidst his
doubts and his love of dialectic, were the providence of
God, and the tendency of virtue in the government of
God to promote happiness. When Plato rises above
the intellectual gymnastic which he so delighted to
·exercise, it is to merge his philosophy in a theology in
which the God is represented as for ever contemplating

eternal ideas, and developing all things according to
them.   Even Aristotle, cold though he be in his
references to divine subjects, falls back on God as the
principle and ground of all things.   In the Stoic system
there was a fiery deity, who pervaded all nature, and
continued unchanged amidst the periodical conflagration
of all things.   Cicero wishes everywhere to be thought
a pure theist; and the later Latin Stoics, such as
the philosophic emperor, were more religious than the
Greek founders of the school.   Mediæval scholasticism
consisted essentially in the application of Logic to
Theology.   In the reaction of the sixteenth and seventeenth centuries, philosophic thinkers delighted to show
that their systems could bear up and confirm true
religion.   Bacon excluded final causes from physics, but
gave them and formal causes a place in the higher field
of metaphysics, which stand next to and support theology at the apex of the pyramid.   Descartes maintained
that the mind has an idea of the infinite and perfect,
which implies the existence of an infinitely perfect
Being.   Locke wrote much on religious subjects, and in
the Fourth Book of his *Essay*, he shows that his system
leads to a reasonable belief in the existence of a spiritual
Being.   The founders of the German School, Leibnitz
and Kant, embraced the existence of God as essential
parts of their philosophies, and in this they were followed
by the ideal pantheists, Fichte, Schelling, and Hegel.
The Scottish School, from Hutcheson to Hamilton, including Brown, has been at great pains to expound and
defend the great truths of natural religion.

It is surely an ominous circumstance, that in this the nineteenth century there should arise a system of philo sophy, supported by very able men, and with very ex tensive ramifications and applications, especially in social science, but which contains within it no argument for the Divine existence, or sanctions to religion. The founder of the school was an avowed, indeed a rabid, atheist ; and I am not aware that any of his French followers have made any profession of religion,—most of them are favourers of a materialism, which does not admit of a spiritual God.[1] The British branch of the school seems, with one accord, and evidently on a system, to decline uttering any certain sound on the subject : they certainly do not pretend that their philosophy, em bracing though it does, all mental, moral, and social problems, requires us to believe in the existence of God, in the immortality of the soul, or a day of judgment. Mr. Mill's method of dealing with the subject is uniform, and evidently designed. Though fond of uttering opinions on most other topics, he declines saying what are his convictions, or whether he has any convictions, in regard to religious truth. He satisfies himself with declaring, that if you believe in the existence of God, or in Christianity, I do not interfere with you. He does not pretend that his philosophy does of itself give any aid or sanction to religion ; but if we can get evidence otherwise, he assures us that he does not disturb us.

[1] A vigorous opposition is being offered to the prevailing Materialism by a number of able French writers, as M. Cousin, M. Remusat, and M. Janet (see his *Matérialisme Contemporain*).

Without saying that it has convinced him, he speaks with great respect of the argument from design in favour of the Divine existence, and advises us to stick by it, rather than resort to *a priori* proof. The advice is a sound one. The greater number, even of metaphysicians, are in doubts whether there has ever been an *a priori* argument constructed by Anselm, by Descartes, by Leibnitz, or by Clarke, which can of itself prove the existence of God, apart from the observation of the traces of wisdom and goodness in the Divine workmanship. The reaction against the argument from final cause, which has been fostered by the German metaphysics for the last age, is far from being a wise or a healthy spirit and sentiment. The proof from design is that which ever comes home with most force to the unsophisticated mind.

But the important question is not about our author's personal predilections and convictions, but is,—Does his philosophy undermine the arguments for the existence of Deity, and the immortality of the soul, and a day of accounts? It is clear that many of the old proofs cannot be advanced by those who accept his theory. The argument from catholic consent can have no value on such a system. That derived from the moral faculty in man, so much insisted on by Kant and Chalmers, is no longer available when it is allowed that the moral law has no place in our constitution, and that our moral sentiments are generated by inferior feelings and associated circumstances. But then, he tells us, that the Design argument " would stand exactly where it does "

(p. 210). I doubt much whether this is the case. I see no principles left by Mr. Mill sufficient to enable us to answer the objections which have been urged against it by Hume. Kant is usually reckoned as having been successful in showing, that the argument from design involves the principle of cause and effect. We see an order and an adaptation in nature, which are evidently effects, and we look for a cause. Has Mr. Mill's doctrine of causation left this proof untouched? Suppose that we allow to him that there is nothing in an effect which of itself implies a cause; that even when we know that there is a cause, no light is thereby thrown on the nature of that cause; that the causal relation is simply that of invariable antecedence within the limits of our experience; and that beyond our experience there may be events without a cause,—I fear that the argument is left without a foundation. And there are other questions pressing on our notice, and demanding an answer. Can God be shown to be infinite on the principles of this philosophy? If so, what are these principles? If God exists as a designer, is He also a moral governor? Will He call His creatures to account, and reward those who do good, and punish those who do evil? Is this world the only world to us, or is there another? It is clear that the argument drawn from the abiding, the substantial, and spiritual nature of the soul is entirely cut off by a philosophy which makes mind a mere series of feelings. The more convincing argument from God's justice calling His responsible creatures to account, can have little or no force in a system which admits no independent morality.

I should like, I confess, to have the proof and the doctrine of natural religion drawn out according to this philosophy. The argument for the being of a God founded on any native principles is unavailable, but we are allowed to weigh the *a posteriori* evidence. It is conceivable that the adherents of the system may thread their way through the series of feelings and possibilities of sensations, and as they do so discover traces of what, if done by man, would be reckoned design and beneficence : but whether these phenomena within our experience entitle us to argue that there is a Being beyond who has caused them, is a question in regard to which some are waiting for light, to come from the head of the school or some other quarter. Those who believe that an effect of itself implies a cause, have no hesitation in concluding that the design in nature implies a designer ; and those who look on man as having a moral nature, and constrained by inward principles to believe in infinity, can clothe the designer with moral and infinite perfections. But there are not a few, both of those who oppose and those who support Mr. Mill, who cannot see that his system warrants us in reaching any such result. And there is the more puzzling inquiry, whether there is proof that the thread or prolonged throb of consciousness exists after its external bodily conditions or possibilities have been evidently dissolved by death. These are questions which some of our youths, who have com mitted themselves to this philosophy, are sporting with in utter levity, and which are wringing the hearts of others till feelings more bitter than tears burst from

them : and what are they to do in this transition state,
with the old undermined and the new not yet constructed ?

I have carefully refrained throughout this work from
urging any argument from consequences, or from religious considerations, against the philosophy I am examining. I have, to the best of my ability, and with
an anxious desire to reason fairly, met my distinguished
opponent on the ground of consciousness, and of legitimate inference from it. But neither he nor I, neither
those who follow nor those who oppose him, can avoid
looking at the results. Scepticism, as Hume delights to
show, can produce no mischief in the common secular
affairs of life, because *there* man is ever meeting with
circumstances which keep him right in spite of his
principles or want of principles. But it is very different
in those questions which fall to be discussed in higher
ethics and theology. A man will not be tempted by
any sophistry to doubt the connexion of cause and
effect when he is thirsty and sees a cup of water before
him ; in such a case he will at once put forth his hand
and take it, knowing that the beverage will refresh him.
But he may be led by a wretched sophistry to deny the
necessary relation of cause and effect when it would
lead him upward from God's works to God Himself, or
to seek assurance and peace in Him. Hence the im
portance of not allowing fundamental truth to be
assailed : not because the attack will sway any one in
the common business of life, but because it may hold
back and damp our higher aspirations, moral and re-

ligious. I put no question as to the religious convictions of its supporters; but I may surely ask—What is the religion left us by the new philosophy?

M. Comte provided a religion and a worship for his followers. He had no God, but he had a 'Grand Etre,' in Collective Humanity, or "the continuous resultant of all the forces capable of voluntarily concurring in the universal perfectioning of the world"—being in fact a deification of his system of science and sociology. In the worship he enjoined he has nine sacraments, and a priesthood, and public honours to be paid to the Collective Humanity; but with no public liberty of conscience, or of education, in sacred or indeed in any subjects. The religious observances were to occupy two hours every day. Mr. Mill tells us, " Private adoration is to be ad-
" dressed to Collective Humanity in the persons of worthy
" individual representatives, who may be either living or
" dead, but must in all cases be women; for women, being
" the *sexe aimant*, represent the best attribute of huma-
" nity, that which ought to regulate all human life, nor can
" Humanity possibly be symbolized in any form but that
" of a woman. The objects of private adoration are the
" mother, the wife, and the daughter, representing seve-
" rally the past, the present, and the future, and calling
" into active exercise the three social sentiments—vene-
" ration, attachment, and kindness. We are to regard
" them, whether dead or alive, as our guardian angels,
" 'les vrais anges gardiens.' If the last two have never
" existed, or if, in the particular case, any of the three
" types is too faulty for the office assigned to it, their

" place may be supplied by some other type of womanly
" excellence, even by one merely historical" (*Comte and
Posit.*, p. 150). The Christian religion surely does not
suffer by being placed alongside this system, which is
one of the two new religions which this century has
produced—the other being Mormonism. The author
clung more and more fondly to this faith and ceremonial
as he advanced in years. His English followers are
ashamed of it, and ascribe it to his lunacy,—as if he had
not been tinged with madness (as his poor wife knew)
all his life, and as if his whole system had not been
the product of a powerful but constitutionally diseased
intellect.

He denounces his English followers, because they did
not adopt his moral and social system ; he characterizes
the conversion of those who have adopted his positivity
and rejected his religion as an abortion ; and declares
that it must proceed from impotence of intellect, or in
sufficiency of heart, commonly from both ! (*Polit. Posit.*,
tome I. pref. p. xv. ; III. p. xxiv.) There is a basis of
wisdom in this complaint. All history shows that man
is a religious, quite as certainly as he is a feeling, and
a rational being. But what has the British School
provided to meet man's religious wants ? As yet they
have furnished nothing. But Mr. Mill, who always
weighs his words, and who is too skilful a dialectician
to say more than he means, evidently points to something which is being hatched, and may some day burst
forth. While he has the strongest objection to the
system of politics and morals set forth in the *Politique*

Positive, he thinks " it has superabundantly shown the
" possibility of giving to the service of humanity, even
" without the belief in a Providence, both the psycholo-
" gical power and the social efficacy of a religion : making
" it take hold of human life, and colour all thought, feel-
" ing, and action, in a manner of which the greatest
" ascendency ever exercised by any religion may be but
" a type and foretaste " (*Util.*, p. 48).   More specifically in
his latest work he says, that " though conscious of being
in an extremely small minority,"—a circumstance which
is sure to catch those ' individualists' who are bent on
appearing original—" we venture to think that a religion
" may exist without belief in a God, and that a religion
" without a God may be, even to Christians, an in-
" structive and profitable object of contemplation"
(*Comte and Posit.*, p. 133).   He tells us, that in order to
constitute a religion, there must be " a creed or conviction," " a belief or set of beliefs," " a sentiment connected
with this creed," and a " cultus."   I confess I should like
excessively to see this new religion, with its creed and
its cultus, fully developed.   It would match the theolo-
gies, with their ceremonial observances, projected by doc-
trinaires in the heat of the French Revolution.   There
is no risk of the British School setting up a religion and
a worship so superbly ridiculous as that of M. Comte,
but I venture to predict that when it comes, it will
be so scientifically cold, and so emotionally blank, as to
be incapable of gathering any interest around it, of ac-
complishing any good—or, I may add, inflicting any
evil.

Leaving the religion to develop itself in the future, let us ascertain what we have without it in the philosophic system. Within, we have a prolonged series of feelings; without, we have a possibility of sensations; both regulated by the most unbending laws of necessity, within the limits of experience and a reasonable distance beyond; and beyond that *beyond*—if there be such—a land of darkness and eternal silence. This is the cold region into which thought, as it moves on in its orbit, has brought us, in the third quarter of the nineteenth century. And is this, then, what is left us after all the dialectic conflicts, and as the result of all the scientific discoveries of the last two thousand five hundred years that have elapsed since reflective thought was awakened? We know how keenly some patriotic and high-minded Frenchmen feel when they are obliged to contemplate the present state of their country, and to confess how great the humiliation implied in the bloody revolutions through which they have passed, ending in a military despotism, which restrains on all hands liberty of thought and action. I am sure that a like feeling will rise up in many noble and hopeful minds when they are made to see that all these discussions, philosophic and religious, in the past, that all these throes and convulsions of opinion and sentiment have left us only a series of feelings and a possibility of sensations, beginning we know not with what, and carrying us we know not whither,— all that we are sure of being, that the sensations and feelings are conveyed along pleasantly or unpleasantly, and ranged into companies suitably or unsuitably, and our very beliefs generated, by a fatalistic law of contiguity and resemblance. Some may be content with this lot, as being caught in the toils and despairing of an escape : but there will be others—I venture to say nobler and better—who feel that they must be delivered from this mental bondage at all hazards, and will hasten to attempt it even at the risk of new conflicts and new revolutions. It should not after all be so difficult for humble and sincere men to escape from this net which sophistry would weave around them. Let them follow those intuitions and ultimate beliefs, the existence and the veracity of which Mr. Mill has acknowledged—while he has declined to pursue them to their consequences ; let them gather around them a body of acquired observations with their appropriate sentiments ; and, as they do so, they will reach a body of truth, practical, scientific, and religious, sufficient to stay the intellect and satisfy the heart,—while what still remains unknown will only incite to further explorations, and lead to new discoveries.

APPENDIX.

SIR W. HAMILTON'S PHILOSOPHY.—*See* p. 13.

I HAVE taken exception to certain doctrines of Hamilton in the *Method of Divine Government* (M. D. G.); in the *North British Review*, Nos. liv. and lix. (N. B. R.); in *Dublin University Magazine*, Aug. 1859 (D. U. M.); in *Intuitions of the Mind* (I. M.); in *Supernatural in Relation to Natural* (S. N.); in Appendix to Stewart's *Outlines* (S. O.); and now in this work (D. F. T.)

1. His Method.—N.B R. liv. 427; I.M. 96; D.F.T. 34.
2. His ambiguous use of Consciousness.—N.B.R. liv. 428; D.U.M. 159, 160; I.M. 96; D.F.T. 25-30.
3. His omission among the Reproductive Powers (*Metaph.* vol. ii.), of the Recognitive Power by which we believe the remembered event to have fallen under our notice in time past.—D.U.M. 160; D.F.T. 174.
4. His view of Time and Space.—N.B.R. liv. 429; I.M. 178, 179.
5. His doctrine of Unconscious Mental Operations.—D.U.M. 161, 162; D.F.T. 196-198.
6. His unsatisfactory way of appealing to Faith without explaining its nature.—N.B.R. lix. 150, 151; I.M. 168-173; S.N. 355.
7. His view of all Knowledge implying Comparison.—I.M. 207-210; D.F.T. 222.
8. His defective view of the Relations which the mind can discover.—D.U.M. 162, 163; I.M. 211.

9. His doctrine of the Relativity of Knowledge.—M.D.G. 536-539; N.B.R. liv. 428-429 ; D.U.M. 163, 164 ; I.M. 109, 340-341; S.O. 132 ; D.F.T. 218-221.
10. His doctrine of Nescience.—M.D.G. 520 ; N.B.R. liv. 430-431 ; I.M. 342-345 ; D.F.T. 219.
11. His defective doctrine as to our idea of the Infinite.— M.D.G. 534 ; N.B.R. liv. 430, lix. 150, 154, 156 ; I.M. 193-197 ; S.N. 141.
12. His axiom that truth lies between two extremes.—I.M. 304, 338.
13. His doctrine of Substance.—I.M. 146, 148.
14. His doctrine of Causation.—M.D.G. 529, 530 ; N.B.R. liv. 430 ; D.U.M. 164.
15. The application by Dr. Mansel of the doctrine of Relativity to Moral Good and Evil.—N.B.R. lix. 157 ; S.N. 356, 357.
16. His view of the Theistic Argument.—M.D.G. 520 ; N.B.R. liv. 431, lix. 152; S.N. 355 ; S.O. 140.

EDINBURGH : T. CONSTABLE,
PRINTER TO THE QUEEN, AND TO THE UNIVERSITY.

WORKS BY DR. M'COSH.

to neglect the great German works. I admire the moderation and clearness, as well as comprehension, of the author's views. While entertaining a great respect for the Masters of the Scottish Philosophy, such as Sir W. Hamilton, this has not restrained his independent judgment, or kept him stationary."—DR. DORNER *of Berlin.*

"The undertaking to adjust the claims of the sensational and intuitional philosophies, and of the *a posteriori* and *a priori* methods, is not only legitimate, but accomplished in this work with a great amount of success." —*Westminster Review,* April 1865.

"No philosopher before Dr. M'Cosh has clearly brought out the stages by which an original and individual intuition passes first into an articulate but still individual judgment, and then into a universal maxim or principle ; and no one has so clearly or completely classified and enumerated our intuitive convictions, or exhibited in detail their relations to the various sciences which repose on them as their foundations. The amount of summarized information which it contains is very great ; and it is the only work on the very important subject with which it deals. Never was such a work so much needed as in the present day. It is the only scientific work adapted to counteract the school of Mill, Bain, and Herbert Spencer, which is so steadily prevailing among the students of the present generation."—*London Quarterly Review,* April 1865.

"Though treating of the intuitions of the mind, and thus labouring in that particular division of philosophy which is most liable to degenerate into imaginative, or at best merely speculative notions, Dr. M'Cosh preserves a clear, calm, and sober intelligence. The history of many philosophic opinions, and the peculiarities of many philosophical schools, are also passed in review in the notes to the work, in a concise yet thorough manner ; and the criticisms that are made upon several of the celebrated theories of the past are candid and exhaustive."—DR. SHEDD, *in Introduction to Second American Edition.*

"When the original edition of this work appeared, we characterized it in terms of strong recommendation, such as we rarely bestow on any work, and pointed out at some length its distinctive merits. We will just say here, that, in regard to all the greatest issues between Mill and Hamilton, indeed all the great issues raised by either of these eminent authors, or their respective philosophical schools ; and in regard to nearly every great issue raised between the philosophic scepticism and the Christian philosophy of our day, Dr. M'Cosh quite generally takes the right side."—*Princeton Review,* Oct. 1865.

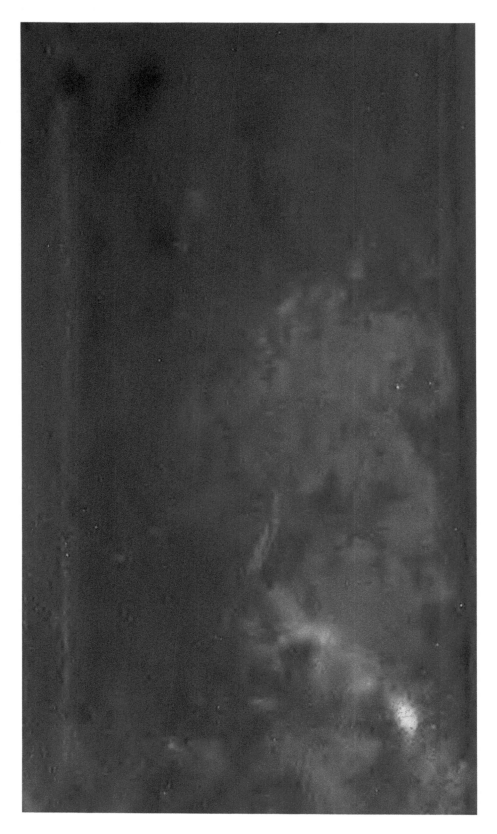

ImTheStory.com

Personalized Classic Books in many genre's

Unique gift for kids, partners, friends, colleagues

Customize:

- Character Names
- Upload your own front/back cover images (optional)
- Inscribe a personal message/dedication on the
  inside page (optional)

Customize many titles Including
- Alice in Wonderland
- Romeo and Juliet
- The Wizard of Oz
- A Christmas Carol
- Dracula
- Dr. Jekyll & Mr. Hyde
- And more...